The City and the World

New York's Global Future

The City and the World

New York's Global Future

Margaret E. Crahan and Alberto Vourvoulias-Bush
Editors

A COUNCIL ON FOREIGN RELATIONS BOOK

The Council on Foreign Relations, Inc., a nonprofit, nonpartisan national membership organization founded in 1921, is dedicated to promoting understanding of international affairs through the free and civil exchange of ideas. The Council's members are dedicated to the belief that America's peace and prosperity are firmly linked to that of the world. From this flows the mission of the Council: to foster America's understanding of its fellow members of the international community, near and far, their peoples, cultures, histories, hopes, quarrels, and ambitions; and thus to serve, protect, and advance America's own global interests through study and debate, private and public.

From time to time books, monographs, and reports written by members of the Council's research staff or others are published as a "Council on Foreign Relations Book." Any work bearing that designation is, in the judgment of the Committee on Studies of the Council's Board of Directors, a responsible treatment of a significant international topic.

THE COUNCIL TAKES NO INSTITUTIONAL POSITION ON POLICY ISSUES AND HAS NO AFFILIATION WITH THE U.S. GOVERNMENT. ALL STATEMENTS OF FACT AND EXPRESSIONS OF OPINION CONTAINED IN ALL ITS PUBLICATIONS ARE THE SOLE RESPONSIBILITY OF THE AUTHOR OR AUTHORS.

Council on Foreign Relations Books are distributed by Brookings Institution Press (1-800-275-1447). For further information on Council publications, please write the Council on Foreign Relations, 58 East 68th Street, New York, NY 10021, or call the Public Affairs Office at (212) 434-9400.

Library of Congress Cataloging-in-Publication Data

The City and the World : New York's Global Future / Margaret E. Crahan
     and Alberto Vourvoulias-Bush, editors.
        p.   cm.
     Includes bibliographical references and index.
     ISBN 0-87609-208-3
     1. New York (N.Y.)—Economic conditions.   2. New York (N.Y.)—
Population.   3. New York (N.Y.)—Commerce.   4. Immigrants—New York
(State)—New York.   5. Competition, International.   I. Crahan,
Margaret E.   II. Vourvoulias-Bush, Alberto.
HC108.N7C49   1997
330.9447'1—dc21   97-31556
                                                                              CIP

Contents

Tables and Figures

Foreword:
New York's Global Future

AMERICANS have become used to the idea that the United States as a nation is the central player and greatest force in the global economy. We can measure the rapid growth of America's international trade, the increasing flows of foreign investment across our borders, and the number of commercial agreements this nation signs. Membership in the United Nations, International Monetary Fund, World Bank, World Trade Organization, plus periodic summits and meetings of foreign, finance, and trade ministers, attest to America's ever-growing global role.

With considerably less fanfare America's cities also have become significant actors in the global economy. The magnitude of their participation in global finance, trade, and information flows cannot be as easily measured. Nor do they participate in frequent international meetings and august international institutions to remind us of their global roles. The primary actors in the globalization of cities are not ministers of finance or trade, or Washington diplomats, or even the mayors of these cities themselves. They are the energetic and international-minded leaders of private industry and finance. They are innovators in telecommunications, computer technology, and entertainment. They are universities and medical centers of global reputation. They are international charities and foundations. And they are the hundreds of thousands of annual immigrants for whom our cities serve as magnets.

Globalization has had an enormous impact on New York, a driving force relentlessly changing the city's economic, cultural, and intellectual landscape. Dating back to the time of the early Dutch settlers, New York has been a major commercial and financial center. Its "high-energy culture" has long been associated with its openness to immigrants and the fresh ideas and entrepreneurial spirit they bring. Sitting in my office, using cyberspace technology to e-mail colleagues in Tokyo or London, I can look out over New York harbor, where my grandparents arrived at the turn of the century after an arduous transatlantic voyage. The technologies, corporations, and arts that drive New York's economy and energize its society have changed greatly since that time, but its openness to new people, new ideas, and new cultures has remained a vital feature.

As the twenty-first century approaches, few cities have as much to gain from continuing to harness the benefits of what promises to be a further acceleration of international flows of technology, commerce, finance, people, ideas, and information. Conversely, few have as much to lose if in the future fiscal mismanagement, ineffective schools, widening income disparities, cultural or racial tensions, and drugs or crime were to lead to a deterioration of economic infrastructure, social disharmony, a decline in living conditions for all of the city's citizens including its most creative and entrepreneurial ones, and loss of attractiveness as a global center of finance, culture, and the interchange of ideas.

This book is a compendium of insightful essays that discuss New York's enormous opportunities in coming years along with its equally enormous challenges. Its authors examine New York's future from many perspectives, relating issues facing the city to those facing the country and the world—finance, commerce, crime, culture, migration, governance, and information flows.

This book focuses primarily on New York City, but it has great relevance to other cities in the United States—and cities throughout the world. Although New York is in many ways America's most "global city," it is far from the only one, nor has it been as proactive in some respects as other cities. As I travel around the country, I am constantly impressed by the degree to which virtually all cities in the United States, and many smaller communities, have become integral and dynamic parts of the global economy. The technological and entrepreneurial centers of Silicon Valley and the Bay area; the dynamic new businesses in Dallas, Denver, Phoenix and the Southwest; the globally minded entertainment companies of Los Angeles; the world-class manufacturing industries of Chicago, Detroit, and much of the Midwest; the growing international business hubs of Atlanta, Raleigh-Durham, and other parts of the South; the international centers of medical excellence in Baltimore, Boston, Cleveland, and Houston; and the great university communities of Berkeley, Cambridge, Chapel Hill, New Haven, Palo Alto, and Princeton—all are major global players.

Through this book the Council on Foreign Relation and the authors and editors of these chapters expand the horizons of knowledge and perceptions of the globalization process. This book addresses New York's circumstances and policy problems, but the methodology and approach applied here can be of considerable value to other cities.

As we approach the turn of the century, America's cities are in a global competition just as individual companies are. Cities around the world are competing with one another for funds, for businesses, for the best people, and for leadership as centers of technology, telecommunications, the media, the arts, medicine, and education. They must constantly make policy adjustments to changing global requirements. This book seeks to remind us of what it will take for New York, and for other cities, to thrive in the future in this global environment.

Robert D. Hormats
Goldman Sachs (International)
New York, New York

Acknowledgments

THIS BOOK, and the Council on Foreign Relations study group from which it was drawn, were made possible by a special grant from the Andrew W. Mellon Foundation aimed at encouraging innovation and a wider participation in our programs. It is also one of the first major initiatives conducted under the auspices of the Nelson and David Rockefeller Chair in Inter-American Studies.

The success of this enterprise rested very much on detailed, preparatory discussions and a series of lively and productive seminars with the active participation of scholars and practitioners from all segments of city life. Margaret E. Crahan of Hunter College of the City University of New York chaired the study group providing intellectual leadership and served as an exacting editor. Her many contributions to this project are reflected in the quality and originality of this book. Alberto Vourvoulias-Bush was the director of this project and coeditor of the volume, and managed all stages of the study group and publication with enthusiasm and tact. Linda Wrigley line edited the volume brilliantly and Michael Weber expertly shepherded it through production.

We are grateful to our advisory committee (Andrea Bonime-Blanc, Armando Bravo Martínez, Roland Leigiarde-Laura, and Benjamin Rivlin), to our distinguished commentators (Albert Fishlow, Arturo Lindo Fuentes, Robert S. Gelbard, Philip Kasinitz, John Mollenkopf, Daniel Mato, Nina Glick-Shiller, and Aristide R. Zolberg), and to all the members of the study group listed in full in the "Participants" section. In particular, we would like to thank James F. Hoge, Jr., editor of *Foreign Affairs* and former publisher of the *New York Daily News*, for his critical reading of the manuscript and Robert D. Hormats, vice chairman of Goldman Sachs (International) and chair of the Committee on Studies of the Council on Foreign Relations during my term as director of studies, for his review of the manuscript and contribution to the volume. Most especially, we would like to thank Stephanie Bell-Rose of the Andrew W. Mellon Foundation for her active encouragement and good will. The project was assisted along the way by Arcadio Casillas, Michael Clough, Rafael Docavo-Malvezzi, Kenneth Keller, Daria Lyman,

Alina Rocha Menocal, James Shinn, Richard Smithy, David Vidal, April Wahlestedt, and Ruth Wedgwood.

As with all Council events, we are continually in the debt of the Council staff who do so much behind the scenes to make everything run so smoothly. Last, but by no means least, we are grateful to the president of the Council on Foreign Relations, Leslie H. Gelb, for encouraging us to undertake this innovative and exciting project.

Kenneth Maxwell
Nelson and David Rockefeller Senior Fellow
for Inter-American Studies,
Council on Foreign Relations
New York, New York

Contributors

Peter Andreas is a doctoral candidate in government at Cornell University, a Guest Scholar at the Center for U.S.-Mexican Studies at the University of California, San Diego, and an SSRC-MacArthur Foundation Fellow in Peace and Security. He is a coauthor of *Drug War Politics: The Price of Denial*.

Margaret E. Crahan is Dorothy Epstein Professor in Latin American History at Hunter College. From 1982 to 1994 she was Henry R. Luce Professor of Religion, Power, and Political Process at Occidental College. Her books include *Africa and the Caribbean: Legacies of a Link* and *Human Rights and Basic Needs in the Americas*.

Josh DeWind is Director of the International Migration Program of the Social Science Research Council. He is on leave from Hunter College, where he is a member of the Department of Anthropology and directs the Latin American and Caribbean Studies and Human Rights Programs. He is the coauthor of *Aiding Migration: The Impact of International Development Assistance on Haiti*.

Jay Kaplan is Executive Director of the New York Council for the Humanities, a nonprofit agency dedicated to bringing the insights of history, literature, and other humanities disciplines to broad, general audiences. In 1992 he launched the New York Council for the Humanities' magazine, *culturefront*, which he edits and for which he writes. He is also Series Editor for Syracuse University Press's forthcoming publications on New York City.

Clifford Krauss was recently the Police Department Bureau Chief for the *New York Times*. He has previously covered the State Department and Congress. He is the author of *Inside Central America: Its People, Politics, and History*.

Carol O'Cléireacáin is an economic consultant and Visiting Fellow in Economic Studies at the Brookings Institution, where she authored *The*

Orphan Capital: Adopting the Right Revenues for the District of Columbia. Under Mayor David Dinkins from 1990 to 1994 she served first as Finance Commissioner and then as Budget Director of the City of New York. She cochairs MEXNY21, a joint project of major universities in New York City and Mexico City on common issues facing these two megacities into the next century. She is a member of the Council on Foreign Relations, where she chaired a recent study group on labor issues in trade policy.

Edward M. Roche is chairman of the International Federation of Information Processing (IFIP) Working Group 8.7 on "Informatics in Multinational Enterprises" and the author of *Managing Information Technology in Multinational Corporations* and *Telecommunications and Business Strategy.* He has edited *Global Information Technology and Systems Management* with Prashant Palvia and Shailendra Palvia; *Information Technology, Development, and Policy* with Michael James Blaine; *Corporate Networks, International Telecommunications, and Interdependence—Perspectives from Geography and Information Systems* with Henry Bakis and Ronald Abler; and *Developments in Telecommunications* with Henry Bakis. He is a visiting scholar at the Institute for Urban and Regional Development, University of California at Berkeley.

Rae D. Rosen is a senior economist with the Federal Reserve Bank of New York, where her work focuses on regional issues. Ms. Rosen's prior positions have included Vice-president, Senior Economist at the Federal Home Loan Bank of New York, where she was responsible for regional forecasts of the economy and the real estate market; and Senior Economist at Merrill Lynch Economics, Inc., where she was a consultant to major U.S. and European motor-vehicle manufacturers and their suppliers.

Joseph J. Salvo and **Arun Peter Lobo** are, respectively, Director and Senior Demographer of the Population Division of the New York City Department of City Planning. They have coauthored *The Newest New Yorkers: 1990–1994; Puerto Rican New Yorkers in 1990*; and a host of articles pertaining to immigration and to population change.

Saskia Sassen is Professor of Urban Planning at Columbia University and also serves on the faculty of the School of International and Public Affairs. Her books include: *The Global City: New York, London, Tokyo; Cities in a World Economy;* and *Losing Control? Sovereignty in an Age of Globalization,* the 1995 Columbia University Leonard Hastings Schoff Memorial Lectures.

Robert C. Smith is an Assistant Professor in the Sociology Department of Barnard College and directs the Transnational Migration module of the Hewlett Program on Mexico at the Institute of Latin American and Iberian Studies at Columbia University. His dissertation "Los Ausentes Siempre Presentes: The Imagining, Making and Politics of a Transnational Community between Ticuani, Puebla, Mexico and New York City" (Columbia University, 1995) was nominated for the Bancroft Prize.

Anthony Stevens-Arroyo is Professor of Puerto Rican Studies at Brooklyn College in the City University of New York and Executive Chairperson of the Program for the Analysis of Religion Among Latinos (PARAL). He is the author of *The Cave of the Jagua: The Mythological World of the Tainos* and of *Discovering Latino Religion*, part of the PARAL series published by Bildner Center Books in New York.

Alberto Vourvoulias-Bush is Research Associate for Latin America at the Council on Foreign Relations and a doctoral candidate in politics at Yale University.

Introduction

The City and the World

MARGARET E. CRAHAN
WITH ALBERTO VOURVOULIAS-BUSH

NEW YORK CITY has long considered itself the center of the world, and even more so of late as globalization has intensified. Globalization—understood here as economic integration and the dramatically increased global flows of money, people, and ideas—has both enhanced the city's status and exacerbated some of its problems. While New York City's role as a center for international finance and related services has expanded, the city's manufacturing base has continued to erode. The gap between rich and poor New Yorkers has widened at the same time that government resources and social programs have narrowed. A new wave of immigrants has brought specialized labor skills and entrepreneurial energy to the city, but has added to the demands made on already overburdened services such as public education. These trends are occurring, moreover, within the context of a technological and telecommunications revolution that is redefining how New Yorkers do business, interact with the world, and identify and form communities. This volume focuses on the interplay of such urban, regional, national, and international developments within the context of an increasingly integrated world.

During the last twenty-five years, global trends have prompted changes in the nature and role of the nation-state as well as that of cities like New York. The sovereignty of nation-states has been eroded as certain traditional functions have been superseded by transnational actors, reassigned to the private sector, or decentralized in favor of regional and local authorities. Lessened nation-state regulation of national economies has meant that cities are integrated more directly into the international economy and are more exposed to global processes—requiring cities to develop the equivalent of a "foreign policy," in addition to revamping municipal policies. As the United Nations Research Institute for Social Development recently affirmed: "At a national level, many state institutions have been eroded or eliminated. And at a local level, the imperatives of market forces and globalization have been undermining communities and families."[1]

At the same time, the transfer of decision-making and spending power from central governments to cities has not been confined to advanced industrial countries nor to global or mega-cities. For example, according to a World Bank official, Latin American municipal governments spend two to four times as much as they did twenty years ago despite central government budget cuts. One result is that "local leaders, not national ones, have emerged from political and electoral reforms to produce scores of innovations in governance that parallel, even exceed, the breadth of change seen in the United States."[2] Clearly globalization is contributing to the transformation of government at all levels, from the nation-state to the municipality.

Among the principal global trends contributing to the transformation of cities and the world are:

- *Rapidly increased integration of the global economy.* Capital, markets, labor, and goods and services have become much more international and mobile. According to United Nations statistics, "between 1980 and 1992 transnational corporations (TNC) sales more than doubled, from $2.4 trillion to $5.5 trillion, and by 1994 there were 37,000 parent corporations with over 200,000 affiliates worldwide. TNCs now control over 33 percent of the world's productive assets, although, since they tend to be concentrated in capital-intensive industries, they employ directly or indirectly only about 5 percent of the global workforce."[3] That workforce is increasingly dispersed and mobile and often has little job security or benefits.[4] The international operations of these corporations are often beyond the legal purview of nation-states with both the General Agreement on Trade and Tariffs (GATT) and the World Trade Organization (WTO) aimed more at facilitating than regulating their activities.[5] Cities are even less equipped to do so. This places a heavy burden on local elected officials to ensure that economic internationalization is more positive than negative for those that they represent.

- *Integration has stimulated the mobility of production.* Such mobility has resulted in increased efficiency in some sectors, as well as more dispersed production facilitated by innovations in transport and communications. In 1950 New York City had an estimated one million manufacturing jobs,[6] a good number in small- and medium-sized plants owned by or employing first and second generation immigrants. By 1995 this sector only employed approximately 216,000,[7] with many jobs having been exported either abroad or elsewhere in the United States where wages, benefits, and other costs were lower. Government has replaced manufacturing as the chief employer in New York. Also critical for the city's economic health are the finance, insurance, and real estate sectors (FIRE), which, while currently accounting for only 15 percent of total employment, contribute 27 percent of wages. As Carol O'Cléireacáin points out in Chapter 1, "The city's tax revenues are highly dependent on a small number of payers, reflecting an income distribution in which the top fifth of the households earn more than half of the total income. The top 1 percent of the city's taxpayers now account for about 65 percent of the property tax revenue, more than half of business income tax revenue, almost half of commercial rent tax revenue, and about a third of the personal income tax revenue. Half of the business income taxes come from the top thousand payers, fully 40 percent of whom are in the FIRE sector."[8] This ties city revenues to fluctuations on Wall Street, as when a bond market crash contributed to a $400 million gap in the city's 1995 budget, while an upswing in the stock market and increase in mergers and acquisitions bolstered the city's 1996 income. While relatively high FIRE salaries have benefited the city, outside of that sector wages have largely declined and there has been substantial growth in the informal sector. This has contributed to a widening gap in income distribution in New York City, a trend present in the rest of the United States as well. According to the Department of Labor, from 1979 to 1995 the income of the poorest 20 percent of families in the United States declined 9 percent, while that of the richest 20 percent rose 26 percent.[9] Widening income inequality is also a global trend, particularly in Africa, Asia, and Latin America.[10] The mobility of production impedes governments, at all levels, from enforcing labor legislation and makes financing public services more difficult. It has also stimulated a resurgence of labor and community mobilization, in which nongovernmental organizations have played crucial roles.

• *Technification of production and communications.* In the last twenty years computers have revolutionized traditional production, as well as a substantial portion of the service sector, contributing to the elimination of jobs in the former and the creation of new ones in the latter. Advances in telecommunications have facilitated moving back-room activities, particularly in the FIRE sector, out of New York, at the same time that the city has become the site of a new high-tech sector—Silicon Alley, a conglomeration of companies developing multimedia software, web sites, online entertainment, and related goods. Employment in this new sector in metropolitan New York rose from 28,500 in 1992 to 71,500 in 1995, with income estimated at $3.8 billion.[11] City officials and others have touted this development as potentially counterbalancing the erosion of manufacturing in the city.[12] However, some experts have expressed reservations. Edward Roche notes in Chapter 3 that the jobs created are frequently relatively low paying, with few benefits and lacking long-term security.

- *Transformation of politics and political structures.* Globalization has had both positive and negative consequences for politics and political structures at national, regional, and local levels. Global integration has helped disseminate democratic ideas and networks more broadly and has contributed to increased mobilization, particularly on behalf of greater enjoyment of civil, political, social, economic, and cultural rights. It has led to a proliferation of nongovernmental organizations (NGOs) that have increased citizen and community input into public and private sector decision making. This trend has been heightened by the erosion of public services and the delivery by NGOs of services once provided by governments. Estimates of the number of nongovernmental organizations worldwide ranges into the millions and include tiny village co-ops as well as such large and well-known organizations as Amnesty International, Green-peace, and CARE, the last of which has a yearly budget of $400 million, larger than that of many cities. NGOs currently provide more development assistance than the United Nations and can mobilize more financial and human resources than some smaller nation-states. NGOs have also demonstrated their capacity to influence the policies and actions of major powers such as the United States on both domestic and foreign-policy issues. Utilizing new technology, they are capable of mobilizing international networks instanta-neously around public policy issues on the international, national, regional, and local levels.[13] In New York City, NGOs have joined ethnic, religious, labor, and other groups to lobby on a variety of is-sues, including neighborhood redevelopment, environmental, and personal-security issues. Hence, government at all levels is much more influenced not only by global economic interests but also by watchdogs, particularly NGOs. Such organizations are not as representative, however, as broad-based citizen participation.

- *Internationalization of crime.* Globalization has facilitated the internationalization of crime, particularly drug trafficking, as Clifford Krauss and Peter Andreas indicate in Chapters 4 and 5. According to the United Nations, illegal drugs generate an estimated $500 billion per year, making the search for means to launder profits a major preoccupation of crime cartels.[14] This has serious implications for the international financial system, as well as for the integrity of governments and their personnel. As Mexico's Ambassador Oscar González recently observed, "With their enormous economic power, modern drug traffickers have increased their technological capacity in areas of communication, laboratories, transportation and in penetrating and corrupting government and business structures, especially the judicial and police sectors, the chemical industry and the financial sector."[15] Virtually all countries have experienced sharp increases in crime. This has not been limited to drugs but also has included the smuggling of arms, vehicles, and illegal immigrants; kidnapping; and money laundering. In New York City an overall drop in crime statistics tends to obscure the plight of neighborhoods such as Jackson Heights, Corona, and Elmhurst, which have borne the brunt of the North American operations of the Colombian cartels, as Clifford Krauss points out in Chapter 4. The internationalization of crime has revealed the inadequacies of nation-states and cities in dealing with such developments, particularly in controlling money laundering and its impact on banks. New York is particularly well suited to laundering profits on a massive scale, given its concentration of financial institutions and import/export companies and the fact that as a world financial center an estimated $2 trillion is transferred there every day. Considering the city's shrinking tax base, the creation and funding of law-enforcement units with the level of expertise necessary to track the increasingly sophisticated and diversified operations of international crime cartels is a major preoccupation. While public pressure for spending on crime control has increased, most programs developed to date do not appear adequate given the complexities of the increased internationalization of crime. Experts differ as to the most effective strategies but agree on the importance of reducing domestic demand if international drug trafficking and its attendant crimes are to be reduced and hence be less destabilizing for nation-states and local communities.

- *Increased migration has contributed to new concepts of citizenship and transnational identity.* As transnationalization has increased, the identification of the citizen with the nation-state has been altered. According to UN statistics, approximately 100 million people are currently residing outside their country of citizenship and another 16 million are refugees in foreign lands.[16] New York has been a primary destination for immigrants to the United States, 563,000 arriving between 1990 and 1994, as Joseph Salvo and Peter Lobo indicate in Chapter 6. Although immigration forms an integral part of the city's history, migrants today have much more opportunity to maintain close contact with their countries of origin. Indeed, as Rob Smith indicates in Chapter 7, this can lead to ongoing involvement in the sending community and the emergence of multiple national identities and dual citizenship. Increasingly, countries are allowing such citizenship and looking to nationals abroad for financial and political support. This means that more and more of the "new New Yorkers" may regard themselves as citizens of more than one country with loyalties to both.

- *Transformation of culture and social institutions.* New York's dual role as a magnet for cultural producers and for setting global trends gives it a major role in determining national and international cultural developments. Some observers, including Jay Kaplan in Chapter 10, argue that globalization has resulted in a greater homogenization and commercialization of cultural production and expression, both in New York and internationally. Local cultural traditions, ranging from popular to high culture, provide a shared arena of experience and identification for an otherwise highly diverse and cosmopolitan city. The replacement of these arenas by less-rooted and more-standardized cultural products weakens community life. Religious and social institutions, particularly the schools, are also central to a shared cultural experience and identification. Many immigrant students, as Josh DeWind and Antonio Stevens-Arroyo note in Chapters 8 and 9, tend to do well in the classroom, where they acquire elements of both American and New York culture while retaining elements of their original culture. New York's ongoing ability to compete in an increasingly internationalized economy will be aided by promoting the cosmopolitan nature of its cultural life embodied in the retained diversity of its human capital.

This brief survey only hints at the impact of global trends on the city and the world and the complexity of the public policy issues they raise.

The latter are explored more fully in the chapters that follow. At the core, however, are changes in the reach of state sovereignty, the international role of cities such as New York, and changing concepts of community and citizenship. Experts, including the authors in this volume, have struggled to analyze these changes in order to suggest some of the implications for public policy on the national, regional, state, and local level. In order to do so, it is essential to explore briefly the changing realities of the nation-state, city, community, and citizenship.

Nation-State

A principal effect of globalization has been to transform the identification of the nation-state with a geographic entity. Increased economic integration has tended to denationalize and deterritorialize the nation-state and, along with population movements and advances in transportation and communications, modified the definition of nationality and citizenship. This has had tremendous consequences for state sovereignty—the traditional basis for the international order in the modern era.

The concept of state sovereignty grew out of the needs of emerging territorial states in the sixteenth and seventeenth centuries. Intent on subordinating both heterogeneous social groups and competing internal centers of authority, principally cities, monarchies promoted central government as the ultimate authority within defined geographical areas—the sovereign state. As nation-states were consolidated in the eighteenth and nineteenth centuries and competition among them intensified, it became apparent that there was also a need to regulate the interactions between states and, as a consequence, there developed supranational mechanisms and organizations. State sovereignty, however, continued to impose substantial limits on nonstate actors. The decline of monarchy and the rise of nationalism in the nineteenth and early twentieth centuries, together with industrialization and the growth of commerce, fortified nation-states and central governments' control of national economies.

Economic developments, among others, in recent decades, however, have undercut the power and sovereignty of nation-states and, along with the concentration of certain financial and support functions in a few urban areas, are resulting in the emergence of cities as critical actors in the new global economy. The traditional monopoly of the state over taxation, information, and the provision of security has eroded. Substantial portions of the global economy are untaxed and this combined with relatively unregulated currency markets can place strains on the fiscal strength of any country. An indication of the dimensions of the problem is provided by the fact that private currency transactions currently account for "$1.3 trillion a day, more than 100 times the volume of world trade. The amount exceeds the total foreign exchange reserves of all governments, and is more than even an alliance of strong states can buck."[17]

Together with the power to tax, the legitimate use of coercive force by the nation-state has traditionally been of the essence of its sovereign powers. Three developments have undermined this power: the limited capacity of governments to deal effectively with expanding social violence and international crime has resulted in an increased sense of personal insecurity on the part of many citizens around the globe; technological and organizational changes have put a virtual end to the government's monopoly on information, allowing nonstate actors to challenge the credibility of state agents and offer alternative explanations for, and solutions to, public-policy issues; and, at least in the United States, there is a growing cynicism about government and politicians. The last of these phenomena has undercut the capacity of civil society, as well as the political system, to build that level of consensus necessary for local, regional, and national policies to address the impact of globalization.

The future evolution of the nation-state is unclear. One vision is that of the "virtual state." As conceptualized by the political scientist Richard Rosecrance, the virtual state is a "tighter, more vigorous unit"[18] better able to compete in a more globalized economy in which land-based production has diminished. He posits:

> The virtual state is a country whose economy is reliant on mobile factors of production. Of course it houses virtual corporations and presides over foreign direct investment by its enterprises. But more than this, it encourages, stimulates, and to a degree even coordinates such activities. In formulating economic strategy, the virtual state recognizes that its own production does not have to take place at home; it may play host to the capital and labor of other nations. . . . The virtual state specializes in modern technical research services and derives its income not just from high-value manufacturing, but from product design, marketing, financing. The rationale for its economy is efficiency attained through productive downsizing. Size no longer determines economic potential. Virtual nations hold the competitive key to greater wealth in the 21st century.[19]

The concept of the virtual state responds to some of the implications of the trends mentioned previously, including the evolution of nation-states from sovereign territorial units to more decentralized entities less rooted, both politically and economically, in national identity. In economic terms, national identity has already blurred, and it is hard to tell the foreign from the domestic. For example, 20 percent of U.S. corporate production occurs abroad.[20] Such seemingly quintessential American companies as Coca Cola, IBM, and McDonalds today earn the bulk of their profits abroad, while the Australian Rupert Murdoch's News Corporation's U.S. holdings include Fox TV, the *New York Post*, Twentieth Century Fox, *TV Guide*, HarperCollins Publishers, and 22 television stations.[21] All these corporations bring a strongly transnational agenda to their relations with any government.

Rosecrance further argues that the evolution of nation-states into virtual states will mean fewer international conflicts since reduced dependency on land-based production in favor of globalized production would reduce the likelihood of conflicts between states. Indeed, he argues:

> If durable access to assets elsewhere can be assured the need to physically possess them diminishes. . . . Free movement of capital and goods, substantial international and domestic investment and high levels of technical education have been the recipe for success in the industrial world of the late twentieth century. Those who depended on others did better than those who depended only on themselves. Can the result be different in the future? Virtual states, corporate alliances, and essential trading relationships augur peaceful times. They may not solve domestic problems, but the economic bonds that link virtual and other nations will help ease security concerns.[22]

While one can debate the likelihood of Rosecrance's projections, the problems he identifies as resulting from global economic integration ring true. He cautions that traditional state processes will not be capable of dealing with all the problems emerging out of globalization since neither decisions by central governments nor domestic citizen participation would be sufficient to resolve them given their transnational scope and complexity.

The United States, Rosecrance notes, has historically tended to be inward turned, and currently some sectors of Congress are not only highly suspicious of greater global integration but are also intent on reducing the authority of the central government precisely at a time when innovative responses are necessary to meet international challenges. The principal way to deal with the latter, he asserts, is to make the United States more competitive in terms of human capital. That can be accomplished only if government gives much higher priority to education at all levels. Without that investment the United States, and New York City, could become much less internationally competitive, and this is likely to aggravate existing socioeconomic inequalities, which the political system, as presently constituted, is not well-equipped to handle.[23]

Similar fears have been voiced by some of the leading partisans of globalization, including Klaus Schwab and Claude Smadja, the founder and director of the Davos Forum. In a recent *International Herald Tribune* article, they asserted that "economic globalization has entered a critical phase. A mounting backlash against its effects, especially in the industrial democracies, is threatening a very disruptive impact on economic activity and social stability in many countries. The mood in these democracies is one of helplessness and anxiety, which helps explain the rise of a new brand of populist politicians. This can easily turn into revolt."[24]

In a city such as New York, the positive and negative aspects of globalization are already apparent. There is a clear and compelling need for innovative policies to cushion the effects of economic dislocation and for a renewed vision for the future of this global city.

Cities

If nation-states are limited in their capacity to cope with globalization, cities are even less able to do so. According to Saskia Sassen, who contributed Chapter 11 to this volume, the growing role of such cities as New York, London and Tokyo has resulted from:

> The spatial dispersion of production, including its internationalization, [which] has contributed to the growth of centralized service nodes for the management and regulation of the new space economy. Major cities . . . have greatly expanded their role as key locations for top-level management and coordination. And the reorganization of the financial industry has led to rapid increases in the already significant concentration of financial activities in major cities. The pronounced expansion in the volume of financial transactions has magnified the impact of these trends. Finally, the reconcentration of a considerable component of foreign investment activity and the formation of an international property market in these major cities has further fed the economic core of high-level control and servicing functions. In brief, alongside well-known decentralization tendencies, there are less known centralization tendencies.[25]

As global cities these urban centers have acquired new functions: "first, as highly concentrated command points in the organization of the world economy; second, as key locations for finance and for specialized service firms; third, as sites of production, including the production of innovations . . . ; and fourth, as markets for the products and innovations produced."[26] Sassen posits, as a consequence, a reconfiguration of the traditional world order focusing on the triangular interaction of nation-states, transnational actors, and global cities, such as New York.[27]

The very process of decentralizing former concentrations of manufacturing in such cities as New York and Detroit has generated growth in management and business services, but not in every city. New York gained more than Detroit in the economic reconfiguration of the last few decades. The demand for more financial and management services was accompanied by an expansion of generalized consumer services, as well as the growth of government. This helps explain why government employment and business services came to replace manufacturing as the principal source of jobs in New York City.[28]

Growth within the United States has increasingly become sectoral and fluctuating with an emphasis on services rather than consumer goods. Even the highly touted growth of the sun belt and decline of the rust belt has not been consistent. As a consequence, national, regional, and local economic developments in the United States in recent years have not always lent themselves to broad public-policy prescriptions. Cities and regions increasingly require nontraditional policies that factor-in global as well as local realities. Public-policy formulation in this realm is made more difficult by changing occupational distribution with growth in high- and low-income jobs, the former helping to generate demand for the latter, particularly in the service sector. Such phenomena are clearly seen in New York City's increasing maldistribution of income, growth of the informal economy, and increase in poverty.

A recent analysis of seventy-four metropolitan regions in the United States suggests that effective responses to inner-city poverty and the erosion of the traditional economic base of many urban areas lies in integrating urban and regional planning. The study, funded by the Haynes Foundation, argues that the most successful respondents to global economic integration have been "regional groupings and business clusters" characterized by

> highly collaborative relationships between economic agents. Businesses are closely linked through supply/demand relationships, and public/private-sector partnerships are common. Continuing interactions lead to "dense" networks—what some analysts call "social capital"—that help a region's competitiveness. For example, the ability to rely on continuing and dependable suppliers helps firms reduce costs, while a high level of trust between economic and social actors allows for consensus on appropriate growth strategies.

In this context, inequality and poverty are anathema. They breed distrust and social tension and lower the skill base, or human capital, necessary for a competitive economy. It is little wonder that studies of regional metropolitan areas in the United States—which, by focusing on one country, control for differences in various nations' social tolerance for inequality—have found that those areas that exhibit more similar levels of income between city and suburb also tend to have faster economic growth across the entire metro region.[29]

The study further posits that community development corporations, which traditionally have been focused on "place based development," ought to become more regionally oriented. Having built up local expertise, bases, and networks, they have the resources that are necessary for informed and effective urban/regional planning. The National Community Building Network has already initiated meetings of community leaders to discuss how best to participate in more regionalized planning.[30] While many analysts argue that globalization is reducing the importance of the nation-state, others are finding an increased role for metropolitan areas in response to the impact of global trends.

Communities

New York has always been a city of neighborhoods and diverse communities—ethnic, religious, artistic, generational, and otherwise. It has also historically been identified as essentially a middle-class city, albeit with a substantial working-class population. The growth of New York as a middle-class city in the earlier part of this century was linked to the expansion of its manufacturing base. It was accompanied by rising wages, strengthening of workers' organizations, expanded government services, and the growth of the suburbs. The gradual shift away from production of consumer goods to specialized services in the last few decades has undercut the security of the middle class and the aspirations of the working class.

While new sectors, such as women, have been largely incorporated into the work force, particularly in the service sector, many such workers have been shunted into temporary or part-time labor, with low wages and no benefits—a far cry from the increased job security, benefits, and social mobility of the late 1940s and 1950s. Moreover, with the decentralization and increased mobility of economic production, workers and local communities have less leverage to influence the decisions of transnational economic actors than they previously did.

As O'Cléireacáin, Rosen, Murray, and Sassen note in this volume, income in New York is increasingly concentrated among senior executives and, to a lesser degree, technocratic professionals. Hence, the city is being molded less by the middle and working classes and more by

> the new high-income workers [who] are the carriers of a consumption capacity and consumption choices that distinguish them from the traditional middle class of the 1950s and 1960s. While their earned income is too little to be investment capital, it is too much for the basically thrifty, savings oriented middle class. These new high-income earners are primary candidates for new types of intermediate investments: arts, antiques, and luxury consumption. The conjunction of excess earnings and the new cosmopolitan work culture creates a compelling space for new lifestyles and new kinds of economic activities. It is against this background that we need to examine the expansion of the art market and of luxury consumption on a scale that has made them qualitatively different from what they were even fifteen years ago—a privilege of elites. The growth of a stratum of very high income workers has produced not only a physical upgrading of expanding portions of global cities, but also a reorganization of the consumption structure.[31]

New York's traditional role as both a commercial and artistic entrepôt has been intensified by such developments. The impact can be seen most clearly, perhaps, in the transformation of SoHo, originally an industrial zone, into an artists' redoubt and again into a center for high-income professionals and the services they desire. Indeed, the burgeoning of SoHo has led the way for an increasingly residential lower Manhattan, as high-income earners take up residence in office buildings vacated by some of the very companies that employ them. As a result of economic decentralization, Manhattan remains highly cosmopolitan and dynamic but is increasingly devoid of middle- and working-class neighborhoods.

The economic and social polarization of cities such as New York may require a new approach to resolving problems, one emphasizing individual engagement with the broader community through shared tasks and involving a more expansive concept of citizenship than one focused largely on the pursuit of individual rights[32]—thus, increasing the citizen's sense of responsibility for the community and contributing to social cohesiveness, tolerance, and the capacity to work together. According to Felix Rohatyn of Lazard Frères & Co., governmental promotion of a more involved citizenry "doesn't mean that government should be more intrusive than it has to be, but the market system on its own is not capable of dealing with all the problems of a very complicated society. You have to have a government that's willing to be intelligent and active in order to offset some of the worst problems that are being created."[33]

Recent research tends to support increased government-community cooperation to solve critical problems. School dropouts, drug use, and crime were found to be less in New York public-housing projects that had the highest degrees of social organization.[34] In addition, the Harvard political scientist Robert Putnam has documented that "social capital embodied in norms and networks of civic engagement seems to be a precondition for economic development, as well as for effective government."[35] Regrettably he has also found that in the United States there has been an erosion of social capital, particularly over the past twenty-five years, as well as a loss of trust among and within communities as well as between people and government.[36]

Community organizers in Chicago and Pittsburgh are experimenting with multilayered cooperative efforts, rather than the more traditional interest- or pressure-group organizing. Programs are devised via deal making among the relevant actors, with each group recognizing that it will probably have to make some concessions. While generally a slower process, the base of support is often broader and more stable and consequently the effort more likely to endure. The approach has sometimes demonstrated better results than more traditional adversarial methods rooted in interest-group politics.[37] It is also consistent with the Haynes Foundation study, which argued that community-based organizations need to help link urban and regional development plans.

The complexity of problems in New York City and elsewhere means a greater need for public and private resource development and creative strategies to encourage more expansive citizen and community involvement. Given the increased number of New Yorkers who are not citizens, any mechanisms developed need to ensure their inclusion as well.

Nationality and Citizenship

National identity has always been a somewhat contested concept in the United States. This is especially so in New York, which prides itself on being a city of immigrants. While nation-states confer citizenship, national identity is more amorphous and shifting. As more and more individuals live outside their countries of birth or citizenship, multiple identities have become common. Multiple identities and nationalities raise issues of civil and political equality and the rights and responsibilities of citizens. Furthermore, as historian Eric Foner has noted:

> The greater the substantive rights of American citizenship, the more important the boundaries of inclusion and exclusion. American history is

not simply the story of a fixed set of rights to which one group after another has gained access. On the contrary, the definition of those rights has changed as a consequence of battles at the boundary over the demands of excluded groups for inclusion. For example, after the Civil War and again in the 1950s and 1960s, the struggle for full citizenship by former slaves and their descendants inspired similar claims by other excluded groups and transformed what it is to be an American.[38]

The influx of immigrants into the United States in recent years has intensified the public debate over who is an American and, hence, who should benefit from governmental services. While new arrivals increasingly obtain citizenship, a good number also retain strong political, economic, and social involvements in their sending communities. These immigrants are better able to maintain such links because of advances in communication and transport. As Rob Smith indicates in Chapter 7, globalization has created more expansive political identities and communities. The question arises of how such developments will affect civil society and its relation to government, particularly if national identities and civic participation are more diffuse.

The question is particularly pertinent for New York City because it has been the destination for close to 15 percent of the immigrants arriving in the United States since 1990. As Joseph Salvo and Peter Lobo note in Chapter 6, 55 percent of New Yorkers are first or second generation immigrants. They have not only filled a substantial proportion of jobs in the service sector but also helped stabilize a number of neighborhoods and renew a good portion of the city's housing stock. Others have suggested that such heavy immigration is placing undue strains on public services as well as on job availability.[39] The mayor of New York, Rudolph Giuliani, has argued that immigration has helped staunch the erosion of the city's population base, enriched the human capital of the city, and made it easier for New York to compete globally. Furthermore, he has asserted: "The people who came through Ellis Island had the same look in their eyes as the people that now come through Kennedy airport. . . . They did the same wonderful things for us that the new people are going to do for us. We can't be afraid of people, then we become a nation and a city in decline."[40]

As the debate over immigration has intensified, more immigrants are becoming citizens and voters. In New York the number applying for citizenship doubled in the years 1992–95 to 141,235.[41] With both national and local elections increasingly being decided by less than 5 percent of the vote, new voters can be critical for a politician's fate. In addition, immigrants are beginning to organize legislative and ballot initiatives as well as run for office. Currently, two immigrants are serving on the New York City Council—Una Clarke from Jamaica and Guillermo Linares from the Dominican Republic.

While more immigrants are becoming U.S. citizens, sending countries are passing legislation allowing for dual nationality. In December 1996, the Mexican Congress passed a law allowing for dual citizenship that will affect some six million Mexicans in the United States. As Robert Smith indicates in Chapter 7, such action reflects the desire of the Mexican government to tap into the Mexican community abroad in terms of political and economic support. Other countries have taken the same step for similar reasons, including Colombia, Ecuador, and the Dominican Republic. The latter country, like a number of others, receives between 10 percent and 15 percent of its national income from its immigrants abroad who are an important source of investment capital.[42] The push by countries of origin to organize immigrant communities abroad will no doubt reinforce transnational and multiple political, as well as cultural, identities.

As Josh DeWind, Antonio Stevens-Arroyo, and Jay Kaplan note in Chapters 8, 9, and 10, the connection between national identity and citizenship raises critical issues for local schools, churches, and cultural institutions. These include not only their role in facilitating absorption, but also retention of one's original culture and identity. It also raises the question of how public institutions will be transformed by an increasingly transnational population. As Josh DeWind suggests, acculturation today is more additive than assimilative. Therefore, a "multicultural" conceptualization of "American," drawn from the diversity of the city, may be displacing more traditional notions and giving the city a competitive edge, economically and culturally, in an increasingly transnational world.

However, Jay Kaplan raises the issue of the degree to which the loss of shared cultural experiences might undercut civic life while at the same time globalization is contributing to a homogenization of culture. Hence, while the new New Yorkers are diversifying the city, culturally and otherwise, the question arises as to the degree to which they will find the common cultural arenas necessary to civic life and sustained involvement in problem solving.

Conclusion

New York City remains both a microcosm of global changes and an epicenter of global trends. The city has been central to the redefinition of international trade, global financial investment, marketing, media, and telecommunications technology. Indeed, in the past twenty years, New

York City has become more important, not less, in terms of global finance, investment, trade, and communications. The growth of the FIRE and new media sectors remains, however, no guarantee of the city's economic health, as competition intensifies in other parts of the country and abroad. In order to keep pace the city needs to increase its existing market shares, which requires a concerted effort in terms of strategic planning on the part of both government and business. The tendency for New York's growth rate to be under 1 percent in recent years suggests the degree to which much more needs to be done in terms of economic development.

Critical for improving New York's financial situation is a rethinking of its relationship with both Washington and Albany, since New York essentially has to play by rules of the game devised in those two cities. The U.S. federal system works to the disadvantage of cities. Hence, while U.S. monetary policy, changes in interest rates, and commercial policy have substantial impact on New York's economy, by and large the city does not participate in the basic decision making concerning them. Add to this federal and state tax policies that often result in less revenue being returned to New York than it provides, and there are clear problems in maintaining not only the city's infrastructure and services but also its human capital in order to attract business. Demand, for example, for highly trained workers in the expanding new media sector is being met primarily by newly arrived New Yorkers rather than by graduates of New York schools.

Recognizing the need for New York City to increase its efforts to attract international business, the authors in this volume believe that this objective requires a revamping of state and national commercial and banking legislation. Currently, banking regulations in the United States and New York state are aimed primarily at protecting the domestic market. As a result, New York is not as well prepared as a city such as London to compete internationally. The latter city benefits from the fact that it is its nation's capital and has a larger role in devising national economic policies than New York does.

Overall New York shares with other cities a series of problems including a tax base that has eroded or does not effectively tap the growth of new sectors of the economy, disadvantages relating to the federal system, particularly with respect to fiscal and commercial policies, and the increasing costs of providing social services. In addition, national political parties and institutions have not yet taken fully into account in their long-range strategies the reordering of the international system as a result of globalization. As a consequence, steps to deal with the impact of globalization on cities have by and large not been sufficiently debated in public-policy forums. Nor have many city governments initiated sufficient long-range planning to deal with the impacts of globalization.

In addition, little has been done to generate policies and programs that take into account the increasing integration of cities and suburbs. Recent studies by the National League of Cities and the Federal Reserve Bank, as well as the Haynes Foundation Solutions Research Program, have suggested that income growth in central cities and suburbs is linked. Successful economic strategies in metropolitan areas, therefore, are those that take into account inner cities, suburbs, and exurbs.[43] Increased coordination around such issues as environmental degradation, the utilization of public spaces, and public transportation could lead to more effective regional economic plans and increased influence with federal and state governments.

New York is a global city, moreover, in more than simple economic terms. Demographic changes and shifts in patterns of immigration have accentuated the links between global and local concerns. Not only is the city home to a large and remarkably diverse set of immigrant communities—which more than in any previous period of history remain linked to their sending communities—but also, as a global cultural and communications center, the political interplay and cultural expressions forged in New York are propagated in turn around the globe.

To date, the federal government treats international and global issues largely in a geopolitical, bilateral, and multilateral fashion and has not substantially integrated into national policy planning the impact of globalization on cities and regions. This places a considerable burden on local leadership, not only to devise innovative policies and programs, but also to push the federal government to think more in terms of integrating the needs of cities into U.S. foreign policy as well as U.S. domestic policy.

At the same time, cities such as New York can be major actors in promoting U.S. foreign policy goals, particularly in ensuring greater economic security for the nation and as laboratories for devising effective responses to global trends such as the growth in financial services, technology exports, and immigration. Advancing the interests of the nation and its cities are complementary and hence should be dealt with via increasingly coordinated strategic planning at the local, regional, state, and federal levels. Indeed, New York should use its convocatory power to call on other cities and regions with common problems and challenges to devise coordinated strategies and practices while recognizing specific local differences. These strategies would serve as a basis for lobbying state and federal governments for greater attention to urban and regional recommendations in terms of domestic and foreign policies. In addition, New York should be in the forefront of increasing coordination with global cities abroad in confronting common problems. Finally, the city should promote more public/private cooperation and greater participation by civil society in building more livable communities. It is time for New York to respond to the challenge of globalization by assuming a leadership role regionally, nationally, and internationally.

Notes

1. United Nations Research Institute for Social Development (UNRISD), *States of Disarray—The Social Effects of Globalization: An UNRISD Report for the World Summit for Social Development* (New York: UNRISD, 1995), p. 8.

2. Tim Cambell, as quoted in "Citadels of Power," *The Economist. A Survey of Cities*, July 29, 1995, p. 17.

3. UNRISD, p. 18.

4. The International Bank for Reconstruction and Development/The World Bank, *World Development Report, 1995: Workers in an Integrating World* (New York: Oxford University Press, 1995).

5. Peter Morici, "Export Our Way to Prosperity," *Foreign Policy 101* (winter 1995–96): 3–17.

6. Matthew Edel, "The New York Fiscal Crisis: Lessons for Latin America," in *Cities in Crisis: The Urban Challenge in the Americas* (New York: Bildner Center for Western Hemisphere Studies, Graduate School and University Center of the City University of New York, 1989), pp. 68–69.

7. O'Cléireacáin, Chapter 1, Table 1.1.

8. O'Cléireacáin, pp. 31–32.

9. David E. Sanger, "'Parting Benediction' by Lonely Liberal: Labor Secretary Reich Offers 'A Last Word' on U.S. Social Policy," *New York Times*, January 9, 1997.

10. Robin Broad and John Cavanaugh, "Don't Neglect the Impoverished South," *Foreign Policy 101* (winter 1995–96): 18–35.

11. Steve Lohr, "New York Forging Ahead in New Media," *New York Times*, April 15, 1996.

12. Michael Krantz, "The Great Manhattan Geek Rush of 1995"; "The New York Cyber Sixty"; James J. Cramer, "Playing the Futures Market"; David S. Bennahum, "Mr. Big Idea," *New York* (November 13, 1996), pp. 34–76.

13. Jessica T. Mathews, "Power Shift" in *Foreign Affairs* 76, no. 1 (January/February 1997): 52–56.

14. UNRISD, p. 13.

15. Washington Office on Latin America, *Mexican Insights: Mexican Civil Society Speaks to the United States* (Washington, D.C.: Washington Office on Latin America, 1995), p. 37.

16. UNRISD, p. 13.

17. Mathews, p. 57.

18. Richard Rosecrance, "The Rise of the Virtual State" in *Foreign Affairs* 75, no. 4 (July/August 1996): 45.

19. Ibid., p. 47.

20. Ibid., p. 52.

21. Steven Pearlstein, "We Are the World, Like It or Not: How the Global Economy Is Blurring the Boundaries of National Politics," *Washington Post National Weekly Edition*, December 9–15, 1996; Thomas L. Friedman, "Big Mac I," *New York Times*, December 8, 1996.

22. Rosecrance, p. 59.

23. Ibid., pp. 56–61.

24. Klaus Schwab and Claude Smadja as quoted in Thomas L. Friedman, "Revolt of the Wannabes," *New York Times*, February 7, 1996. For a critical view of economic globalization see William Greider, *One World, Ready or Not: The Manic Logic of Global Capitalism* (New York: Simon & Schuster, 1996).

25. Saskia Sassen, *The Global City: New York, London, Tokyo* (Princeton, N.J.: Princeton University Press, 1991), p. 324. These same processes have contributed to the migration of manufacturing from the Northeast and Midwest to the South and the West, and particularly to the border regions that are benefiting from the increase in production for export in Mexican plants. Hence, from 1970–92, "average manufacturing growth was 2.67% in California border cities and 3.38% in Texas border cities, compared to 0.65% in the state of California, 1.17% in the state of Texas, and −0.41% in the nation as a whole." Gordon H. Hanson, "Economic Integration, Intraindustry Trade, and Frontier Regions" in *European Economic Review*, 40 (1996): 945. The formation of the European Union has also stimulated a revival of provincial and urban networks in order to respond more effectively to the pressure of globalization and transnational actors.

26. Sassen, pp. 3–4.

27. For a somewhat different perspective, see John Mollenkopf and Manuel Castells, eds., *The Dual City: Restructuring New York* (New York: Russell Sage Foundation, 1991).

28. Sassen, p. 13.

29. Manuel Pastor, Jr., Peter Drier, J. Eugene Grigsby III, and Marta López-Garza, *Growing Together: Linking Regional and Community Development in a Changing Economy* (Los Angeles: Occidental College International and Public Affairs Center, 1997), p. 4.

30. Ibid., pp. 5–6, 15.

31. Sassen, p. 335.

32. Vickey Maier, "Strengthening Society through Citizens: The Legacy of the New Deal," *The Woodrow Wilson Center Report* 8, no. 3 (December 1996): 3.

33. Ibid.

34. Adele Simmons, "Restoring the Social Fabric: The Case for Collaboration," *The John D. and Catherine T. MacArthur Foundation Report on Activities, 1994* (Chicago: The John D. and Catherine T. MacArthur Foundation, 1995), p. 4.

35. Ibid., p. 5.

36. Ibid., pp. 5–6.

37. Ibid.

38. Eric Foner, "Who Is an American?" *culturefront* (winter 1995–96): 7.

39. Roy Beck, "Unfettered Immigration Has Costs, Too," *New York Times*, January 11, 1997.

40. Clyde Haberman, "Ellis Island Still Vexes Its Neighbors," *New York Times*, January 10, 1997.

41. Celia W. Dugger, "Immigrant Voters Reshape Politics," *New York Times*, March 10, 1996.

42. Somini Sengupta, "Immigrants in New York Pressing Drive for Dual Nationality," *New York Times*, December 30, 1996.

43. Manuel Pastor, Jr., "Growth Strategies Must Include the Poor," *Los Angeles Times*, December 8, 1996.

Chapter 1

The Private Economy and the Public Budget of New York City

CAROL O'CLÉIREACÁIN

NEW YORK CITY at the close of the twentieth century is the preeminent global financial marketplace. It is also America's media capital and boasts the nation's largest concentration of international corporate headquarters. As home to the United Nations, it attracts the world's most influential political leaders to the annual General Assembly. New York City's thriving entertainment industry and the world's largest collection of cultural institutions make it the most popular tourist stop for Americans and a major destination for foreign visitors.

Immigrants flock to New York from around the globe, producing an ethnic diversity unparalleled anywhere on earth. As a result local politicians and members of New York's congressional delegation feel entitled to thrust themselves equally into the U.S. foreign policy-making process and the domestic affairs of sovereign nations across the globe—from the "three Is" (Italy, Ireland, and Israel) to Haiti, the Philippines, Korea, and South Africa. Unlike many Americans, New Yorkers, most of whom have recent ties to the immigrant experience, view immigration as positive for the economy. Although viewing it as a source of strength for the city, New Yorkers question a national policy that leaves their city on its own to bear the huge service costs associated with this immigration.

The economic linkages between New York City and the rest of the world are, perhaps, less visible than the human ones, but they are just as important. National policy determining interest rates and the exchange rate of the dollar affect key sectors of the city's economy to a greater extent than they affect the economies of other U.S. cities. In the mid-1980s, the combination of President Reagan's loose fiscal policies and Federal Reserve Chairman Volcker's tight monetary policies generated an overvalued dollar. The resulting decline in the price of U.S. (dollar-denominated) assets attracted a flood of foreign investment into New York City real estate, sending commercial property values soaring to historic heights. In 1994 the hike in U.S. interest rates and resulting bond market crash cost New York City jobs, income, and significant tax revenue. At present, tourism, retailing, and theater are benefiting from a dollar whose (trade-weighted) value in 1995 was about 40 percent below the 1984 peak.

In the global twenty-four hour daily capital market, New York City is the Western Hemisphere's capital. It is home to the prime markets and the major institutions, to traders, analysts, and financial firms. Foreign banks must maintain a presence here. In the recent Mexican financial crisis, while policy decisions were made in Washington and Mexico City, the financial deals and new market instruments designed to deal with the crisis came out of New York City. The proliferation of multinational enterprises introduces the problem of extraterritoriality into local policymaking. Specifically, state and local business tax bases are being eroded rapidly by the ability of corporations, through intricate accounting, to shift their costs and profits to the sites in their global operations that minimize their taxes.

The expansion of global trade has thrust the city's major industries— banking, securities, insurance, accounting, publishing, film production, management consulting, and law—into the forefront of international commercial competition. These sectors make major contributions to overall U.S. exports of services. A new center for interactive information technology and services is emerging in New York, fostered by entrepreneurs looking to ride the next wave of global outreach from the tip of Manhattan, which has been a vantage point for global involvement since the arrival of the Dutch in the seventeenth century.

Nevertheless, New York City is finding it increasingly difficult to stay ahead of the competition and to foster its advantages, especially in providing a broadly skilled work force. While rapid technological changes are providing opportunities in some areas, they are also reducing the city's private- and public-sector job bases, particularly in commercial banking, which has lost 55,000 jobs (31 percent) since 1988.[1] It is becoming more difficult for the city's government to budget within its means. Both the city and state governments are overextended and are increasingly looking to nongovernmental organizations and institutions to provide needed services. There is a widening disparity in the wage distribution as well as in the earnings of residents. The city's rates of poverty and homelessness are among the highest in the nation.

The Private Economy

New York City's economy provides employment for about 3.3 million people and stands at the center of a thirty-county regional economy of about 10.5 million jobs. Every day hundreds of thousands of workers cross county and state borders to crowd into midtown and lower Manhattan, two of the nation's top three office districts.

Where the Jobs Are

New York City accounts for about 3 percent of all nonfarm U.S. employment, 4.5 percent of U.S. output and, as a high wage area, almost 5 percent of nonfarm U.S. payrolls. (See Table 1.1.) The city's economy has a leading share of the U.S. finance, insurance, and real estate (FIRE) sector, as well as of professional business services, with 43 percent of the national payroll in the securities industry, 24 percent of the advertising, 14 percent of the banking, 10 percent of the legal service, and 5 percent of the accounting and managerial consulting national payrolls.[2] However, these shares have been declining over the past twenty years.[3] Since all these are services the city "exports" to the rest of the country and to the world, growth is heavily dependent on outside factors. In addition to the FIRE sector, business services, culture and media, tourism, and most manufacturing constitute the city's "export" sector, while construction, retail and wholesale trade, transportation and public utilities, and health and human services constitute its "local market" sector.[4]

Predating national trends, the city's manufacturing sector has been in decline and its service sector on the ascent during the entire postwar period. Manufacturing job losses began as a trickle in the 1950s, accelerated to a hemorrhage at the rate of 5 percent yearly from 1969 to 1977, and continued downward throughout the booming 1980s and the stagnant 1990s. Manufacturing now accounts for about 225,000 jobs, roughly the size of business services, while a third of the jobs in the city are in the service sector. Service-sector job growth has resulted in increases in both high- and low-wage jobs. Legal, accounting, medical, and other professional and business services provide a number of highly paid jobs; personal and hotel services offer some of the lowest paid. The FIRE sector provides some of the highest paid employment in the country; roughly a quarter of the workers in this sector commute from the suburbs.[5]

**Table 1.1   New York City Employment by Sector, December 1995
(thousands of jobs, seasonally adjusted)**

Sector	Employment		
Total Private			2,789.2
Export		1,285.5	
Securities	144.9		
Hotels	34.1		
Culture and Media*	170.5		
Banking, Insurance, and Real Estate	325.5		
Manufacturing	216.0		
Business Services	231.4		
Professional Services	163.1		
Local Market		1,503.7	
Health Services	308.0		
Social Services	152.8		
Construction	87.6		
Retail Trade	365.1		
Wholesale Trade	194.6		
Transportation	125.3		
Other Services	218.0		
Utilities	52.3		
Total Government			534.7
Local	415.5		
State	51.8		
Federal	67.4		
Total Employment			3,323.9

*Publishing is included in Culture & Media, not in Manufacturing.
Source: Data from New York State Department of Labor. Seasonal adjustment and export/local sector by New York Office of the State Deputy Comptroller for the City of New York.

The current decade has not been a particularly good one for New York City's economy. From 1988 through 1992, during the most serious recession since the 1970s, the city lost almost 350,000 private-sector jobs. The effects of the protracted downturn, which started earlier, lasted longer, and was more damaging than the national recession, have proven hard to shake off. This slow recovery has resulted in the city regaining, from December 1992 through December 1995, less than a third of these lost private-sector jobs. Moreover, the government shed 45,000 jobs over this period, with the result that the city's total employment has increased by fewer than 65,000 jobs (18 percent) since the recovery.[6] With the majority of economic forecasts predicting a slowdown in the national economy as the millennium approaches, New York City will be lucky if its employment base holds steady.

For those at the bottom of the labor market, there is not much good news from the formal sector of this economy. About half of employed New Yorkers work in industries where the real wage is lower than it was five years earlier.[7] The government has ceased to be the employer of last resort and the source of new capital construction projects. New York's unemployment rate remains persistently high, at times exceeding the national average by as much as three full percentage points.[8] The proportion of the adult population active in the labor force, about 56 percent, is significantly below the national average of 67 percent. Indeed, it took almost a full decade of economic boom to lift the labor force participation rate of the city's residents to a peak of 59 percent in 1989. The rate has been declining ever since.

Yet, the city attracts a population that remains and does flourish thanks in part to a number of networks and ways of living that have come to be known as "informal." A lack of dependable data makes it very difficult to document the "informal" sectors of the economy, other than with partial and anecdotal observations. It is clear that a variety of informal economies existing in the city are linked through the flow of people, money, and goods to all corners of the globe. New Yorkers can testify to a thriving cash economy, much of which is off the books, though not attached to a criminal network, which provides jobs and services in both richer and poorer neighborhoods. In addition, the city has become increasingly aware of the more sinister side of globalization, including links to a world-wide illicit drug trade, bringing the drug economy and its impact into the city's neighborhoods, as detailed in the chapters by Peter Andreas and Clifford Krauss in this volume. Through its effects on family life, street, and school safety, this global link makes significant demands on the legitimate and formal economy as well as on the deployment of public (and police) resources.

Wall Street—The Hometown Industry

How well the city does in absolute terms or compared to the overall U.S. economy depends on international, national, and industry-specific developments. For example, the city's recent relatively slower employment growth compared to the nation's is explained in part by the fact that national growth in the 1990s was driven largely by residential construction and the manufacturing of consumer durables and capital goods, production not common to New York City.

Wall Street is New York City's hometown industry and dominates its economic fortunes. According to one recent economic analysis, "The securities industry has been the single most important determinant of short-term volatility and cyclical change in the New York City economy because of the substantial size and rapidity of changes in its profits, incomes and employment."[9] The 81,700 jobs gained in the securities industry in the 1980s alone accounted for a third of the private sector's new jobs. When the stock market crashed at the end of 1987, the rapid securities job losses from 1988 through 1991 spearheaded the downturn, while the jobs regained since 1992 have contributed strongly to the recovery, notwithstanding the pause caused by the turnaround in interest rates that devastated the industry during 1994. In 1996 the securities industry remained 9,000 jobs (6 percent) below its 1987 peak.

Despite the slow recovery in employment, the city's payrolls and tax revenues have been buoyed by strong income growth for the high earners. As Wall Street profits go, so go New York City's incomes. However, the likely longer-term impact of technology on the finance, insurance, and real estate sector should not be ignored. In the ongoing recovery, the role of the FIRE sector, generally, and of its highest paid component, the securities industry, specifically, on wage and income growth has been strong and positive. In 1993 the FIRE sector accounted for 15 percent of the city's jobs, but 27 percent of the wages; its securities component, which was responsible for only 4 percent of jobs, accounted for 14 percent of wages. Every securities job in the city, with an average salary of $130,456, is equal to 3.3 jobs in other sectors.[10]

The growth of wage income of city residents depends on changes in employment and average salaries. With little employment growth, the city's mix of high- and low-paying jobs has had, until 1994, a negative effect on wage growth. At the margin, the city is losing higher-paid jobs and gaining lower-paid ones, resulting in a declining average salary outside the FIRE sector.[11] Except for a short period of hiring in the securities industry, the changing job mix has been a drag on wage growth. This should continue to be the case into the foreseeable future, particularly with the expected loss of jobs in commercial banking as a result of bank mergers and consolidations. If the Wall Street profits and bonuses are strong enough, however, they can swamp the job-mix effect, resulting in a rise in the average wage.[12] For workers outside the FIRE sector, however, such a rise will have no direct effect.

The Public Sector

Under the U.S. Constitution, the powers not delegated to the federal government are reserved for the states. The framers made no mention of cities. Over time, however, the various states devolved powers, through home-rule arrangements, upon more than 80,000 local governing entities—cities, counties, school districts, and the like. The division of responsibilities and the delineation of services to be provided by all such local governing bodies varies widely from state to state, and even within states. In short, there is no standard definition of what constitutes a "city" as a public jurisdiction.[13]

A Creature of the State

There is no other city in the United States that compares to New York City in size, organization, and municipal authority. Most American cities share considerable authority and responsibilities with either overlapping or contiguous counties. New York City comprises five counties (called "boroughs"). It has sole authority over general municipal services (police, fire, sanitation, health, parks), as well as over public education. The only significant local authority it shares is with several regional transportation entities.[14]

New York State has the constitutional responsibility for the quality of life for all New York City's residents. Through municipal home-rule legislation, it delegates certain responsibilities to the city. As a legal "creature" of the state, the city is tied to Albany, the state capital, through a complex web of legal and fiscal arrangements.[15] The state controls all city tax rates, defines base growth, charges fees to administer the city's income and sales taxes, and has consistently prohibited anything other than a small flat tax on nonresident earnings in the city. The state provides funding for elementary and secondary education through a formula set each year, although the city's share of education aid is at least three percentage points less than its share of the state's students. The state sets standards for spending on education, criminal justice, and health and welfare services that the city must meet or face fiscal penalties and sanctions. Further, the health of the state's economy is strongly related to the strength of the city's economy: half of state tax revenues come from economic activity within the city and about 40 percent of the all jobs in the state are located in the city.

The City's Budget

New York State imposes fiscal burdens on New York City through mandates that are imposed in very few other states—largely for major redistributive programs. For example, welfare and Medicaid, the major income and health programs for the poor, cost the city more than $3.5 billion annually. The benefit levels for both programs are set by the state and federal governments. The federal government pays half the costs; New York State, in turn, passes half of its burden on to New York City. New York is one of only thirteen states requiring any local share for Medicaid and one of only ten states requiring a local share for welfare. New York City's local share, at 50 percent, is the highest in the country for both programs. To enable the city to fund these and other mandated programs, New York State has granted the city an unusual amount of local taxing power. As a result, local tax burdens are high, and New York has the lowest ratio of state taxes to local taxes of any state in the United States (except for New Hampshire)—only 94 cents for every dollar of local taxes.[16]

The city's $32 billion annual budget is the fourth largest in America, after the federal government and the state budgets of California and New York. Excluding intergovernmental transfer payments specifically targeted for welfare and Medicaid, the city's own funds, raised through a variety of taxes, fees, fines, and water charges, amount to almost $22 billion, or about 70 percent of the budget.

About *half* of this $22 billion is earmarked for nondiscretionary items, about $3.5 billion for the city's share of welfare and Medicaid; $3 billion each for debt service and education; and about $1.3 billion for pensions. The other "discretionary" half is allocated in roughly equal thirds of about $3.5 billion each for criminal justice (police, courts, prisons, probation); core neighborhood services (such as fire protection, sanitation, water, roads, bridges, public health, and parks); and to government administration (tax collection, salaries of elected officials, lawyers, and planners, and the upkeep of public buildings).

"Discretionary" and "mandated" are somewhat slippery terms when it comes to the city budget. To some degree, all of local government is mandated. Spending required by state or federal law and court orders, as well as bond covenants entered into with creditors, are all mandates. Certain other costs, such as wages and benefits, may be fixed in the short run but subject to change over the longer term; labor agreements entered into by one administration bind those that follow and may be categorized as self-imposed "mandates."

The city raises its own funds through a wide array of taxes, fees, fines, and miscellaneous revenues. The single largest revenue source is the real property tax, which brings in about $7 billion annually. In addition, New York City levies a number of taxes that are much more commonly imposed by state governments and are strongly linked to economic activity. The city collects almost $4 billion annually from a graduated personal income tax on residents; about $2.5 billion in sales taxes; and about $2 billion from a variety of business income taxes. Over the past two decades, city taxes have averaged about 10 percent of personal income, fluctuating in a narrow band, from a low of 9.2 percent in 1973 to a high of 10.3 percent in 1987.

Declining Federal Aid

With the rise of categorical federal aid to state and local governments in the 1960s, and the implementation of the program of General Revenue Sharing in 1972, federal aid became a significant source of revenue for New York City. Federal money paid for some basic city services, including police and fire protection, during the city's fiscal crisis of the mid-1970s. The Reagan administration (1981–89) cut federal aid dramatically, however. In 1980 one out of every five dollars New York City spent came from the federal government; ten years later, only one dollar out of ten came from the federal government. The cumulative loss of federal aid to the city's expense budget over the decade, controlling for inflation, was about $12 billion.[17]

Both New York City and State worked to replace much, although not all, of these lost funds. In the booming financial and real estate economy of the 1980s, the city was able to borrow to replace lost federal revenues. However, the strong recession that began at the end of 1988 closed off this option. If the city were able to count on the level of federal aid provided only fifteen years ago, it would have about $2.7 billion more per year in revenue—enough to cover the structural budget imbalance. That amount would be enough either to fund the entire police, housing, health, aging, and youth services departments combined or enable the city to eliminate all of its business taxes.

As the city approaches the new century, it faces four years of yawning budget gaps of from $2 billion to $5 billion annually. With one million residents on welfare (and Medicaid), and public school enrollment exceeding one million children and growing by 20,000 each school year, spending is rising significantly faster than the city's revenues. The persistence of this structural budget gap over three city administrations has resulted in two downgradings of the city's credit rating already in this decade. On notice that another downgrade is possible, and bumping up against the state constitution's limit on the amount of outstanding debt, the city's costs of adding to and servicing its large debt contribute seriously to the structural budget problems. The key to resolving this structural imbalance lies in reconciling the unfunded spending mandates that the state and federal governments place on the city with the limits on the city's competitive ability to tax.

Tax Policy: The Intersection of the Economic Base and the Public Budget

The health of the public sector is dependent upon the health of the private sector. In New York City's case, government revenues have become increasingly vulnerable to global economic forces. The city's major industries—banking, securities, insurance, accounting, publishing, film, management consulting, and law—operate in a global marketplace, as Saskia Sassen has aptly pointed out in her chapter in this volume. This means that the rules for trade and commercial licensing are being written elsewhere, leaving local policymakers to play catch-up.

The recent history of the property market is illustrative. In the 1970s the recycling of petrodollars had a significant impact on the London property market, producing a boom-and-bust cycle that was repeated in New York City's property market in the 1980s with the recycling of Japanese current account surpluses into dollar-denominated asset markets. The market for prime office space and significant properties, such as Rockefeller Center, is now a global one, with changes to foreign ownership representing an important element in the flow of foreign direct investment into New York and the United States. The city's revenues swell as property values soar and crash as they plunge, in fluctuations of billions of dollars. Flight capital from Hong Kong, directed at strategic purchases in lower Manhattan, as well as purchases of property in Flushing, Queens, has had an impact, along with decisions by major foreign-owned banks to demonstrate their presence in New York by putting up skyscrapers in midtown Manhattan, even though cheaper, prime space has been vacant downtown.

The city's revenue base has also become increasingly dependent on Wall Street—a rich, narrow, volatile, and mobile sector. Accounting for less than 15 percent of the city's jobs, Wall Street provides about a third of its tax revenues.[18] The city's tax revenues are highly dependent on a small number of payers, reflecting an income distribution in which the top fifth of households earns more than half of the total income.[19] The top 1 percent of the city's taxpayers now account for about 65 percent of property tax revenue, more than half of business income tax revenue, almost half of commercial rent tax revenue, and about a third of personal income tax revenue. Half the business income taxes come from the top thousand payers, fully 40 percent of whom are in the FIRE sector.[20]

These tax collections from the FIRE sector are as volatile as Wall Street profits. A significant share of personal earnings in this sector comes in the form of annual bonus payments. From the short-term perspective of the budget, revenue forecasts and collections are thus hostage to a small number of firms' annual bonus payout decisions, made in December, midway through the budget year. The importance of the finance sector derives not only from employment, but also from the high levels of profit and compensation. For example, the bond market crash of 1994 and the resulting cut in firms' profits was a major cause of the sudden $400 million revenue shortfall in the city's budget in the middle of fiscal year 1995, while the 1995 surge in the stock market and galloping mergers and acquisitions activity boosted fiscal year 1996 revenues.

Rapid technological advances permit a high degree of mobility in the financial services sector, with the result that city taxpayers are increasingly foreign businesses. Annual foreign investment averaged almost 4 percent of gross city product during the boom of 1985–89, and foreign ownership of businesses rose to $60 billion. More than 7 percent of private sector employees work in foreign-owned establishments and foreign banks account for 60 percent of city bank tax revenue. This high degree of mobility means that policymakers will have a hard time predicting where business growth is going to be and they will have to face increasing competition from other locations seeking this business.

The city's financial services firms have benefited enormously from the role of the dollar as an international currency. However, the dollar's international role as a means of payment, unit of account, and store of value is declining. The dynamic growth of the Asian economies may be expected to enhance the regional and global role of the yen at the expense of the dollar, while the European Union's planned monetary union will have a similar effect with respect to that part of the world. Both Japanese and European financial service firms may be expected to benefit and New York City's role to diminish. This element of changing market shares is beyond the city's, and perhaps even the U.S. Treasury's, control. While city-based firms are strategically positioning themselves in all markets, both employment and profits will likely be more globally diversified than they are now.

Taxes paid to the city are in addition to similar taxes paid to the state. And while the state legislature passes both city and state tax laws, it is only responsible for balancing the state budget. As a result, the state looks to the city for a significant portion of its personal income, corporate, and banking tax revenues.[21] Tension between the state and the city over tax policy and administration has been constant over the years. The state has all the power, setting the tax laws and rates, as well as collecting, for a fee, the personal income and sales taxes. The state, possessing equal constitutional standing with other states, must sign multistate tax agreements and deliver on voluntary cooperative arrangements reached through organizations such as the Federation of Tax Administrators. The city, although the country's fourth largest taxing jurisdiction, lacks constitutional standing and struggles to be heard on the national stage, facing the inability of some states to sign agreements with an entity other than another state. And, in dealing with other states, the city's tax specialists must first convince Albany as to the soundness of the city's case, strategy, or interpretation.

The global changes in banking and finance—the city's hometown industry—make close cooperation on taxation within New York crucially important. Unfortunately, Albany has often proved to be slow and reactive on international and bank tax issues. In part, the governor has generally avoided sending complex issues of business taxation to a legislature not controlled by his political party. In part, too, the bank tax status quo is a smaller problem for the state, which is less dependent than the city on the taxation of banking and finance, a tax base under fierce pressure from other states' predatory practices. And, too, the fair and efficient taxation of banks is a complex issue. Nevertheless, as this century closes, it is an issue that cannot be ignored. The competitive pressures on the ability of New York City to continue to rely on significant tax revenues from the taxation of banks and other financial firms engaged in growing global activity needs to be on the agenda of policymakers in Albany.

The city has become increasingly dependent on a narrower and more mobile tax base than is healthy. In addition, technology is reducing jobs and challenging the locational advantages of the city in many sectors of the economy, particularly in business services. Until significant new economic development takes place, it will not be easy to predict alternative sources of economic activity that might generate the taxes presently supplied by the large FIRE, law, accounting, architecture, and management consulting firms. The sales tax, as an alternative, is constrained by the open nature of the city's economy and by the tax policies of surrounding jurisdictions. The bordering states have lower sales tax rates. New Jersey exempts a number of popular items, such as children's clothing, and has created tax free zones for large retail development. State sales tax revenues throughout the country are suffering from slow growth and erosion because of increases in mail-order, cata-log, and, now, Internet shopping. Every state that has attempted to in-crease revenues by extending the sales tax to include significant types of services, such as advertising, has been forced to back down by fierce political opposition.

Increases in the residential property tax—the mainstay of local gov-ernments everywhere—have been put out of bounds in New York City, so far, by history and politics. Long-standing protection of homeowners from assessment increases has turned the nation's largest and richest stock of property value ($300 billion) into a wasting asset. The city's property tax is one of the least fair in the nation. Under state law, there are four classes of property in New York City, each of which may be as-sessed at a different fraction of market value and each of which pays a different tax rate. As a result, homeowners, who possess about 40 per-cent of the value of all property, pay about 12 percent of the bill. Com-mercial buildings, half of which are office buildings, represent about 30 percent of the value of all property but carry fully half the tax load. As a result of the built-in protections for residential property owners, a sharp drop in commercial property values, and a freeze on tax rates, the city will collect about $7 billion in property taxes in fiscal year 1996—$800 million less than it collected in fiscal year 1993, at the depths of the property market recession, and almost $200 million more than it expects to collect in fiscal year 1997.[22] Neither a series of administrative reforms that have highlighted the problems inherent in New York's property tax structure, nor the report of a 1993 study commission, presenting an agenda for change, has moved property tax reform onto any elected official's agenda, however.[23]

Conclusion

Cities are small, open economies. They are small in relation to the economies of the surrounding area, and they are open to the movement of people, goods, and money. This is as true of New York City as of other cities. Moreover, New York's economy is particularly vulnerable to rapid technological change, the globalization of financial markets, and new waves of immigration. New York City is now more than ever captive to forces beyond its control.

Yet, the advantages of location in New York City can be fostered by the public sector. In this task, New York City's government is increas-ingly on its own.[24] A new era of regionalism is not around the corner; rather, recent attempts at détente, if not actual cooperation, between New York, New Jersey, and Connecticut appear to have ended. Federal and state resources are not on the way, either, as those governments focus on balancing budgets as they cut taxes, and enter a new era of fiscal federalism marked by the devolution of significant spending responsibilities to local governments.

The city's best hope to affect its own economic destiny lies in building a public-private strategy for job creation based on global competitiveness. The public contribution takes three forms. First, a competitive state and city tax policy. Second, the city provides value in its public services. Third, city government, working with the private sector, serves as a facilitator for private economic growth. One mechanism has been the establishment of business improvement districts (BIDs). Another is to identify the areas for growth and provide a reasonable strategy to make it happen. A good place to begin is with the recommendations in *Strong Economy, Strong City*, issued by the Office of the Deputy Mayor for Finance and Economic Development in 1993.[25] A four-year strategy to create 25,000 new jobs, the focus is on the city's competitive advantages in the global marketplace—its highly specialized pools of skills, technology, and infrastructure that are tailored to the needs of particular businesses; its local suppliers of specialized inputs; its sophisticated and demanding local customers who pressure firms to innovate; the vigorous local rivalries; and, in the case of software, biotechnology, and other advanced industries, the presence of leading academic institutions. From these bases of strength, job creation would be targeted on nine industries that national forecasts indicate are expected to grow: biotechnology, software, apparel, jewelry, film and television production, recycling, health care, nonprofits, and retail.

These industries offer a wide range of jobs, skills, space requirements, and geographic location in the city and add different value to the city's economy. Biotech, multimedia, and film and television production blur the line between manufacturing and services, requiring blue- and white-collar skills. High-end apparel and jewelry already have demonstrated higher than national productivity, promising returns to be reaped by owners and workers (even, perhaps, the tax collector). High-end apparel and software have needed an industry focus in the city to raise their visibility nationally and locally. All of these industries need help to be globally competitive. This can be accomplished by strengthening trade associations, intervention at the federal level for export promotion resources and the creation of city-based export promotion programs, and by taking advantage of bilingual skills in the city's labor force.

Significantly, the private sector is recognizing its role in such a partnership. The New York City Partnership/Chamber of Commerce and several BIDs, particularly in the garment district and downtown, have been active in setting up new industry associations and helping to locate space and facilities to serve as the apparel industry and the new media/software industry focal points. Furthermore, the New York City Partnership has spent two years raising $100 million to capitalize a new investment fund to help finance specific projects that the private sector determines, usually in combination with significant public policies, will generate economic development.

More than anything else, the demands of globalization require flexible responses and adaptable, fleet-footed institutions and individuals with the necessary, specific skills. The foundation of that adaptability is the education system, as the corporate sector now recognizes. Since the late 1980s, more than two billion people have been injected into the global economy through the end of communism in eastern and central Europe and the reorientation of many countries, including China and India, toward more open economic systems. These changes are enlarging global investment flows and labor markets. With rapidly changing technology, these influences are working to widen the wage gap between the skilled and the unskilled. For example, in the United States in 1979, males aged 25–34 years old with a college degree earned 15 percent more than those with only a high school education. By 1993, the gap had widened to 55 percent. In the same period, the difference for women grew from 43 to 74 percent.[26]

While the skill premium has been rising, the city's high school performance has, unfortunately, been falling. New York City employers face a labor market filled with the growing ranks of city high school dropouts and unqualified graduates. Taking action to improve the quality of city schools must be a top public and corporate priority. Only then will New York City be working on all fronts to assure its place in the globally competitive economy.

Notes

1. During this same period, the rate of job losses in commercial banking nationwide was 7 percent (Office of the State Deputy Comptroller for the City of New York [hereafter OSDC], *The New York City Economy: Recent Trends and Implications for Income Distribution*, Technical Memorandum 3-96, March 1996 [hereafter Tech Memo 3-96], pp. 5–6).

2. OSDC, *Analysis of the City Economy*, Technical Memorandum 2-95, October 1994 [hereafter Tech Memo 2-95], p. 7.

3. See Rae Rosen and Reagan Murray's chapter in this volume.

4. This is the standard distinction made for regional economic analysis. The term "export" is used in place of the term "tradable." For a discussion of these sectors in the tri-state region, see Hugh O'Neill and Mitchell Moss, *Reinventing New York: Competing in the Next Century's Global Economy* (New York: New York University Urban Research Center, Robert F. Wagner School of Public Service, 1991); for a discussion of these sectors in New York City, see OSDC, *Recent Trends in the New York City Economy*, Technical Memorandum 2-96, November 1995 [hereafter Tech Memo 2-96].

5. *Tech Memo 2-95*, p. 32.

6. *Tech Memo 3-96*, p. 3.

7. Ibid., p. 13.

8. In 1995, for example, the average New York City unemployment rate was 8.2 percent compared with 5.9 percent for the nation as a whole.

9. *Tech Memo 2-95*, pp. 12–13.

10. Ibid., p. 36.

11. The jobs gained had an average salary of $38,500 while jobs lost had an average salary of $43,000. (*Tech Memo 2-96*, pp. 47–49).

12. *Tech Memo 2-95*, p.36, and *Tech Memo 2-96*, p. 45.

13. For example, in California, San Francisco is a coterminous county and city, with both sets of responsibilities, while Los Angeles and San Diego have overlying city and county boundaries. Chicago and Detroit are each part of larger counties; New York City comprises five counties. These states—California, Illinois, Michigan, and New York—specify very different city and county service responsibilities, taxing authority, grant revenues, and fiscal institutions.

14. The Metropolitan Transportation Authority covers some, but not all, commuter trains and the city subway system. The Port Authority of New York and New Jersey covers the harbors, airports, bridges, and tunnels.

15. Most state legislation handles New York City separately by referring to "cities over one million in population."

16. U.S. Advisory Commission on Intergovernmental Affairs, *Significant Features of Fiscal Federalism 1992*, vol. 2 (Washington, D.C., 1991), pp. 160, 172.

17. Over the same period, the federal government's budget priorities shifted. Washington went from spending $7 on the military for $1 spent on housing, to spending $46 on the military for every $1 spent on housing. The cumulative loss to the city's capital budget housing program was $27 billion.

18. This applies to taxes on economic activity only: the general corporation tax, banking corporation tax, unincorporated business tax, commercial rent tax, and personal income tax. It excludes the property tax.

19. *Tech Memo 3-96*, p. 12.

20. New York City Department of Finance, "Selected New York City Tax Revenue Information," mimeograph, 1991.

21. Until recently, the state levied a number of taxes directly on the city's base, including a statewide tax on gains from property transfers in excess of $1 million, and another on hotel rooms renting for more than $100 per night. Ninety percent of the revenues for both taxes came from the city. They resulted in significant losses of business, and both have been recently repealed.

22. The freeze was instituted by Mayor David Dinkins and the City Council at the depths of the property recession in 1992 and continued by Mayor Rudolph Giuliani. The Dinkins administration faced a pipeline of phased-in assessment increases that stabilized the tax base, so freezing the rates did not mean sacrificing significant revenue. That is no longer the case.

23. See New York City Department of Finance, *Final Report of the New York City Real Property Tax Reform Commission*, December 1993.

24. In this respect, many cities are in the same situation. The MEXNY21 project of the CUNY Graduate Center, for example, has found identical issues of matching the local, regional, and national politics to the needs of the changing economic base to be at the forefront of the problems confronting Mexico City's government and budget.

25. Economic Policy and Marketing Group, Office of the Deputy Mayor for Finance and Economic Development, *Strong Economy, Strong City: Jobs for New Yorkers. Job Creation Strategies for the Global City of Opportunity*, September 1993.

26. Richard J. Murnane, "The New Basic Skills," as reported in the Summer Newsletter of the Jerome Levy Economics Institute of Bard College, p. 19.

Chapter 2

Opening Doors:
Access to the Global Market
for Financial Sectors

RAE D. ROSEN WITH REAGAN MURRAY

NEW YORK CITY has long been the financial capital of the United States, the country's corporate headquarters, and the nation's center for news and media. Globally, it ranks with Tokyo and London as a leader in international finance. The city's businesses are known for their national and international orientation; New York is not a city of small shopkeepers focused on small local markets. Immigration and international tourism provide a constant influx of foreign-born residents and visitors, contributing to a diversity unequaled in most parts of the world. The volume of immigration is such that local officials frequently make their voices heard in Washington's foreign policy circles, and elected officials often attempt to influence the domestic policies of sovereign nations from Ireland to Haiti to Egypt.[1]

However, city and state officials must also begin to make their voices heard in Washington with respect to international trade negotiations on financial services. Beyond simply proclaiming the preeminence of the city's financial services, they must ensure the city's access to foreign markets even as they welcome foreign competition to their environs. This must be done because the city's share of the domestic financial services market is slowly eroding. The international markets for financial services are typically shielded by highly effective trade barriers. New York City and, consequently, New York State are likely to benefit more from changes in the regulatory structure and from the removal of barriers to international trade than are most other areas in the United States.

Therefore, city and state officials should focus on the international trade in financial services as a primary goal of economic development. Washington's negotiations in these areas will be critical to New York City's future growth—the policy results are potential large and far reaching.

At present, policies to enhance international trade in financial services are noticeably absent from the economic programs of the city and state. There are policies that address major "industrial clusters"—the latest term for such groups as the optical-related industries in Rochester, the computer-related industries in and around Poughkeepsie, and the fashion-related industries in New York City—and there are general policies to promote domestic economic growth, but little or no attention is being given to increasing access to international financial markets.

The Importance of Financial Services in New York's Economy

Financial services and related supporting businesses are the primary engines of growth, an important source of new jobs, revenues, and output for both New York City and New York State. These services account for 25 percent of the $500 billion gross output of New York State and closer to 30 percent of the output of New York City.[2] Significantly, finance is not only the dominant sector; it is also the fastest-growing sector. Over the past twenty-five years, the growth rate of financial output in New York State averaged 8.9 percent per year—the fastest growth rate of any major sector—compared to 6.6 percent for total gross state product excluding finance. The importance of this sector can also be demonstrated in terms of wages. Over the 1968–95 period, nominal wages in the city's financial sector grew 8.1 percent per year—the fastest growth rate of any major sector of the city's economy—compared to 5.6 percent for all other sectors.

These high rates of growth are not the only measure of the importance of financial services to New York City's economy. The effect of the faster growth rate is intensified by the level of wages in this sector, which surpasses all other sectors. In the first half of 1996, the average wage in the financial sector in New York City was $99,700, compared to an all-industry average (excluding the financial sector) of $37,600. Within the financial sector, securities employment wages averaged $169,500. A single job in securities generates 4.5 times more income than a single job in any other sector. Such wages are possible because the financial sector is characterized by wide profit margins, barriers to entry, and high productivity: just 14 percent of the labor force typically produces 26 to 30 percent of the city's total output. Moreover, because the financial sector is sensitive to fluctuations in interest rates, most of the variance in city and state income can also be traced to this sector—another measure of its impact on the economy.

Many business services are closely tied to the financial services industry. For example, New York City has the nation's largest legal industry. Each merger, acquisition, hostile takeover, new issue, or initial public offering undertaken by Wall Street and the commercial banks requires extensive legal work. Accounting, public relations, advertising, insurance, and commercial real estate firms also provide major support services to the financial sector. Even the city's printing industry is tied to the financial sector through the demand for prospectuses.

New York's Decreased Market Share

Depending upon the indicator, New York's share of the domestic market for financial services is stagnating or declining. The financial sectors of other U.S. cities are growing at a faster pace than New York City's as the city cedes market share to midsized cities as well as large metropolitan areas. Measured simply as a percentage of national employment, financial employment in New York City has dropped from 13 percent to under 7 percent over the past thirty years. As seen in Table 2.1, the largest and generally older industrial cities have lost market share while the share of the smaller metropolitan areas has grown (the shaded section of the table).

Although this decline has been a slow one, the cumulative impact has been significant. Other cities are adding financial jobs at a faster pace than New York City, and some are attracting whole industries or parts of industries. For example, thirty years ago, New York City was the nation's headquarters for the insurance industry, accounting for more than 12 percent of all insurance employment in the country; by 1996, it accounted for just 2.3 percent. Now the banking and securities industries are increasingly relocating their back-office operations from the city to South Dakota, New Jersey, and Florida. Other older industrial cities like Chicago, Los Angeles, and Philadelphia have also lost market share to fast-growing areas of the Sunbelt—Orange County, Fort Lauderdale, Atlanta, San Diego, and Phoenix—and to "newer" cities such as Seattle.

A more refined measure of the concentration of employment is the location quotient or relative market share. For example, if 3 percent of New York City's labor force were employed in hat making compared with 1.5 percent of the nation's labor force, the location quotient for New York City's hat industry sector would be 2. For its size, the city would have a hat industry that is twice as large as would be expected.

Table 2.1   **Distribution of Financial Employment, 1965–1996**
             (percentage of total U.S. financial employment)

	1965	1975	1985	1995	1996
New York	13.1	10.1	8.5	7.0	6.8
Los Angeles-					
Long Beach	4.8	4.4	4.2	3.3	3.1
Chicago	5.3	4.7	4.4	4.4	4.4
Philadelphia	2.9	2.6	2.4	2.3	2.2
Detroit	2.0	1.9	1.6	1.6	1.6
Houston	N/A	1.4	1.8	1.4	1.4
Boston	N/A	2.2	2.2	2.2	2.2
Nassau-Suffolk	0.8	1.0	1.1	1.2	1.1
Orange County	0.4	0.7	1.2	1.2	1.2
Miami-Hialeah	0.8	1.0	1.1	1.0	1.0
Fort Lauderdale	0.3	0.4	0.6	0.6	0.6
Atlanta	N/A	1.4	1.5	1.7	1.8
Seattle	0.9	0.9	1.1	1.1	1.1
Minneapolis-St. Paul	N/A	1.3	1.4	1.6	1.6
San Diego	0.4	0.6	0.8	0.8	0.8
Tampa-St. Petersburg-					
Clearwater	N/A	0.7	1.0	1.0	1.0
Sacramento	0.3	0.3	0.5	0.6	0.6
Columbus	0.6	0.8	0.8	1.0	1.0
Charlotte-Gastonia-					
Rock Hill	N/A	0.4	0.5	0.7	0.7
Salt Lake City-Ogden	N/A	0.4	0.4	0.6	0.6
Middlesex-Somerset-					
Hunterdon	N/A	0.2	0.5	0.6	0.6
Orlando	N/A	0.3	0.5	0.6	0.6
West Palm Beach-					
Boca Raton	0.2	0.3	0.4	0.4	0.4
Austin	N/A	0.2	0.4	0.4	0.4

Calculations: Federal Reserve Bank of New York.
Source: U.S. Department of Labor, Bureau of Labor Statistics.

The larger the number, the greater the intensity of New York's employment relative to the nation as a whole. So, the impression of a casual observer that New York City has an unusually large number of people employed in the securities industry is correct, in the sense that it has proportionately 9.5 times as many people employed in securities as does the nation as a whole. Over time, the location quotient may rise or fall as employment grows more rapidly or slowly in the city, compared with elsewhere in the nation (as illustrated in Table 2.2).

Table 2.2 New York City's Relative Concentration of Employment, 1975–1996[1]

	1975	1985	1995	1996
Supporting Services				
Business Services				
(Public Relations,				
Computer Services, etc.)	2.57	2.08	1.18	1.20
Legal Services	2.42	2.42	2.63	2.64
Engineering and Management Services	N/A	1.26[2]	1.21	1.23
Financial Services				
Depository	N/A	2.26[2]	2.19	2.15
Securities	9.20	9.92	9.73	9.52
Insurance	1.71	1.43	1.24	1.24

[1] Represents the ratio of the market share of financial employment in the metropolitan area to the market share of U.S. financial employment.
[2] Figures are for 1988.
Calculations: Federal Reserve Bank of New York.
Source: U.S. Department of Labor, Bureau of Labor Statistics.

The relative concentration of financial jobs and supporting service employment has declined from 1975 to 1996. The legal sector does not fit neatly into the table as concentration peaked in 1996 at 2.64. But the sector began to shrink in relative importance in late 1996, and the relative concentration had declined to 2.57 as of May 1997.

Yet another way of looking at the importance of the city and state financial sectors is to calculate the city and state share of the nation's gross domestic output of financial services. As is clear in Table 2.3, New York State's share of U.S. financial output has declined since 1969. Be-

Table 2.3 Market Share of Financial Output, 1969–1996

	1969	1975	1985	1995	1996
Financial Earnings					
New York City Primary Metro-					
politan Statistical Area as a					
percent of U.S.	16.2	13.6	15.9	15.8	16.0 (est.)
Gross Domestic Product Financial					
New York State as a percent of U.S.	14.3	11.6	13.0	12.9[1]	—
Financial Earnings					
New York State as a percent of U.S.	19.4	16.7	18.9	17.9	18.1

[1] 1994.
Calculations: Federal Reserve Bank of New York.
Source: Bureau of Economic Analysis.

cause of lack of industry detail and problems with the timeliness of gross product data at the city level, it is more useful to make comparisons on the basis of industry wage data, a close substitute for gross city output.

Here, too, despite the unusually high level of wages in the city noted earlier, the city's share of all U.S. financial wages has stagnated or slowly declined over the longer term. As would be expected, a comparably slow decline is also evident in state wages. In short, New York State's and New York City's share of the nation's financial paycheck is not growing. Taken together, the long-run data on financial wages and output suggest that New York City's market share of financial services is stagnating or slowly deteriorating compared with the market share of other major cities.

Why Has New York Lost Market Share?

The factors that underlie the erosion of New York City and New York State's financial market share are both regional and national. Moreover, they are so strong that even a major gain in aggregate U.S. financial employment—an unlikely occurrence—would not significantly increase financial employment in New York City. The United States, with more banks per capita than most European nations, has more banks than it needs, and the banking industry is contracting. Mergers, acquisitions and, more recently, the establishment of bank branches within supermarkets are accelerating the job losses in this sector. As a result, New York City and New York State, which are home to a disproportionate number of banking headquarters, are encountering a disproportionate loss of banking employment. Advances in technology have also boosted productivity and reduced employment requirements of banks in general. The cumulative effect of these changes is a 6.2 percent loss in bank jobs nationwide since 1990, but a 32 percent decline in New York City— a loss of 34,900 jobs, equal to 1 percent of the city's total employment.[3] Regional analysts and industry analysts expect the job losses to continue through the end of the century, albeit at a slower pace, as banks prepare for increasingly intense competition.

Securities firms, investment banking firms, and legal firms are following the banking industry's lead. The *Red Book*, a directory of security dealers, has shrunk over the years from a thick book to a slim volume as closures, mergers, and acquisitions have reduced the number of securities firms. Over the past ten years, the number of member firms in the New York Stock Exchange has fallen more than 20 percent. Each completed merger or acquisition reduces demand for other business and financial services, such as outside legal counsel, accountants, and real estate. Most notably, legal employment has declined sharply, falling 10 percent in New York City since 1990.

There are also regionally specific factors depressing financial employment. The high level of competition among financial services firms mean that they must continually look for ways to innovate and reduce costs. The high cost of doing business in the city also puts constant pressure on firms to consider relocating as advances in communications and computer technology make it possible for firms to relocate staff functions far from New York City. If the function can be mechanized, making routine what was formerly unique, the function is a candidate for relocation to low-cost operating areas such as South Dakota, Florida, and New Jersey.

Two other regional factors contributing to New York City's diminished market share are the faster growth and increasing sophistication of smaller metropolitan areas, and the maturity and slower growth of the city's business community. As smaller cities have come into their own, their need for sophisticated local financial services and related businesses has increased. Fast-growing populations in such places as North Carolina, Arizona, and Florida also stimulate local demand. In contrast, New York City has a mature economy with a large established industrial structure that can fill incremental demand through additions rather than wholesale new provision of services. These trends are clear from the data in Table 2.1, which point to the growing market share of financial services and related business employment in midsized cities across the United States.

Structural factors and factors of taste and preference also limit growth in New York City. Population growth has been slow to negligible, and in recent years has occurred only because of large-scale immigration from other countries. Large corporations continue to leave the city seeking cheaper labor or different amenities. The slow growth of the local population means that local demand for financial services is also growing slowly, while the decline in the number of corporate headquarters means that nationally oriented demand for New York's financial services is also declining. If the local demand for financial services were growing in tandem with a rapidly rising local population, as in Florida or North Carolina, local demand might offset the loss associated with the relocation of major corporations, but such is not the case.

Tapping the Global Markets

In order to grow, individual financial firms can cannibalize the domestic market and prosper, but New York City and New York State have a stake in the prosperity of the industry overall—simply because of the number and kinds of financial services firms located in the city and the state and the number of other business services that are dependent upon the financial services sector. When the prospects for job growth in the domestic financial markets are weak, the city and state could improve the job outlook by increasing the access of domestic firms to international markets.

The advantages in doing so would be numerous. Increased financial business abroad would increase the need for financial and business headquarters staff in the United States, particularly in New York City and New York State. Size counts in financial transactions. Institutions with the largest asset base and greatest access to capital are in a stronger position to market their products. In growing their international business, domestic firms are also likely to improve their competitiveness in the domestic market.

Moreover, the prospects for growth in international financial services are strong. The conversion of the command economies of the former Soviet Union and Eastern Europe to market economies and the continued development of emerging economies will require major investments in infrastructure that in turn will require large-scale financing. The growth of the monied classes and the ongoing structural adjustments such as pension reform in developing countries promises increased demand for private financial services in insurance, mutual funds, stocks, and brokerage. These opening markets are tailor-made for the financial services and products that have been developed by New York City's financial institutions. A focus on gaining access to international financial markets would play to the strength of the city's financial services sector, which excels in the creation, marketing, and delivery of sophisticated financial products by drawing on the city's skilled financial labor force—the talented supporting pool of accountants, advertising executives, and marketing personnel—as well on its advanced technological infrastructure.

Obstacles to Access

Historically, U.S. trade policy has been primarily concerned with manufactured goods. Recognition of the importance of service exports and of the potential volume of financial and business services abroad has been slow in coming among state and local officials. In addition, the impediments to international trade in financial services—such as restrictions on the number of U.S. banks permitted to operate in a country, the prohibition against U.S. insurance companies and pension funds, and the restrictive limitations on U.S. market share in many foreign countries—are just becoming apparent to many elected officials.

Even though the New York region has the dominant share of the nation's financial institutions, these institutions do not speak for the region. Competitive issues usually keep the commercial banks, life insurance companies, and investment banks at cross-purposes, so they are unlikely to lobby free-trade issues jointly, and they have no particular reason to view problems from a regional perspective.

In the fall of 1995, the Uruguay round of the General Agreement on Tariffs and Trade negotiations addressed the subject of trade in financial services but no consensus was reached. Today, U.S. financial institutions and related businesses encounter trade barriers in developed nations, such as Canada and Japan, as well as in developing economies, such as Mexico, Chile, Argentina, and India. When trade negotiations resume, the negotiations on international trade in financial services will be characteristically slow, lacking definitive timetables for implementing change and maintaining purposefully vague transition periods.

However, these trade negotiations are of critical importance to the economies of New York City and New York State. It is therefore imperative that the city and the state broaden their economic development programs to include international trade in services. City and state officials must be able to speak knowledgeably about the complex issues involved, both to spur negotiations and to keep them focused.

Business, political, and media leaders tend to take the international prominence of New York's financial services sector for granted. As the economy of the nation, state and city made the transition from a manufacturing base to a service base, the financial sector was typically profitable and a source of job growth. Manufacturing, while generally profitable, was a major source of job loss. And job losses tend to garner political attention. Until recently, little thought was given to the promotion and development of financial services, possibly because financial services seemed to be doing "okay," and few thought to ask if the financial sector could do better. Today neither the city nor the state has a plank in its economic development plan aimed at increasing access to international trade in financial services. Trade policy remains firmly rooted in manufactured goods. While the city and the Port Authority of New York and New Jersey run international trade missions to promote the sale of manufactured goods, they do little to promote the foreign purchase of financial services in mutual fund management, underwriting, insurance, and commercial banking, all areas in which New York City excels.

Regulatory restrictions also impede the competitiveness of U.S. financial firms in the global marketplace. Policymakers routinely need to consider not only the domestic but also the international implications of their regulatory policies. The U.S. regulatory structure largely reflects domestic concerns. However, a greater sensitivity to the implications of such regulations for international trade in financial services could well lead to changes in regulatory policy that would enhance the competitiveness of U.S. firms abroad without compromising domestic concerns. For example, Alan Greenspan, chairman of the Federal Reserve, has spoken out in favor of repealing the Glass-Steagall Act and is attempting to ease the regulatory restrictions on the amount of revenue a bank can make from a securities affiliate. Such a change would improve the competitiveness of U.S. banks in both the national and international markets.

Given the importance of the financial services sector and related businesses to the economies of the city and the state, city and state officials should take an active role in the development of international trade policy in this area. New York's economic development officials should push for faster transitions to free operations, less open-ended resolutions, and more timely meetings in the trade policy discussions. As we have noted, the region's financial institutions cannot themselves adequately represent regional interests in trade policy. Now the GATT negotiations have been superseded by the negotiations of the World Trade Organization, but the noticeable absence of regional representation continues. Yet, the city and the state stand to benefit more from increased access to international financial markets than almost any other city or state in the country.

Leveraging New York's Strengths

New York City's financial institutions offer unparalled depth and liquidity. By depth and liquidity we mean the ability to transact financial business regardless of the size of the loan, the new issue, or the block of stock. The financial institutions in many countries cannot handle the very large transactions that move smoothly through the large U.S. markets. New York's stock exchange offers both, plus anonymity (which is important to organizations that do not wish to reveal their strategic goals). These characteristics are not duplicated in the Hong Kong, Singapore, Frankfurt, or Paris markets. In theory, online trading would permit the functions of New York's financial exchanges to be relocated almost anywhere in the world. However, during the stock market corrections of July 1996, there were numerous reports of people unable to contact their electronic exchange for several hours. Of those who made contact, many were unable to verify that their transactions had been executed and, indeed, some transactions were apparently placed but not executed. Clearly, the issue of the depth and liquidity of the new electronic exchanges is still an open question.

New York City also has the specialized labor force necessary to create, support, and effect sophisticated financial transactions. There are twice as many financial specialists and related business service professionals in New York as there are in London.[4] Tokyo lacks the supporting staff of business professionals with expertise in British and American law under which most international business transactions are negotiated.[5] Comparisons with Paris, Frankfurt, Hong Kong, and Singapore are equally favorable to New York. For example, the number of New York City's business and financial employees exceeds the entire population of Frankfurt.

The fact that most business transactions are negotiated under British or American law is an additional factor in New York's favor since international business transactions tend to be negotiated where the legal experts in British and American law are concentrated. As a result, follow-up transactions requiring financing are also likely to be negotiated in the same place. This also means that, in practice, the New York courts are frequently the adjudicators when problems arise. To the extent, therefore, that the law governing these transactions can be made more transparent, a greater number of contracts are likely to be negotiated in New York. For example, New York State's law was recently rewritten to narrow the basis for third-party liability in workman's compensation lawsuits. This was a step in the direction to improve the competitiveness of New York corporations. Under the old law, an injured worker could generally sue both his employer and a typical tangential, but deep-pocketed, third-party. This broad basis for liability discouraged some would-be New York corporations and helped boost the rates for workman's compensation to among the highest in the nation.

The issues surrounding international trade in financial services are too critical to the future of the state and the city for local officials to abdicate the setting of timetables and agendas for negotiations in this area to federal officials. New York's leaders, city and state, must take an active role in this process so that such negotiations not only do not falter but are continued with greater urgency. Only then will New York be able to build on its strengths in financial services as it enters the twenty-first century.

Notes

The views expressed in the paper are those of the author(s) and are not necessarily reflective of views at the Federal Reserve Bank of New York or the Federal Reserve System. Any errors or omissions are the responsibility of the author(s).

1. See Carol O'Cléireacáin's chapter in this volume.

2. Gross state product and gross city product are comparable to national gross domestic product. These figures and the wage data are from the U.S. Bureau of Economic Analysis.

3. United States Department of Labor.

4. The City Research Project, "The Competitive Position of London's Financial Services" (London Business School, March 1995), p. xi.

5. Japan Center for International Finance, "Options and Strategies of Foreign Financial Institutions, Regarding the Tokyo Money and Capital Markets" (December 1995), p. 8.

Chapter 3

"Cyberopolis":
The Cybernetic City Faces
the Global Economy

EDWARD MOZLEY ROCHE

TODAY the city faces two major challenges—the cybernization of organizations and the globalization of the world's economy. How the city of today responds to these challenges will determine how it fares in the daunting competitive struggle it faces as a single economic unit in a rapidly globalizing market.

Cybernization is driven by the ongoing rapid advances in computer and telecommunications technologies. According to Moore's law, the price/performance of microelectronics halves every eighteen months. This provides a strong stimulus for the proliferation of information technology. In addition, the astounding growth of the Internet has started a wave of innovation as profound as that resulting from the invention of the telephone. Improvements in data-processing methods promise to revolutionize delivery of services and introduce more flexibility into the tired bureaucratic structures that characterize most city governments.

Globalization has had enormous impact on multinational corporations (MNCs), which now account for more than 70 percent of world trade. Although these international business enterprises have existed since the foundation of the *Verenigde Oostindische Compagnie* in 1602, the twentieth-century expansion of a liberal international trading regime and the development of technologies permitting real-time management coordination between headquarters and subsidiaries have vastly accelerated globalization.[1] Multinational corporations continue to restructure their administrative machinery, avoiding the need to duplicate functional areas in each country.

The scale of their operations make MNCs difficult to regulate at the international level.[2] At the local level, also, these global enterprises pose a regulatory challenge to even the most powerful cities in which they operate. The survival of cities such as New York is tied to the development of a regulatory framework more cooperative and farsighted in its linking of interests between such enterprises and local government—relations that will result in benefits for both business and the public. In order to accomplish this, the capacity for New York to respond effectively to the needs of existing enterprises, as well as cutting-edge sectors, needs to be frankly assessed and pragmatic recommendations made. This requires analysis of recent developments in the cybernization of business and city government, as well as identification of the requirements and costs of taking advantage of opportunities such as the emergence of technologically advanced sectors related to the Internet. In this way, the city will be able to compete effectively in an increasingly global economy.

Cybernization of Business

One far-reaching result of cybernization is the breakdown of that traditional Weberian hierarchy, which in both the private and public sectors has so long been the dominant organizational paradigm. Based on an information model in which reporting flows upward and control flows downward, with information creation at the bottom and information consumption at the top, the accuracy of Weber's model is such that traditionally we have seen this type of hierarchy with its fixed spans of control in almost every human institution, including taxpaying businesses and city governments. The hierarchical form, however, is by no means the only possible paradigm available to organizations.

In contrast, the emerging "networked" organizations are able to utilize intensive arrays of information technology to simplify internal business transactions and decision-making processes so that middle management's role is diminished and the Weberian structure is passé. In some cases technology has such force that the organizational structure is itself transformed into a confederation of flexible "islands" of decision making with managerial control arranged horizontally along a value-added chain.[3] As the network firm matures, the classical Weberian hierarchy is no longer needed for functional control of the organization. In contrast to traditional arrangements, the networked organization is able to work effectively while employing a considerably smaller number of persons. From the point of view of the city, however, the networked firm may mean less employment creation and even massive layoffs.

The Virtual Firm

At the end of the process of cybernization lies the "virtual firm"—a new form of industrial organization in which the firm has broken down even further into legally separate companies that act together as a business utilizing a complex web of contractual arrangements.[4] Only the "core competencies" of the firm remain "inside," everything else is "subcontracted" to others.[5] A good example is Nike shoes, which neither manufacturers nor distributes shoes, these functions being subcontracted out.

The virtual firm is not a passing phenomenon; rather, it appears to be an emerging and possibly more successful economic form. The failure of the Massachusetts-based Route 128 companies, Digital Equipment and Wang Computers, in contrast to the stunning success of California's Silicon Valley companies, Hewlett Packard and Sun Microsystems, reveals the strengths of this model of organization.[6]

The success of the virtual firm model has been attributed to several factors:

1. The *pace of innovation* is increased because quick alliances can be set up to take advantage of the most advanced technologies and methods in use at other firms—rather than having to duplicate these innovations internally.[7]

2. The *supply of labor* is improved since outsourcing of work to lower-cost regions is the norm. This guarantees a wider choice of employees without the same level of commitment. Labor is more easily "imported" from low-wage, high-skill areas;[8] this can damage the employment base in the city whose employees are replaced by remote workers.

3. The *cost model* of the virtual organization is radically different. Not being forced to rely on internal resources, it is able constantly to search the market for least-cost solutions, many of which are found overseas in developing countries.

4. *Flexibility* is enhanced because it requires less time and costs less to restructure a virtual firm than a traditional firm. Rapid build-up and tear-down of organizations becomes possible, resulting in a type of agile instability better able to respond to competition. This organi-

zational churn inevitably influences the metropolitan tax base, particularly if it is based on assumptions no longer valid about the stability of firms.[9]

Cybernization of City Government

Information technology has also provided great opportunities for city governments to reengineer how they operate and deliver services.[10] Salem, Oregon, for example, has created a computerized bidding system for government purchasing, radically simplifying the request for proposal (RFP) and bidding processes. Orange County and Palm Springs, California, are adopting similar mechanisms. Automated eligibility systems for Aid to Families with Dependent Children (AFDC), Medicaid, and food stamps, for example, have saved millions of dollars.

Financially hard pressed cities and states have turned to technology for major cost savings. Los Angeles has instituted fingerprint identification to verify eligibility for benefits, thereby saving millions of dollars within months. St. Paul, Minnesota, is replacing checks with electronically coded cards, which can be used in regular bank-cash machines. Ohio is developing a "smart card" for identification purposes that will include a digital driver's license and enable holders to register vehicles and order license car plates at public kiosks.[11] New Orleans is using an automated voice-response system to handle more than 1,200 calls per day by its citizens making queries regarding public services. Phoenix has developed a comprehensive plan to use computers to "reduce the cycle time" for providing services to the private sector.[12] Hawaii has implemented an online system using public terminals to give citizens access to legislative information, electronic mail, and bulletin board services, as does Arizona's "Aztel" system. Alabama is using an imaging system to scan birth certificates and supporting documentation, thus lowering the costs of retrieval. Waiting times in Kentucky have been reduced from five hours to less than 30 minutes through the use of artificial intelligence to aid in delivery of public services such as taxation inquiries, licensing (renewals), and general inquiries for forms. Jacksonville, Florida, has improved its tax collection system.[13] (For a summary of ways in which new technologies may help city governments, see Table 3.1.)

Despite these pilot efforts, governments on the whole lag far behind in adapting innovative technology, particularly at the state and municipal levels. For example, although automatic teller machines (ATMs) were created in 1971, they are only now coming into wide-

Table 3.1   New Technologies Benefiting City Governments

Artificial Intelligence
Use of expert systems to help make routine decisions using standardized information

Client/server computer
Movement away from mainframe computers toward more flexible and decentralized systems[14]

Electronic data interchange
Replacement of trade documents with electronic standardized messages transmitted between nodes

Geographic information systems
Electronic mapping databases used to model the structure of a city

Image processing
Use of scanners to file and retrieve documents electronically using "workflow" software

Interactive broadband networks
Substantially increase the amount of information that can be transmitted

Kiosks
Automatic teller-like machines in public places give citizens access to public services and information[15]

Object-oriented databases
New programming techniques and modular construction

improve applications development

Smart cards
Provide better tracking of benefits without having to build large-scale interactive online networks

Videoconferencing
Improves coordination between agencies in providing services to citizens and private enterprise

Voice-recognition systems
Automation of routine telephone calls that interface with computer records

Wireless communications
Increase the mobility and geographic distribution of computer database access

Groupware
Group decision support systems for issue analysis and brainstorming[16]

Intranet
"Internal Internets" simplify delivery of complex multimedia information

Internet
Opens city government databases to the public and promotes "electronic democracy"[17]

spread use in the public sector. Governments have been slow to innovate and deserve the criticism they receive for not taking advantage of the savings and greater efficiency that would result.[18] Few city governments have confronted the challenge of reengineering because of the costs and massive layoffs such reorganization imply.[19] Nevertheless, by privatizing large portions of their data-processing operations, some cities had some success in holding down their systems-development costs.[20]

Even though they lag behind in the adoption of leading-edge technology, cities are under relentless pressure to improve the delivery of services not only to individuals but also to businesses. On a global scale cities are competing against one another to attract investments from multinational corporations.

The City as a "Node" in the Global Economy

Cybernization has allowed the MNCs to engage in complex strategic arrangements spanning the globe. Communications technology allows it to locate economic activities in historically remote places while maintaining tight headquarters-to-subsidiary and subsidiary-to-subsidiary coordination. For example, while Intel's corporate headquarters are in California, it designs and manufactures chips in Israel, assembles them in Malaysia, and sells them in Silicon Valley. Automobile manufacturers have long relied on discrete manufacturing arrangements—electronics from Germany, glass from Britain, motors from Japan, and fuel-control systems from South Korea may end up in a car assembled in the American Midwest. For company after company, distributed manufacturing is facilitated by multisite coordination through the computer communication networks we now call "cyberspace."

As a consequence, the city becomes simply another "node" for potential investment. Multinationals have concluded, in their calculation of location economics, that cities can be played off, one against the other. Like restless apartment dwellers who keep moving to the newest complex, multinational corporations move from one city node to another in order to take advantage of the incentives offered.[21] As a result, an important strategy of economic development for cities is the reengineering of their factor endowments to attract investments by multinational corporations.

The Technopolis and the Teleport

The technopolis and the teleport[22] represent two attempts to engineer a change in factor endowments of cities. Teleports are geographically concentrated clusters of satellite up-links and other high-capacity telecommunications channels. They are designed to accommodate the global operations of multinational corporations by providing quantum improvements in telecommunications capacity and simplifying provisioning of heretofore complicated and difficult to install wide-area computer-communication services.[23] Singapore, for example, is a city-state that has made a substantial public investment in its telecommunications infrastructure to attract the regional (Asian) headquarters of multinational corporations.

Teleports are multiplying and have emerged as an accepted strategy for cities to improve their factor endowments with an eye to international competition to attract and keep business. Cities building teleports[24] include: New York,[25] Moscow,[26] Sophia Antipolis,[27] Singapore,[28] Seattle,[29] Denver,[30] Alameda,[31] Boston, San Antonio, Minneapolis, Metz, Bremen, Amsterdam, Osaka, Cologne, and Tokyo. In some cases, the existence of teleports elsewhere may be a determining factor in the decision of firms to abandon a city or its downtown area.[32]

Other cities have gone beyond teleports by setting up industrial parks, free tax zones, special economic zones,[33] and export zones to attract international businesses. In order to attract high technology industries, policymakers have created the *technopolis*.[34] Like industrial parks, these areas frequently are set apart from older neighborhoods and are designed to service a specific type of business. The new multimedia corridor being built in Malaysia is a good example of this. Other examples are listed in Table 3.2.

Besides teleports and technopolae, cities are exploring other means to upgrade their factor endowments. These include lowering taxes for specific periods of time; for example, granting tax "holidays." Cities can also provide direct or indirect subsidies in the form of buildings, land, advisory assistance, and other input requirements and ease traditional financial burdens such as medical insurance costs. Some cities have attempted to control labor costs through mandated arbitration between labor and capital. Sophisticated infrastructure can be provided, such as high-speed telecommunications linkages, wired neighborhoods, and wired buildings. Human resources can be improved through specialized schools and training programs. Regulatory barriers can be eliminated through the streamlining and "fast tracking" of bureaucratic obstacles to setting up and operating a business.

Differences in national regulatory structures permit some cities to engage in this type of competition better than others. New York faces many impediments at the state and national levels not encountered by a city-state such as Singapore, in which all authority, including that for the conduct of foreign relations, can be coordinated through the same set of policymakers. In this respect, Singapore has more potential for devising integrated policies and strategies to deal with global competition than does New York.[35]

Table 3.2   Specializations of Technopolis Centers

Cologne	Media industries
Edinburgh	Financial services
Roubaix	Textiles
Sophia Antipolis	High-technology R&D
Le Havre; Bremen	Maritime, ports and logistics
Tsukuba	High-technology R&D
Kuala Lumpur	Multimedia super corridor

The New York "Node"

Once the data-processing capital of the world, New York City has experienced a serious erosion of its position. Technical developments in computer operating systems and networking have made it possible to transfer large chunks of mainstream data-processing activity out of New York. Citibank has recently moved its online banking support to Austin, Texas, having previously moved its credit card processing to North Dakota. Metropolitan Life has moved its claims processing to Ireland. Many Wall Street firms have moved their "back office" activities to other states. Airlines have moved their ticket receipt processing to the Caribbean and their corporate headquarters elsewhere. Many companies have moved their computer-programming and data-entry operations for legacy mainframe systems to India and the Philippines or otherwise outsourced them away from New York. A large newspaper is moving away much of its data processing. There are many such examples across different sectors involving traditional data processing.

Several factors are driving this transformation of New York City's cyberscape. First, the overall cost structure (electricity, property taxes, real estate) in other locations is considerably lower. Second, many corporate headquarters have left the city, taking their data processing with them. Third, there is not a large enough supply of local talent to meet needs, as New York does not "manufacture" or import enough talented people in this field. Fourth, better talent can be acquired elsewhere for less cost. While in the past the city depended on immigrants to supplement its labor force,[36] the irony is that advances in telecommunications have made it possible for organizations based in New York to "import" information workers who never leave their home countries because they are connected to their jobs via telecommunications links. Nevertheless, although New York has faced a long-term decline in mainstream data processing, the new multimedia industry is experiencing rapid growth and has started to transform the cyber-scape of Manhattan.

Silicon Alley

Silicon Alley is the name given to the concentration of new media companies clustered in lower Manhattan.[37] These companies are engaged in creating multimedia software. Examples include:

1. Reference and educational CD-ROMs such as multimedia dictionaries and encyclopedias or reference books.

2. Computer games or other interactive entertainment.

3. Design, production, and maintenance of corporate World Wide Web (WWW) sites hosted on the Internet.

4. Generalized electronic publishing activities designed to take advantage of the marketing potential of the Internet.

5. Creation of sophisticated support companies related to advertising placements and response measurement on the Internet.

These companies are taking advantage of several developments in technology that have coalesced to create a new industry:

1. The growth of the Internet has simplified interorganizational linking and thereby reduced the barriers to subcontracting information-intensive work.

2. Personal computers have acquired multimedia capabilities; for example, the ability to process graphics, sounds, and video, thus making possible:
    (a) new forms of electronic publishing;
    (b) new generations of computer games and entertainment;
    (c) desktop teleconferencing and other forms of sophisticated groupware for complex task coordination.

3. The World Wide Web has transformed the economics of publishing by revolutionizing the distribution, production, and manufacturing process for information, including advertising.

There are more than a *thousand* new media companies in Silicon Alley, many of which are single-person firms. Through subcontracting, such companies act as a support sector for large media and publishing conglomerates operating in New York. This parallels the relationship between the movie industry in Hollywood and its large network of support companies, the automobile industry in Detroit and its network of parts suppliers, and the computer industry in Silicon Valley and its large number of component and software suppliers. (See Figure 3.1.)

A key difference between Silicon Alley and other talent and support clusters is that its technology is able to service multiple industry markets, most of which are located in close proximity in Manhattan. Multimedia and Internet-related products and services are not industry-specific as is, for example, the manufacturing of car parts.

New York is blessed in that it is home to four major sectors: Wall Street, publishing, television and radio, and advertising. This gives Silicon Alley companies more than one market for their services. In other cities, new media support companies often have only a single major local industry to support. As a result, the geographical concentration of available markets has made possible the birth of a new industry at the cutting edge of technology—in the middle of Manhattan.

This advantage for Silicon Alley has been further magnified by some intelligent policies involving private and public sector collaboration with respect to infrastructure. The development of the old Drexel Lambert headquarters at 55 Broad Street[38] into a mecca for multimedia design, as well as changes in zoning regulations to allow other underused Wall Street buildings to be reinvigorated, are examples of how collaboration between city government and private entrepreneurs helps provide an adequate infrastructure for the growth of new sectors such as Silicon Alley. Although 55 Broad Street houses less than 1 percent of the reported 1,350 new media companies, it has served as the focal point for much media attention and represents the type of effort needed to stimulate this new economic sector in New York.

A popular view regarding factor endowments is that high-speed data access is a key element encouraging the growth of Silicon Alley. After all, provision of telecommunications access is an important issue for new media companies focusing their business on the World Wide Web. Until recently, twisted-pair lines using "plain old telephone service" (P.O.T.S.) could be used for up to 33.6 kilobits per second (kbps) modem traffic, which is slow, while with Integrated Services Digital Network (ISDN) service speeds could reach 128 kbps. Unfortunately, ISDN tariffs are prohibitively expensive in the New York area for any company that requires constant connection to the Internet. The new X2 modem standard from U.S. Robotics, however, provides 56 kbps over twisted pair lines. In addition, AT&T Paradyne has just released the Asymetric Digital Subscriber Line (ADSL) modem that will transmit 6.14 megabits

Figure 3.1 Mono and Quadsectoral Markets

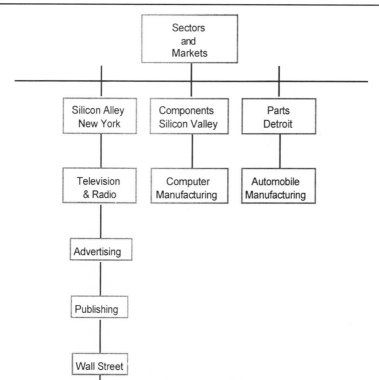

per second (mbps) over a standard twisted-pair line in one direction. These technical developments wipe away any geographical advantage to being near high-speed network access. The effect of this is to remove a possible leverage point for public policy since it makes it less useful to subsidize special network circuits to satisfy Silicon Alley businesses.

A problem that can be addressed by public policy is the cost of telecommunication services. Small, start-up companies, including the twenty-five Internet Service Providers (ISPs) located in Manhattan, find it difficult to pay the very high New York prices for T-1 highspeed access of 1.544 mbps.[39] There are no special tax incentives or subsidies to Silicon Alley, and in a litigious society such as New York, it might be difficult to enact legislation awarding such special favors. However, if the city is to reinvent itself as a center for advanced multimedia, it needs to take aggressive steps to meet the challenge of lowering telecommunications charges.

Another issue is the need to upgrade substantially the technological education and preparation of New York workers. To date the city's educational system has not played a substantial role in the creation of Silicon Alley. Now it must do so through the training of students. Developments in software and hardware emerge and are made obsolete with such rapidity that the adaptation of any public educational system is extremely problematic. Nevertheless, one of the continuing challenges facing New York is the development of educational resources responsive to the needs of cutting-edge industries.

The emergence of Silicon Alley holds out the possibility of increased economic security for New York in the twenty-first century. New York has demonstrated an encouraging tendency to meet the needs of four major markets that purchase services by providing a rich variety of social networking opportunities and infrastructure.[40] These include:

1. Strong social networks for cultural interaction, for example, "Cybersuds" and "Supercybersuds" galleries.

2. Associations of professionals and semiprofessionals including:
   (a) New York New Media Association
   (b) International Interactive Communication Society
   (c) World Wide Web Artist's Consortium
   (d) New Media Forum.

3. Access to high speed networks, particularly important to Internet Service Providers.

4. Presence of some educational institutions that are teaching the new technology, including the New York Institute of Technology, Brooklyn Polytechnic, the New York University Center for Digital Technology, and, to a degree, the Bronx High School of Science, which has become active in this field. The quality of this preparation will be tested in the years to come as graduates enter the job market.

5. Mobility of labor, which is enhanced by the physical proximity of many different firms.

6. The i.MAGIC Cyber Star Awards.[41]

7. Availability of Wall Street area buildings that can be converted to multimedia production centers because of the migration of many Wall Street firms to midtown.

One of the greatest ironies is that in the very sector where geographical distances theoretically should matter the least, it is the physical proximity of many different companies and human resources that appears to have played a key role in Silicon Alley's development. This relatively unforeseen "social factor" helps to explain the birth and sustainability of Silicon Alley, but it also complicates public policy making because it is difficult to "engineer" such communities without aggressive and imaginative policy planning and coordination by city government and the private sector.

Silicon Alley as "Neo-Medievalism"

Some critics might regard Silicon Alley as a form of neo-medievalism—a system in which purchasers demand an endless stream of "intellectual migrant workers" existing in rented spaces and having to get by with no job security and minimal social benefits. Wages in Silicon Alley, for example, are low by New York City standards.[42] (See Table 3.3.)

Many Silicon Alley workers have no health, pension, or disability benefits. Locked out of the crumbling Weberian hierarchies with their semblance of protection and left to the mercy of oligopolistic purchasers and quasi-monopolistic suppliers of telecommunications, new-media workers are to a great extent self-financing in terms of office space and their rapidly obsolescing computer equipment, which generally must be replaced every eighteen months. Lacking the minimal protections of the medieval guild, much less the modern labor union, and operating in a city with one of the world's highest costs of living, they may take their valuable skills elsewhere in the future if better opportunities and security are offered.

Does this mean, in effect, that further efforts to stimulate this new media sector are roughly equivalent to working to create more secretarial or McDonald's supervisor jobs? If not, then how can public policy be directed at the building of a vibrant and sustainable new-media sector in Silicon Alley?

Table 3.3   Average Annual Wages in New Media and Other Media Sectors[43]

New Media	$31,421
Books	$47,824
Movie/Video	$48,907
Cable	$51,592
Newspapers	$53,758
Periodicals	$60,620
Advertising	$62,559
TV	$63,261

New York City and the Global Economy

Although the development of Silicon Alley is certainly a positive step, it is a dangerous myth that New York City can rely on Silicon Alley to fuel its growth into the next century. Silicon Alley may be a creative beacon, but it is not an economic engine (at least not yet). If New York is to meet the challenge presented by the global economy, its policymakers and planners must effectively respond to a series of major issues including:

1. *Coordination with national policy.* Can the city compete internationally in the mainstream data-processing sector without the support of the national and state governments? What can be done if the priorities and practices of national and state policy are in conflict with those of the city?

2. *Financing infrastructure.* What types of computer-related infrastructure should be financed? Should the city provide public telecommunications in the same way it builds bridges and roads? Should private corporations be required to make bandwidth available for public use, much as television companies are required to do? Should the city make computer equipment available to information workers or entrepreneurs just as city parks provide swings and other pieces of equipment to families?

3. *Industrial policy.* Can the city define an industrial policy using the policies of other cities around the world such as Singapore and Kuala Lumpur as a benchmark? What should the goals be? How can the city's people thrive in an economy often defined by the needs of multinational corporations? Can the new-media sector transform itself into a powerful economic engine for New York thereby increasing the city's global reach?

4. *Service dumping.* Foreign-service providers in India, the Philippines, and in other low-wage regions can now use telecommunications networks to export data processing, programming, and data-entry services to New York City. This undercuts wages and takes away jobs. Is there a way to regulate those who engage in this type of activity?

5. *Intellectual migrant workers and protection of labor.* There have been reports of a widespread practice of "importing" temporary intellectual migrant workers (programmers, systems analysts, etc.) under tourist visas. How can such practices be regulated to maintain the city's competitive edge?

6. *Government purchasing.* Can government purchasing be used to strengthen the Silicon Alley phenomenon? Alternatively, can the Internet and the World Wide Web be used to help revolutionize delivery of public services? How could a localized government purchasing policy be reconciled with international treaties and obligations?

7. *Telecommuting and ecology.* Should the city encourage telecommuting in order to protect the environment and reduce air pollution? Over what geographical distance should the city extend its involvement in telecommuting? Should it give a tax break to telecommuters because they are reducing pollution and congestion? Should telecommuters pay city taxes?

These are only a few of the many questions that must be answered in the near future as the traditional data-processing bases of New York and other cities decline and new sectors emerge, thereby generating critical policy challenges. Failure to respond could very well eliminate major economic possibilities necessary for the flourishing of the city as it enters the twenty-first century.

Notes

1. See Peter Hägstrom, *The "Wired" MNC: The Role of Information Systems for Structural Change in Complex Organizations* (Stockholm: Institute of International Business, Stockholm School of Economics, 1991); Edward M. Roche, *Managing Information Technology in Multinational Corporations* (New York: Macmillan, 1992).

2. See Dennis J. Encarnation, *Beyond Trade: Foreign Investment in the U.S.-Japan Rivalry* (Ithaca, N.Y.: Cornell University Press, 1992).

3. See Julia King, "Network Tools of the Virtual Corporation" *Network World* 11 (1994): 28–30.

4. See Mark M. Klein, "The Virtue of Being a Virtual Corporation," *Best's Review* 95 (1994): 88–94.

5. For a review of strategic partnerships, see Charles S. Raben, "Building Strategic Partnerships" in David Nadler, Mark S. Gerstein, and Robert B. Shaw & Associates, eds., *Organization Architecture* (San Francisco: Jossey-Bass, 1992).

6. See Anna Lee Saxenian, *Regional Advantage: Culture and Competition in Silicon Valley and Route 128* (Cambridge: Harvard University Press, 1994).

7. See, for example, Beth Schultz, "A Real Virtual Network Corporation," *Network World* 13 (1996): 13–15; for the effect on research and development, see

Joseph F. Coates, "Managing Scientists in the Virtual Corporation," *Research-Technology Management* 37 (1994): 7–8.

8. On layoffs in the virtual corporation, see Melanie Menagh, "Virtues and Vices of the Virtual Corporation," *Computerworld* 29 (November 13, 1995): 134.

9. Jeannie Coyle and Nicky Schnarr, "The Soft-Side Challenges of the 'Virtual Corporation,'" *Human Resource Planning* 18 (1995): 41–42.

10. Sharon L. Caudle and Donald A. Marchand, "Managing Information Resources: New Directions in State Government," *Information Management Review* 5 (winter 1990): 9–30.

11. "Ohio Food Stamp System Becomes a Success Story," *Government Computer News*, December 5, 1988, p. 69.

12. See interview with Carl Myers, MIS Director of Phoenix, in John Kador, "One on One," *Midrange Systems*, April 15, 1994, p. 46.

13. "Metropolitan Area Avoids 'Government by Crisis,'" *Industrial Engineering* 10 (April 1978): 33–34.

14. On downsizing, see Barbara Macrea, "Inside Government Computing," *Canadian Datasystems* 23 (December 1991): 16–20; on decentralization, see Ravi Gupta, "Why Centralized Financial Systems Fail to Deliver," *Computing Canada* 15 (March 30, 1989): 22–23.

15. New Jersey is going to use ATMs for license renewals for cars. See Jeffrey Schwartz, "ATMs to Speed NJ Motorist Registration," *Communications Week* 395 (March 23, 1992): 32; Brad Bass, "Gov't Looks to Coordinate Kiosk Efforts," *Federal Computer Week* 8 (May 9, 1994): 14.

16. For a review of the Arizona group system in city government, see Paul Saffo, "Same-Time, Same-Place Groupware (the Prototype Electronic Meeting Room at the University of Arizona's College of Business and Public Administration)," *Personal Computing* 14 (March 20, 1990): 57.

17. See "Network Provides Public Access to Government Database (Public Electronic Network)," *Computer Reseller News* 304 (March 6, 1989): 104.

18. Martin S. Putterill, "Developing an Intervention Strategy to Promote Enhanced Public Service Performance by Agent Institutions," *Information & Management* 9 (October 1985): 161–87. In the National Performance Review, initiated under the leadership of Vice President Gore, IT training was made mandatory for all nontechnical managers. See Bureaucratus, "NPR Efforts Will Empower Fed Employees," *Federal Computer Week* 7 (Oct. 18, 1993): 28. See also *The Information Government*, developed by the National Academy of Public Administration, reviewed in Kevin Power, "Execs to Clinton: Start Walking Your IT Talk; NAPA Wants to See White House Endorse its Ideas on Improving Service to Clients," *Government Computer News* 12 (August 16, 1993): 96.

19. A good example is provided by the Housing and Urban Development (HUD) system, which has more than 250 legacy (old) information systems that are not well integrated. See Vanessa Jo Grimm, "HUD Infrastructure Is Solid, but Legacy Systems Aren't," *Government Computer News* 13 (August 29, 1994): 14. Paul Strassman has argued that IT organizations strongly resist change. See Joyce Endoso, "Strassman: 'Fiefdoms' Thwart IT Control: Lack of Structure Hinders Sensible Management of Information Technology at Department of Defense Says Information Director Paul A. Strassmann," *Government Computer News* 11 (Dec. 7, 1992): 3. It is not difficult to see similar patterns at the city level.

20. For a review of the dismal experience in London, see Chris Gibbs, "Council Proposes IT Buy-Out," *Computer Weekly* 1224 (July 26, 1990): 80.

21. For further analysis of the city in the world economy, see Saskia Sassen's chapter in this volume.

22. See Robert Annunziata, "What Is a Teleport?" *Telecommunication Products & Technology* 4 (November 1986): 24–28.

23. Teleports in the United States are provided by private corporations. For a description of teleport communications based in New York, see Vince Vittore, "Teleport's Growth Puts Management Center on the Spot," *America's Network* 99 (August 1, 1995): 24–28. Other companies include Metropolitan Fiber Systems (MFS).

24. See William A. Blazar, Mary Ellen Spector, and John Grathwol, "The Sky Above, the Teleport Below," *Planning* 51 (December 1985): 22–26.

25. For early views of the prospects of New York's teleport, see John F. Naughton, "Designing Urban Telecom Networks: 'The Teleport,'" *Telecommunications* 17 (September 1983): 139–42; and Charles G. Seliga, "The Teleport: The First Satellite Communications Office Park," *Satellite Communications* 7 (February 1983): 30–32.

26. See Vladimir E. Teremetsky, "SOVAM TELEPORT: Telecommunicati Russia and Abroad," *IEEE Transactions on Profenal Communication* 37 (June 1994): 68–69.

27. Sophia Antipolis has more than 700 companies starting up in the area based on its new telecommunications services. It is claimed 10,000 jobs have been created as a result of this French effort to "build a European equivalent of California's Silicon Valley." See Steven McClelland, "Sophia Antipolis: A Mediterranean Teleport," *Telecommunications* 26 (June 1991): 67–68.

28. Singapore was an early adopter of ISDN (Integrated Services Digital Network). See Stephen McClelland, "Singapore: The Asian Teleport," *Telecommunications* 24 (September 1990): 108–13.

29. See Walter Sweet, "Seattle Considers Feasibility of Building Area Teleport," *Network World* 7 (July 2, 1990): 19, 22.

30. See Rex Bowman, "Future Looks Bright for Teleport Denver," *Network World* 5 (June 20, 1988): 9–10. Denver was planning to build as many as fifteen satellite uplinks.

31. See John Harrison, "Teleport by the Sea," *Telephony* 213 (July 13, 1987): 28–32.

32. Bruce Hoard, "Teleport: An Office Park Offers Satellite Services to Firms Fleeing New York," *Computerworld* 17 (September 28, 1983): 75–80.

33. For a review of the situation in Europe, see Martin Richardson, "Tariff Revenue Competition in a Free Trade Area," *European Economic Review* 39 (August 1995): 1429–37; for a look at China, see Chip E. Miller, James Reardon, Rajesh Srivastava, and Su-Wei Hu, "Special Economic Zones of the People's Republic of China: An Examination of Entry Strategies by Taiwanese Investors," *International Journal of Management* 12 (June 1995): 247–54, and Xiangming Chen, "The Changing Roles of Free Economic Zones in Development: A Comparative Analysis of Capitalist and Socialist Cases in East Asia," *Studies in Comparative International Development* 29 (Fall 1994): 3–25.

34. For views of the technopolis in Southern California, see Sabina Deitrick, "Planning and Its Subfields—Technopolis: High Technology Industry and Regional Development in Southern California," *Journal of the American Planning Association* 61 (Autumn 1995): 534–35; Gordon H. Hanson, "Technopolis: High-Technology Industry and Regional Development in Southern California," *Journal of Economic Literature* 33 (June 1995): 882–83; Michael L. Lahr, "Technopolis: High-Technology Industry and Regional Development in Southern California," *Journal of Regional Science* 35 (May 1995): 338–39; Richard Florida, "Technopolis: High-Technology Industry and Regional Development in Southern California," *Growth & Change* 25 (Fall 1994): 528–32. For a general overview, see Michael J. Enright, "The Emergence of Technopolis: Knowledge-Intensive Technologies and Regional Development," *Business History Review* 67 (Summer 1993): 347–49. For a look at Australia, see Vinod Gupta, "MFP: The Proposal for an Australian Technopolis," *Tokyo Business Today* 59 (October 1991): 60–61. And for Texas, see Raymond W. Smilor, David V. Gibson, and George Kozmetsky, "Creating the Technopolis: High-Technology Development in Austin, Texas," *Journal of Business Venturing* 4 (January 1989): 49–67. For Japan, see Neil W. Davis, "MITI's Technopolis Project," *Japan Marketing/Advertising* 2 (Spring 1984): 40–41.

35. See Carol O'Cléireacáin's chapter in this volume.

36. See Joseph J. Salvo and A. Peter Lobo's chapter in this volume.

37. See Amy Cortese, "Manhattan Turns into 'Silicon Alley': How the City Is Snaring Multimedia Startups," *Business Week* 3409 (January 30, 1995): 82; and Richard Brandt, "How Skid Row Is Changing to 'Silicon Alley'," *Business Week* 3038, Industrial/Technology Edition (1988): 20D, H.

38. Timothy Harper, "High-Tech High-Rise," *Sky* (April 1996): 35–39.

39. T-1 access is 1.544 million megabits per second.

40. See Trip Gabriel, "Where Silicon Alley Artists Go to Download," *New York Times*, October 8, 1995, and Joe Queenan, "Silicon Alley: Getting Away from My Computer Geek Neighbors," *Washington Post*, May 21, 1993. For women's issues in Silicon Alley, see John Marks, "Wired Women Make the Cyberspace: New York's Silicon Alley Is a High-Tech Happening," *U.S. News & World Report* 119 (October 15, 1995): 75.

41. See Anya Sacharow, "Cyber-World Stars Get Theirs," *Mediaweek* 6 (1996): 30. Winners have been the creators of "Project-Cool" (http://www.projectcool.com) and "MigraineBoy" (http://www.visualradio.com/migraineboy).

42. On health issues concerning "silicon workers," see "Take Out: Small Business," *Crain's New York Business* 11 (1995): 17.

43. Adapted from Steve Lohr, "New York Area Is Forging Ahead in New Media," *New York Times*, April 15, 1996.

Chapter 4

The Cali Cartel and
the Globalization of Crime
in New York City

Clifford Krauss

W HEN ONE thinks of cities steeped in international intrigue, wartime Tangiers and Cold War Vienna and Panama City come to mind, as does Miami, known for its militant Cuban exile groups and banks that, only a little more than a decade ago, more or less openly welcomed the laundered money of international drug traffickers. New York City, one of the world's centers of foreign-based organized crime, also belongs on the list.

The internationalization of crime in New York is not a new phenomenon. Nor is it surprising given the city's position as a major international port and global financial center. But it is a growing problem, not least because the newest wave of immigrants to New York is made up of truly global citizens who continue to participate in a wide variety of activities—legal and otherwise—in their homelands, even as they make new lives for themselves in America. Local Dominican gangs ship stolen cars to their cousins back in the Dominican Republic for resale. Chinese gangs smuggle in illegal aliens from China. Albanian organized crime groups have tapped into the heroin routes between Istanbul and Belgrade to supply the New York metropolitan markets. In the dawning era of cybercrime and cybercurrency, the connections such immigrants weave between their old homes and their new ones will proliferate.

Globalization, especially as expressed in immigration and trade, plays an overwhelmingly positive role in the life of the city. New immigrants are resuscitating entire neighborhoods. New restaurants offer cuisines from every corner of the planet, and schoolchildren learn about the world from their classmates. But when it is expressed in criminal activity, globalization puts enormous strains on the city's resources and presents a new challenge to local and federal law enforcement agencies. The New York City Police Department, for example, faces a particularly difficult job in breaking up organized crime networks in Chinatown because few of its undercover agents speak Chinese dialects and because of the widespread fear among the Chinese-American population of assisting law enforcement. Russian organized crime cadres, who typically come from a highly educated stratum of the former Soviet Union, concoct innovative banking, credit, and insurance fraud schemes that long-established, more traditional Mafia families are unlikely to have dreamed up. Local and federal law enforcement agencies would like to be able to coordinate their efforts with their counterparts in Nigeria to root out the drug-trafficking and money-laundering networks that stretch between New York and Africa, but this has not been possible, in part because of the tense relations between Lagos and Washington.

Meanwhile, transnational criminal enterprises create working arrangements with one another, making law enforcement even more complicated. Take the traffic in heroin, the consumption of which is once again becoming a serious problem in New York (the city is frequently ahead of the rest of the country by a few years when it comes to drug fads). While the opium poppy is cultivated from Colombia to Burma to Afghanistan, a sizeable amount of the finished narcotic derived from it is trafficked by Nigerian networks utilizing hundreds, perhaps thousands, of carriers operating through such far-flung places as South Africa and Brazil.

Each of the foreign- and immigrant-based organized crime groups represents a particular challenge to law enforcement agencies. But none does more business—and thus more damage—than Colombia's Cali cartel, which, with estimated yearly revenues of $5 billion or more, is the richest organized crime organization in the world. No U.S. president has spoken publicly about it, and no mayor has made a speech acknowledging it, but New York City—particularly northern Queens—is probably the cartel's most vital international wholesale hub, serving nearly the entire eastern half of the United States, as well as one of its important money-laundering centers. Local and international law enforcement agencies have been largely ineffective in making inroads against the cartel over the last twenty-five years, and it appears that to acknowledge the problem would be to acknowledge failure. It is clear, however, that if the residents of New York had any idea how deeply entrenched the world's richest crime organization is in the neighborhoods of Jackson Heights, Corona, and Elmhurst, the Cali cartel would become a hot political issue.

The Extent of the Problem

The New York metropolitan area is the most important center of Cali activities in the United States for geographical, economic, and demographic reasons. Metropolitan New York is one of the largest and most densely populated markets in the world. Its ports and airports and its complex highway grid offer superior transportation facilities for cocaine trafficking throughout the city and to the suburbs and beyond. In addition, the large resident Colombian and Dominican communities offer ample manpower.

The Cali cartel handles 80 percent of the cocaine brought into New York City for consumption or resale. And as heroin makes a comeback, the cartel is playing an increasingly important role in the trafficking of that drug as well. The value of this drug traffic is anybody's guess, but it is a multibillion-dollar business.

The Cali cartel began operating in New York in the early 1970s, under the leadership of the two most important Cali leaders, José Santacruz Londoño and Gilberto Rodríguez Orejuela. New York became so important to the Cali cartel that, when the competing Medellín cartel began to encroach on its turf in the late 1980s, Cali operatives gave vital intelligence assistance to Colombian police authorities in their successful efforts to wipe out the Medellín cartel in the early 1990s. There were other reasons for the rivalry between the cartels, but the competition for the control of New York was a critical factor.

Cartel operations are spreading into New Jersey and the suburbs. Local cartel organizations, known as cells, usually deal only at the highest wholesale levels. They primarily sell to local trafficking groups led by resident Colombians who have family members back in Colombia. This virtually guarantees that they will not testify in court against their wholesalers. Dominican groups based in Washington Heights and Harlem in Manhattan and in parts of the Bronx and Brooklyn typically come into play at the middle and lower wholesale levels.

Two events that occurred in 1992 demonstrate how brazen the Cali cartel has become in recent years. The first of these was the discovery by federal agents of two cocaine production laboratories in Brooklyn that had been set up by Santacruz Londoño. Thirty people were arrested, including one of the cartel's leading chemists. In the larger of the two laboratories, located in an industrial warehouse in Greenpoint, Brooklyn, trained technicians were refining up to 200 pounds of cocaine a day, with a wholesale value of $2 million. The laboratories were said by law enforcement officials to have been set up because of a shortage of refining chemicals like acetone and ether in South America at the time. Officials say they doubt such laboratories exist anymore, but continue to be on the lookout for them.

The second event was the murder of a crusading Cuban-American journalist, Manuel de Dios Unanue. He was shot and killed in a restaurant in Elmhurst, Queens, by a teenage hitman who had been paid $1,500 on the direct orders of Santacruz Londoño, according to papers filed in federal court. The Cali cartel had been responsible for the assassinations of dozens of journalists in Colombia itself, but the murder of Manuel de Dios was the first of a journalist working in the United States. The editor and publisher of two Spanish-language weekly magazines, de Dios was the only journalist writing in any language who had pieced together even a partial portrait of the cartel's New York operations. Half a dozen people have since been brought to justice for his murder, but under Colombian law at the time Santacruz Londoño could not be extradited to the United States to face murder charges. Santacruz Londoño was subsequently killed in a shoot-out with police after escaping from prison. Manuel de Dios's death spurred a flurry of stories about the Cali cartel in New York in 1992 and 1993, but journalistic interest was short-lived.

Because both the cartel and law enforcement agencies alike are so secretive, it is difficult in the extreme for an onlooker to discover the exact nature or extent of the cartel's activities in New York. Court documents on cases such as the de Dios murder provide only an incomplete picture of criminal conspiracies hatched years ago. And, obviously, there are no public documents on the presumably greater number of crimes that have either not been unearthed by government investigators or for which there is insufficient evidence. Studying the cartel is something like stargazing, in that the stars we see on a clear night do not reflect the universe as it now exists since what we see is light generated eons ago.

The Cartel's Operations

A dozen or more Cali cartel cells—whose leaders are handpicked by the kingpins in Colombia and take their orders from them—operate independently of one another in New York. Some cells are responsible for trafficking, others for money laundering. Each cell includes about seventy-five full-time members, who usually are unaware of the operations of other cells. Cell leaders are rotated out of the city and back to Colombia every six to twelve months. Such measures maximize security and ensure that the takedown by law enforcement of one group will not impede the workings of the others. One nine-month investigation of two Cali cells by federal and local law enforcement agencies in 1994 revealed that these two cells alone were distributing over 7,000 pounds of cocaine—worth $62 million in an average month.

The cartel has been much in the news of late, but almost all the stories are datelined Bogotá or Cali. The cartel was seriously, if temporarily, damaged in 1995 with the imprisonment of six of its seven top leaders. The Colombian government's campaign against the cartel was in part the result of the hard work of honest officials in the national police and special prosecutor's office, and in part a reaction to American pressure.

One only has to walk down Roosevelt Avenue in Jackson Heights, Queens, beneath the rusting subway tracks, to see how powerful the Cali cartel remains in New York. Here are the scores of travel agencies, wire-transfer operations, and restaurants that are so necessary to the cartel's money-laundering activities. Storefronts are equipped with rows of telephone booths for the many immigrants who do not have telephones at home. But these telephones are also useful to cartel operatives as a means to evade wiretaps. Cartel workers need an endless supply of beepers, fax machines, and cellular telephones because they must dispose of them constantly to frustrate the surveillance efforts of law enforcement agencies. Stores selling such equipment are more common in Jackson Heights than cappuccino bars in Greenwich Village. Law enforcement officials say the owners of these businesses know they offer vital services to the cartel, and in many cases have received seed money from dealers to start or expand their businesses. Along this same strip are numerous legal offices and private security firms that also offer their services to the cartel, as well as real estate brokers who knowingly find safe houses for cartel traffickers and money launderers. Moreover, the cartel has had some limited success in infiltrating more mainstream local institutions. Bank tellers and perhaps even some local bank supervisors have been enlisted in recent years, according to law enforcement officials. The ability of Cali operatives to tamper with their driver's licenses to camouflage their addresses suggests that they also have corrupted bureaucrats in the city's Motor Vehicle Bureau.

Storefront money-transmitting and check-cashing operations in inner city neighborhoods around the country send billions of dollars to drug dealers in Latin America and Asia. However, the greatest concentration of such operations is in the Colombian neighborhoods of northern Queens. New York bank regulators have classified the operations of over 130 money transmitters in the city as suspicious. These businesses typically operate out of storefront offices that bear a resemblance to regular banks, with tellers protected by bulletproof glass. The transmitting business accepts the proceeds of drug deals and deposits it in legitimate banks, frequently under the names of fictitious individuals or corporations. Once this money is transferred electronically to another bank, there is no trace of the real depositor. In most cases, the fact that the money was tied to drug trafficking is hidden because the banks report to regulatory authorities only the names of the money-transmitting companies. New York's understaffed state bank regulatory apparatus does not have the resources to track the literally millions of such transfers each year.

Money-laundering vehicles are spread throughout the metropolitan area. Local and federal prosecutors believe that dozens of small costume-jewelry exporters operating along Broadway below midtown and in the Times Square area as well as many electronic and furniture companies around Manhattan knowingly accept Cali drug money. Scotland Yard is working with federal and local prosecutors to uncover money-laundering schemes in which cartel operatives buy and sell art at galleries in London and New York.

While the money-laundering schemes can be complex, the overall concept is simple. Cartel intermediaries typically contact companies in Colombia that import goods from the United States. These intermediaries offer to pay the American exporters in dollars. In return, the Colombian importers pay the cartel intermediaries an equivalent amount inside Colombia, but at slightly less than the true exchange rate, which is their reward for their participation.

Drug traffickers also ship dollars back to Colombia from regional U.S. ports and airports in everything from used cars to dolls to television sets. When a forklift operator accidentally punctured a shipping pallet in a warehouse on West 32nd Street in 1995, workers were amazed to see hundreds of thousands of dollars in one-dollar bills tumble out.

A Money-Laundering Tale

A routine traffic stop by police on the Sprain Brook Parkway three years ago led to a major break in one of the Cali cartel's money-laundering schemes. Inside a black 1985 Chevrolet Camaro a state police trooper discovered $40,000 in small bills, postal money orders worth $16,000, and records of extensive financial transactions with Colombia. The driver of the Camaro, Hector Fabio Gualteros, told police the money and records were part of his work as an independent distributor of health-care products manufactured by Herbalife International.

Suspecting the records were from a money-laundering operation, agents with the New York State Organized Crime Task Force and the Federal Customs Service placed Gualteros under surveillance, eventually monitoring twenty-two telephone lines, eight beepers, and thirteen fax lines. Within weeks, their suspicions were confirmed. As described in court papers and interviews with law enforcement officials, Gualteros and his associates collected drug money for the Cali cartel and paid it to small New York companies exporting costume jewelry and watches to Colombia. Cash was often dropped off in brown paper bags. Seven exporters were identified in court papers as receivers of drug money, although none has been charged yet with wrongdoing. Three of these companies are located in cramped, nondescript offices along Broadway and Seventh Avenue in New York City. The other four were located in Miami and Los Angeles.

The investigation concluded early in 1996 with the arrest of six people, including a prominent Colombian importer. Court records show that payments were directed to the companies by coded fax and beeper messages from Cali bosses in Colombia. Authorities say the operation laundered about $4 million in six months. And, not surprisingly, the scheme also had a violent side.

On September 1, 1994, midway through the inquiry, state investigators seized $157,000 in suspected drug cash and arrested two men. To keep the investigation alive, Cleofe Ojeda, who had delivered the money to the men, was not arrested. Two weeks later, she and two others were found dead in her Forest Hills, Queens, apartment, gagged with duct tape and showing signs of torture. Investigators believe she was punished for losing the money.

The Impact of Recent Cali Problems

The year 1995 was punctuated with fluctuating cocaine prices and a spate of murders—the direct result of the on-again, off-again repression of the Cali cartel by the Colombian government. The Clinton administration, skillfully using the mounting evidence that Colombia's president, Ernesto Samper, had accepted Cali cartel money to finance his 1994 election campaign, forced his government to crack down on the cartel. Nearly all of the organization's top leaders were arrested. For most of 1995, the cartel was in turmoil, with middle-ranking Colombian kingpins jockeying to take control of the organization. While drug trafficking in the western United States was taken over by Mexican cartels, no organizations were in a position to challenge the Cali cartel in New York.

The leadership vacuum in Colombia led to disruptions in supplies and in communications with local cells. Tensions between the cells over the hoarding of supplies and the competition for control of New York's shrinking cocaine markets led to dozens of murders and kidnappings in northern Queens, perpetrated by three "enforcer" gangs working out of bars and pool halls on Roosevelt Avenue. Between January 1 and November 19, 1995, there were 109 murders in northern Queens (including homicides unrelated to the cartel), compared to 107 over the same period the year before. This occurred during a period in which the homicide rate for the city as a whole declined by 27 percent. Meanwhile, in the most precipitous shift in almost six years, the wholesale price of cocaine increased by nearly 50 percent between May and September 1995 because of decreased supply.

The rash of homicides and kidnappings suddenly ceased just before Christmas, not coincidentally as Colombian enforcement efforts were eased. There were reports that the Cali kingpins were directing their organizations from prison, using messengers and cellular telephones. Wholesale cocaine prices dropped to their previous levels—all in a matter of weeks and with almost no comment from law enforcement officials or local politicians.

If the government is serious about controlling drug trafficking, political leaders as well as local and federal law-enforcement officials need to speak more openly about the threat the Cali cartel and other international organized crime organizations pose to the well-being of New Yorkers. I am not suggesting that investigations be jeopardized, but the public should be made aware of the dimensions of the problem. This is particularly important at a time when government resources are scarce.

Law enforcement officials engaged in the war against illegal drugs are always requesting more manpower and increased resources to inspect international commerce in harbors and airports, to set and monitor wiretaps, and to develop new and innovative ways to interrupt money-laundering flows. But much more could be accomplished with the available resources if the various local and national law enforcement agencies involved coordinated their efforts better, especially in complex money-laundering cases. There is some hope in this regard. The New York City Police Department has launched a new antidrug initiative in northern Brooklyn, northern Manhattan, the Lower East Side, and parts of the Bronx and Queens that has enlisted the active support of the Secret Service, the Customs Service, the FBI, and the DEA. As a result, the crime rate has plummeted in many areas of the city. But if such efforts are to bear fruit permanently, intelligence gathered at the street level must be developed and acted upon all the way up the drug-trafficking ladder from the Cali cells in New York to the kingpins in Colombia.

Chapter 5

Policing the Clandestine Side of Economic Integration

Peter Andreas

MANY OBSERVERS of current trends stress that we are living in a "borderless world" connected by "global cities" that are populated by "transnational communities." We are told that subnational units, particularly global hubs such as New York City, are playing an ever-more prominent role with the apparent decline of the national state.[1]

Yet partly in response to these great transformations, in at least one policy sphere—the policing of clandestine cross-border economic activity—the pivotal role of the national state and territorial politics not only persists but may in fact be increasing. This is particularly true with respect to controlling illegal drugs and migrant labor.[2] Even as there is a loosening of state regulation over the flow of goods, services, information, and capital in an integrating world, there is a tightening of state prohibitions against migrant labor and drug flows. The economist J. N. Bhagwati has noted that immigration controls are "the most compelling exception to liberalism in the operation of the world economy."[3] Drug controls are an equally clear exception. In both cases, the advice of otherwise influential free-market proponents has failed to penetrate the policy debate.[4]

Market liberalization is about rolling back the state: deregulation, privatization, the opening up of the national economies, and the erosion of boundaries. Market prohibition, on the other hand, is about rolling the state forward: economic regulation through the criminalization and sharpening of boundaries. As a result of this process, some state functions are promoted even as others are demoted. The status of state intervention in the market is therefore ambiguous: strong support for market deregulation is apparently matched by equally strong support for (and surprising faith in) increased regulation of prohibited markets through the state's policing apparatus. Consequently, this core function of the state appears to be expanding—from the streets of New York, to the U.S.-Mexico border, to the coca fields of South America—as a coercive form of economic regulation.

The twin dynamics of deregulation and re-regulation are in some respects intimately connected. The loosening of national controls over the flow of goods, services, information, and capital has unintentionally facilitated and encouraged not only legal economic activity but illegal economic activity as well. Indeed, as all forms of cross-border activity have become more extensive and intensive, so too have state efforts to weed out the illicit from the licit. This task falls primarily on the law-enforcement apparatus.

New York City, for example, is not only integrated into the legal global economy but also increasingly into its clandestine side.[5] As James Kallstrom, assistant FBI director in charge of the New York office, notes "international communications and business play a key role in the life of this city." Additionally, "money, goods and services flow all around the world at an ever-increasing rate. Criminals always go where the money is and today the money is in the global economy. That's why global crime is such a big problem for this city. It's like any other international business—New York is the place to be."[6]

The most visible target of law enforcement, of course, has been the drug trade, in large measure because the people involved often resolve business disputes by killing rather than suing each other. According to the New York City Police Department, about 25 percent of all homicides in New York between 1989 and 1994 were drug related.[7] Equally popular and visible targets of law enforcement are the boundaries that separate developed and less-developed regions—such as the United States and Latin America, southern Europe and northern Africa, and western Europe and eastern Europe—where the state plays the role of both liberalizer and criminalizer of cross-border economic flows.

The dynamics of liberalization and criminalization are transforming the 1,951-mile U.S.-Mexico boundary, where the United States is trying both to open the border to legal economic flows and to close the border to illegal economic flows. The geographer Lawrence Herzog has argued that "the internationalization of the world economy . . . has led to an inevitable reshaping of boundary functions. The most obvious change has been the shift from boundaries that are heavily protected and militarized to those that are more porous, permitting cross-border social and economic interaction."[8] However, along the U.S.-Mexico boundary, the intensification of cross-border economic activity has been matched by an intensification of border policing. The border is increasingly fortified—not to deter invading armies, but to deter a perceived invasion of "undesirables." The U.S. Border Patrol apprehends more people than any other law enforcement agency in the world.

The "hardening" of the southwestern border is reflected not only in a significant increase in the deployment of law-enforcement personnel but also in the growing reliance on surveillance technology to spot clandestine border activity. Border enforcers are under intense pressure to deter unwanted cross-border flows but not to impede legitimate flows. As Alan D. Bersin, the U.S. Attorney for the Southern District of California (who has been appointed to the new post of "border czar"), explains: "Our border is intended to accomplish twin purposes; on the one hand, it is intended to facilitate trade in order to bring our nation the significant benefits of international commerce and industry. At the same time, it is geared to constrain and regulate the free movement of people and goods in order to block the entry of illegal migrants and unlawful merchandise. The key to resolving these apparently contradictory purposes lies in the strategic application of modern technology. We can and must have a border that is both secure and business-friendly."[9]

Part of this effort involves making use of military technology and equipment for law enforcement purposes. For example, magnetic footfall detectors and infrared body sensors, first used by the U.S. military in Southeast Asia during the Vietnam War, are placed along points of the southwestern border. Along the border south of San Diego, army reservists have constructed a steel wall made up of 180,000 metal sheets that were originally used for temporary landing fields in the desert during the Persian Gulf War.[10] Mexicans call it the "iron curtain."[11]

These developments along the southwestern border are part of a broader redefinition of inter-American relations after the Cold War. Much of U.S. foreign policy is driven by the twin goals of promoting market reforms and enforcing market prohibitions. In particular, the United States encourages the free flow of virtually everything except two of the region's leading exports: migrant labor and drugs.

Strategies to deter the clandestine flow of labor (especially from Mexico, but from many other countries as well) and illicit drugs (primarily cocaine, heroin, and marijuana) focus largely on curbing the supply and secondarily on targeting the source of demand (consumers of drugs and employers of migrant workers). In the case of drug control, this involves intensified law enforcement efforts to curb the supply at the point of production abroad, at the point of entry at the border, and at the point of domestic distribution and sales in cities such as New York. Federal spending on drug control has increased from less than $1 billion in 1981 to over $14 billion in 1996, with about 70 percent of the total devoted to law enforcement. Funding for immigration control has also expanded significantly. For example, the 1996 budget for the Immigration and Naturalization Service (INS) reached $2.6 billion, a remarkable 72 percent increase since 1993.

While the primary focus of immigration control is on domestic and border enforcement, the U.S. government is also expanding operations beyond the nation's boundaries. For example, the INS is reportedly working inside Mexico to apprehend organizers of migrant smuggling rings. This is part of a broader process of reconceptualizing and internationalizing immigration control. As sociologist Robert Bach, now a senior INS official, has observed, "in order to control events in countries which export migrants, receiving states are increasingly connecting their migration regulatory efforts with new methods of international law enforcement and changes in post–Cold War military doctrine."[12]

The awkward reality in the Americas, however, is that both drugs and migrant labor are significant exports for many countries. During a period when the value of traditional exports has fluctuated, the boom in these illegal "goods" (or "bads," depending on your perspective) is a vital source of revenue for many debt-burdened economies. The remittances generated from migrant workers (many of them illegal) in the United States is a crucial source of foreign exchange for a number of countries. Illegal drugs are Latin America's most successful export industry, serving as a generator of foreign exchange for such countries as Peru, Bolivia, Colombia, and Mexico.[13] From Chile to the Cayman Islands, countries take part in the region's thriving drug trade—ranging from crop production and processing to shipping and money laundering. Illegal migration and the drug trade help cushion the unemployment crisis in some countries, since hundreds of thousands of the unemployed find work through these clandestine alternatives.

As the United States pushes to expand market forces and the private sector throughout the hemisphere, too often overlooked is the fact that the drug-export industry is a leading market force and an entrenched part of the private sector in some countries. Indeed, the drug trade is in many ways the purest example of the kind of aggressive entrepreneurialism advocated by the United States. Liberalizing economies through market-based reforms undermines the state's ability to withstand external market pressures—licit and illicit. This should not be surprising. Neoclassical economic theory, after all, suggests that countries should specialize in exports in which they enjoy a comparative advantage. For some, this means exporting labor and/or drugs. This should be viewed as part of what political scientist Robert Cox has called the "internationalization of the state": the process whereby national policies are adjusted to the exigencies of the international economy.[14] The illegal side of the international economy should be seen as an integral part of this process.

While they should not be overstated, there are parallels between these developments in the Americas and trends elsewhere, particularly between the European Union and its neighbors to the south and the east. For example, along Europe's southern boundaries there has emerged what one observer calls a "European Mexico syndrome—a border-zone where economic, political, cultural, religious and demographic differences accumulate to create a gap between worlds, a zone of confrontation."[15] Spain and Morocco, for example, are separated by only fourteen kilometers at the Straits of Gibraltar. According to one group of researchers, Morocco's sweeping market reform program "has required sharp cutbacks in social spending and in the level of support for export agriculture, with dramatic social consequences: a crisis of the traditional peasantry, internal migration to and overcrowding in urban areas, and a generally deteriorating standard of living. A portion of Morocco's displaced populations is forced to emigrate, often to Spain as illegal workers."[16]

Displaced workers there have also sought work in a leading Moroccan export industry: cannabis products. Morocco is now the largest supplier of marijuana to Europe and a leading hashish producer.[17] The Moroccan port city of Tangier has reportedly experienced "unprecedented prosperity and a construction boom fueled largely by enormous profits from running drugs and immigrants across the strait [of Gibraltar]."[18] In an attempt to appease the Europeans, the Moroccan government has periodically announced major crackdowns on the traffic in drugs and people. In early 1993, for example, Morocco's interior minister claimed that "our war against the smugglers is nothing less than draconian." He noted that "the crackdown has seriously affected the livelihoods of about 3 million Moroccan citizens."[19] Meanwhile, Spain has been tightening its border controls, partly in response to pressures from other members of the European Union. The European Union is developing plans to create a free-trade zone with Morocco. The parallels to Mexico are not overlooked by European officials, some of whom refer to Morocco as "Europe's Mexico."[20]

The boundary between Poland and Germany (marked by the Oder and Neisse rivers) has been referred to as "the Rio Grande of Europe."

"Like it or not," notes Heinrich Vogel of the Cologne-based Institute for East European and International Studies, "there are strong economic and social parallels" between the U.S.-Mexico and German-Polish relationship.[21] Border crossings—both legal and illegal—have increased significantly in recent years. In 1994, 147 million people reportedly crossed the German-Polish border—a 250-percent increase over 1991.[22] Along with the expanding economic ties between Poland and Germany and the liberalization of the Polish economy, there has been a major increase in illegal cross-border activity.[23] According to the United Nations, Poland is one of the primary transshipment routes for illegal drugs into western Europe. Poland is also a leading world producer of methamphetamines.[24] Germany, not surprisingly, is in the process of implementing tighter border controls along its eastern frontier (and Germany also pays Poland to patrol its side of the border).[25]

The enormous growth of the underground economy in Poland is partly driven by criminal organizations operating out of the former Soviet Union, which use Poland as an entry point to western Europe. Organized crime in the former Soviet Union has thrived as the economy has been privatized. As criminologist Louise Shelley observes, "privatization of the former Soviet economies invites participation by organized crime. . . . Organized crime groups exploit the privatization of the legitimate economy by investing illicit profits in new capital ventures, by establishing accounts in banks that have little regulation or do not question the source of badly needed capital and by utilizing new (and ancient) trade routes for the movement of illicit goods."[26] Russia's ministry of the interior estimates that 30 percent of the business privatized under market reforms between 1992 and 1994 is controlled by organized crime.

Rising alarm over these developments on or near the boundaries of the EU has revived the notion of creating a "fortress Europe." Thus, even as internal border controls are being dismantled under the Schengen Agreement (as part of the process of European integration), resources and personnel are being shifted to tighten external border controls. It may be more accurate to say, therefore, that borders are being relocated rather than dismantled. The EU countries are also attempting to harmonize parts of their criminal justice systems, and policing collaboration has also become more institutionalized.[27]

The aim of European collaboration is to create a "security surplus" instead of a "security deficit." This means establishing a "'cordon sanitaire' to keep out drug traffickers, terrorists and other criminals, refugees together with unwanted immigrants. Greatly increased cooperation between police and judicial authorities, shared intelligence and stricter internal controls would offset the consequences of permitting these undesirables—if they have breached the perimeter fence—to circulate freely around Europe."[28]

The trends briefly examined here may provide some initial clues regarding the changing purpose and character of the regulatory state, the function of borders and boundary maintenance in an integrating world, and the (re)definition of security as we approach the twenty-first century.

Many clandestine cross-border activities are increasingly perceived as a threat to the autonomy, social cohesion, and sometimes even the identity of national political communities.[29] And it is the state that is expected to enforce "law and order" abroad, at the border, and on city streets. Through this process, the very concept of security is being redefined to encompass perceived transnational threats posed by nonstate/nonmilitary actors. As the status of policing missions grows and traditional military threats decline, the coercive apparatus of the state is being redesigned and redeployed. This may ultimately be the true meaning of "reinventing government." While some parts of the regulatory state are being dismantled under the pressures of globalization and integration, the policing apparatus of the state is expanding. These developments will, no doubt, have a profound impact not only on international politics and border politics but also on the politics of global cities.

Notes

Research for this chapter was made possible by a Brookings Foreign Policy Studies Research Fellowship and an SSRC-MacArthur Foundation Fellowship on Peace and Security in a Changing World. I also wish to acknowledge the support of the Institute for the Study of World Politics. Some of the ideas in this chapter appear in an expanded form in "U.S.-Mexico: Open Markets, Closed Border," *Foreign Policy*, no. 103 (summer 1996): 51–69.

1. See, for example, the chapters by Saskia Sassen and Robert Smith in this volume.

2. While a large number of people obviously migrate for noneconomic reasons (for example, those fleeing war, political persecution, etc.), the cross-border migration flows examined here are primarily economically driven.

3. J. N. Bhagwati, "Incentives and Disincentives: International Migration," *Weltwirtschaftliches Archiv*, 120, no. 4 (1984): 680.

4. For example, Milton Friedman and the *Economist* promote drug legalization, and the *Wall Street Journal* advocates open borders for labor flows.

5. See, for example, Clifford Krauss's chapter on the activities of the Cali cartel in New York in this volume.

6. Quoted in George Winslow, "Global Warning," *Brooklyn Bridge*, May 1996, pp. 37–38.

7. Ibid., p. 43.

8. Lawrence A. Herzog, "Changing Boundaries in the Americas: An Overview," in Lawrence A. Herzog, ed., *Changing Boundaries in the Americas*, U.S.-Mexican Contemporary Perspective Series 3 (San Diego: Center for U.S.-Mexican Studies, 1992), pp. 5–6.

9. Prepared statement of Alan D. Bersin, United States Attorney, Southern District of California before the House Appropriations Subcommittee, March 29, 1995.

10. Tom Barry et al., *Crossing the Line: Immigrants, Economic Integration, and Drug Enforcement on the U.S.-Mexico Border* (Albuquerque: Resource Center Press, 1994), pp. 43, 77.

11. *Wall Street Journal*, January 6, 1995.

12. Robert Bach, "Processes of Migration," in Peter Smith, ed., *The Challenge of Integration: Europe and the Americas* (New Brunswick, N.J.: Transaction Publishers, 1993), pp. 217–18.

13. It is impossible to provide more than rough estimates of the size of the illegal drug trade. Commonly cited figures for the size of the U.S. drug market range between $40 and $100 billion annually. For a useful analysis of estimates of the size of the drug export sector in Colombia, Bolivia, and Peru, see Humberto Compodonico, "La Politica Del Avestruz," in Diego Garcia Sayan, ed., *Coca, Cocaina, y Narcotrafico* (Lima: Comisión Andina de Juristas, 1989).

14. Robert Cox, *Production, Power, and World Order* (New York: Columbia University Press, 1987).

15. Jan Nederveen Pieterse, "Fictions of Europe," *Race and Class* 32, no. 3 (1991): 5.

16. Colectivo Ioe (Carlos Pereda, Miguel A. de Prada, and Walter Actis), "Bringing International Political Economy into the Immigration Picture," in Wayne Cornelius et al., eds., *Controlling Immigration* (Stanford, Calif.: Stanford University Press, 1994), p. 372.

17. Marlise Simons, "Signs in Wind of Morocco Drug Crop," *New York Times*, June 18, 1995.

18. William Drozdiak, "Morocco Bars Smugglers' Gate to Europe," *Washington Post*, January 24, 1993.

19. Ibid.

20. Howard La Franchi, "Forging New Ties across the Mediterranean," *Christian Science Monitor*, January 27, 1993.

21. Quoted in Tyler Marshall, "Europe's New Wall: The Rich and the Poor," *Los Angeles Times*, September 1, 1991.

22. Peter Gumbel, "European Unity Sits and Waits on the Oder," *Wall Street Journal*, May 10, 1995.

23. Raymond Bonner, "Poland Becomes a Major Conduit for Drug Traffic," *New York Times*, December 30, 1993.

24. *Polish News Bulletin*, July 25, 1994.

25. Marcus Stern, "Germany Slows Flow of Illegal Immigrants," *San Diego Union-Tribune*, September 27, 1994.

26. Louise Shelley, "Transnational Organized Crime: An Imminent Threat to the Nation-State?" *Journal of International Affairs* (winter 1995): 482.

27. See Ethan Nadelmann, "Harmonization of Criminal Justice Systems," in Peter Smith, ed., *The Challenge of Integration: Europe and the Americas* (New Brunswick, N.J.: Transaction Publishers, 1993), pp. 247–77.

28. House of Lords Select Committee on the European Communities (1989):5, cited in Eugene McLaughlin, "The Democratic Deficit: European Union and the Accountability of the British Police," *British Journal of Criminology* 32 (autumn 1992): 481.

29. The term "societal security" refers to "the ability of a society to persist in its essential character under changing conditions." (Ole Waever et al., *Identity, Migration, and the New Security Agenda in Europe* [London: Pinter Publishers, 1993], p. 23.)

Chapter 6

Immigration and the Changing Demographic Profile of New York

JOSEPH J. SALVO AND ARUN PETER LOBO

THROUGHOUT its history, New York City has been shaped by the ebb and flow of migrants. These migratory movements are a result of linkages—economic, political, social, and cultural—that connect the city to the surrounding region, to the rest of the nation, and to the world. Over time, however, as the geographic focus of these linkages has changed, so has the ethnic profile of the people entering and leaving the city, fundamentally altering the city's population. In every era, new population groups have helped reinvent the city economically, politically, socially, and culturally, in turn modifying the city's relationship with the rest of the world. Thus, migration has both mirrored and influenced the city's evolution.

The earliest settlers were the Dutch, who established the city in the seventeenth century as an outpost for trade and commerce. The British, who followed the Dutch, were responsible for the city's rise as the new nation's commercial hub.[1] The Irish, Germans, and Scandinavians who began to arrive in significant numbers in the 1830s constructed and worked in the factories of an industrializing New York and established its craft guilds. As a result of these inflows, by 1860 the city had a population of over one million, 42 percent of which was foreign-born.

The 1880s marked the arrival of southern and eastern Europeans. By the first decade of this century, when these huge flows peaked, manufacturing was thriving and the construction of the subways and skyscrapers had begun. With a population of nearly 4.8 million in 1910,

41 percent of which was foreign-born, New York had solidified its place as the nation's premier city.

While immigration drove the city's population growth throughout the early twentieth century, domestic migration also played an important role, particularly in the second quarter of this century. With the mechanization of agriculture, surplus labor from rural areas was drawn to the manufacturing jobs available in the city. During the 1930s and 1940s, migrants from other states and from Puerto Rico kept New York City's population growing, despite huge declines in the number of arriving immigrants.[2] By 1950, the city's population had reached 7.9 million, 24 percent of which was foreign-born.

The 1950s saw large numbers of New Yorkers leave the city for its mushrooming suburbs. While this phenomenon actually began in the nineteenth century with the development of extensive transportation networks, it was not until the mid-twentieth century that it became a mass phenomenon.[3] It is only because of a resurgence in immigration that the city has been able to maintain its population base in the second half of the twentieth century. These continuing outflows, combined with the entry of immigrants, have proved to be a watershed for New York, dramatically changing the city's racial and ethnic composition. The foreign-born proportion, which reached a low of 18 percent in 1970 has been steadily increasing, reaching 28 percent in 1990. (See Table 6.1.)

Immigration Policy and Immigrant Flows

While the linkages between New York and the rest of the world pull immigrants to the city, the flow is regulated by immigration statutes. In the 1920s, for example, Congress established quotas that discriminated against southern and eastern Europeans; their darker pigmentation and non-Protestant faiths were seen as impediments to assimilating.[4] These quotas, coupled with the effects of the Great Depression, resulted in a sharp drop in the number of immigrants. While data for the city are not available, immigration data for the state of New York show that flows declined from 266,000 in 1921 to a low of 8,000 in 1933. The first group to experience the sting of exclusion was the Chinese, beginning in 1882. But the impact of the earlier restrictions on the city was minimal, since most Asians immigrated to the West Coast. The legacy of discriminatory immigration legislation was repealed with the passage of the 1965 Immigration and Nationality Act, which opened the doors to non-European immigrants.

Table 6.1 Immigrants Admitted to the United States and New York City, 1946–1994

	United States			New York City			New York City as a Percent of the United States
	Admissions	Annual Average	Percent Change	Admissions	Annual Average	Percent Change	
1946–49	614,900	153,725		129,077	32,269		21.0
1950–59	2,499,268	249,927	62.6	470,597	47,060	45.8	18.8
1960–69	3,213,749	321,375	28.6	575,570	57,557	22.3	17.9
1970–79	4,336,001	433,600	34.9	783,248	78,325	36.1	18.1
1980–89*	5,853,404	585,340	35.0	856,020	85,602	9.3	14.6
1990–94	3,849,159	769,832	31.5	562,988	112,598	31.5	14.6
Total	20,366,481			3,377,500			16.6

*Data are not available for New York City for 1980 or 1981. The city figure for 1980–89 is extrapolated from 1982–89 data.
Sources: Immigration and Naturalization Service unpublished data, 1946–81, and Annual Immigrant Tape Files, 1982–94.

The 1965 Immigration and Nationality Act

Although the McCarran-Walter Act of 1952 abolished race as a barrier to immigration, it retained some forms of national bias. Only with the passage of the 1965 Immigration and Nationality Act were national origins quotas abolished and all sending countries placed on an equal footing. Family reunification became the cornerstone of immigration policy. The act also provided for the entry of those with specified occupational skills and the admission of refugees and asylum seekers. While the law established numerical caps for most admission categories, "immediate relatives" of U.S. citizens—defined as minor children and spouses of U.S. citizens, and parents of U.S. citizens over the age of 21—were not subject to numerical limits. The 1965 law led to a marked increase in the number of immigrants entering the U.S. in general and to New York City in particular. This increase was partly a result of the growth in immediate relatives and refugees. Average annual immigration to the city climbed from 47,100 in the 1950s, to 78,300 in the 1970s, to 85,600 in the 1980s.

With less than 3 percent of the nation's population, New York City absorbed 15 percent of all immigrants in the 1980s. (For a comparison of the city's native-born versus foreign-born population from the 1850s to 1990, see Figure 6.1.)

Given the concern in some quarters over the size of recent flows, it is instructive to compare them to flows at the turn of the century. The annual average number of immigrants entering New York State (data for the city are unavailable) around the turn of the century was larger than the number at any point since 1965. (See Figure 6.2.)

During the first decade of this century, New York State absorbed 2.6 million immigrants, or 260,000 persons annually, compared to 170,000 annually in the 1990s. Moreover, since the state's population increased from 7.3 million in 1900 to nearly 18 million in 1990, immigrants accounted for a much larger proportion of the overall population in the earlier period. The number of immigrants in the 1900–09 period was equivalent to 36 percent of the 1900 population; the projected flows between 1990 and 1999, in comparison, will be equivalent to just 9 percent of the 1990 population. (See Figure 6.3.)

There have also been remarkable changes in the origins of immigrants to the city. There has been a dramatic shift in source countries, from the nations of Europe to those of Asia, the Caribbean, and South America. In the first decade of this century, 93 percent of immigrants to the United States were from Europe (again, data for the city are not

Figure 6.1   Total Population by Nativity—New York City, 1850–1990

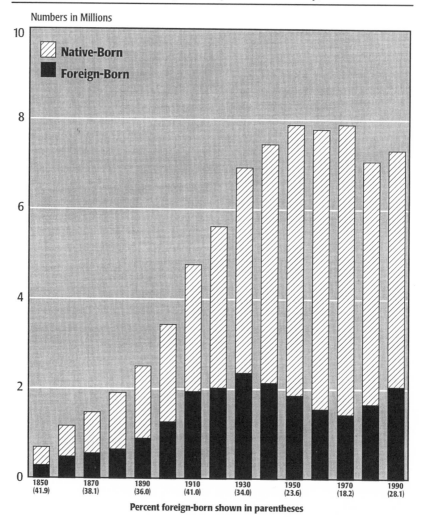

Source: Decennial census data.

available); in the 1980s the percentage of Europeans dropped to just 11 percent. (See Figure 6.4.)

This decline was also seen in New York City, where Europeans constituted only 9 percent of the flow in the 1980s. However, New York's current immigrant profile is still distinct from that of the nation. The city's immigrants are disproportionately from the Caribbean and South

Figure 6.2   Average Annual Immigration to New York State, 1900–1999

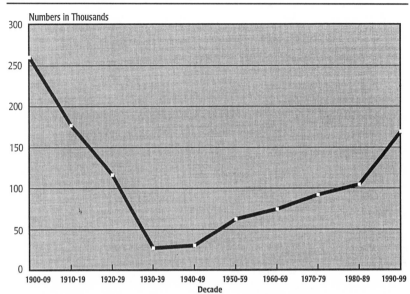

Note: Projected flows for 1990–99 assume a continuation of 1990–93 immigration levels.
Source: Immigration and Naturalization Service.

**Figure 6.3   Immigration to New York State by Decade as a Percentage of
Population at Start of Decade, 1900–1999**

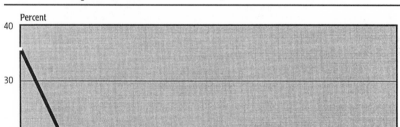

Note: Projected flows for 1990–99 assume a continuation of 1990–93 immigration levels.
Sources: Immigration and Naturalization Service; Decennial Population Censuses.

Figure 6.4   Immigrants by Area of Birth, 1980–1989

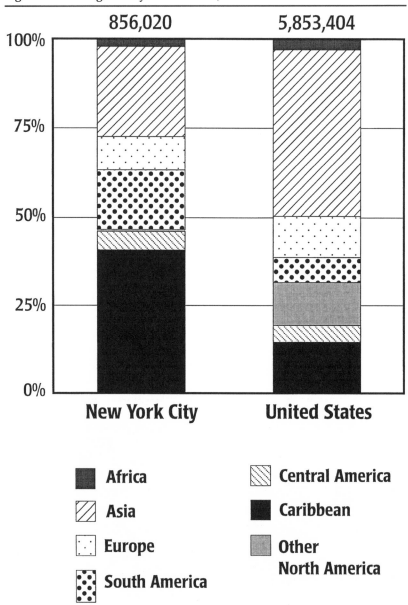

Source: Immigration and Naturalization Service.

America, while Asians are underrepresented. In the 1980s, for example, 40 percent of the city's immigrants were from the Caribbean, compared with just 14 percent for the nation. In contrast, 26 percent of the city's immigrants were from Asia, although Asians accounted for 46 percent of the nation's immigrants. The Dominican Republic sent the most immigrants to the city during the 1980s (145,000), followed by Jamaica and China (90,000 each), Guyana (67,000), and Haiti (51,000). No European country was among the top ten source countries of immigrants to the city during this period.

These changes in the source countries of immigrants were not foreseen by the authors of the 1965 law. They believed that the large number of visas set aside for those with family members already in the United States would ensure that immigrant flows would remain primarily European. However, low demand for visas from Europeans allowed others, many with needed occupational skills, to enter the United States. The diversity of recent immigrant flows is also a reflection of New York's global links and its role as a strategic node in an increasingly global economy.[5]

The 1986 Immigration Reform and Control Act

The flow of undocumented immigrants is also an outgrowth of economic and other structural links between societies.[6] While it has been illegal for undocumented immigrants to work in the United States, prior to 1986 no action could be taken against employers of undocumented immigrants.[7] The Immigration Reform and Control Act (IRCA) of 1986 sought to curb this flow by levying penalties against employers of undocumented workers. It also called for increased enforcement along the Mexican border. The act sought to address the problem of undocumented aliens already residing in the United States by legalizing those who had resided continuously in the United States since January 1, 1982. It also legalized undocumented workers who performed farm labor for at least 90 days during the year ending May 1, 1986. The 2.76 million people legalized under IRCA were mostly residents of western and southwestern states; only 126,000 were from New York City.[8]

However, IRCA did have a major impact on New York in one respect. Many of those amnestied were from countries that had not previously had a large documented presence in the city. This was especially true for immigrants from Senegal, Ghana, Nigeria, and Egypt as well as from Mexico and Guatemala. IRCA allowed these nations to gain a foothold in the city from which further immigration would be attracted.

The 1990 Immigration Act

By placing an emphasis on family reunification, the authors of the 1965 law unwittingly locked out potential immigrants who were more than one generation removed from United States citizens. This inequity was alleviated with the passage of the 1990 Immigration Act, which instituted a "diversity program," initially aimed primarily at Europeans, to provide a path of entry for those with no close relatives in the United States. While family reunification remained the crux of United States immigration policy, the new law placed greater emphasis on the entry of skilled immigrants, nearly tripling the total number of visas available in their category. The law also authorized the entry of "legalization dependents"—the spouses and minor children of immigrants amnestied under IRCA.

As a result of the 1990 act, immigration to the city in the 1990–94 period increased by nearly one-third over the previous decade, averaging 112,600 annually. Thanks to the diversity program and refugee flows, the proportion of European immigrants to the city jumped from 9 percent in the 1980s to 22 percent in this period.[9] The former Soviet Union and Poland broke into the top ten source countries. While the Dominican Republic remained the largest source country, accounting for one in five immigrants to the city, the former Soviet Union was second, accounting for 12 percent of the flow to the city. This represented a major change from the 1980s, when the Soviet Union was only the twelfth largest source country. China (11 percent) remained in third place, followed by Jamaica and Guyana (6 percent each).

Undocumented Immigration

The flow of undocumented immigrants has continued despite employer sanctions and the emphasis placed on increased border enforcement under IRCA. Cross-border flows from Mexico are the most problematic. Peter Andreas notes in this volume that the United States has moved simultaneously to open its border with Mexico to the legal flow of goods while closing it to the illegal flow of labor. However, this gatekeeping is unlikely to halt the flow of undocumented immigrants to the city, since a substantial proportion enter with a valid visa; only by staying beyond the required departure date do they become part of the undocumented population. Of those amnestied by IRCA in New York, for example, over 40 percent were visa overstayers.

Using data developed by the U.S. Immigration and Naturalization Service, the New York City Department of City Planning estimates that the undocumented population in the city in 1992 exceeded 400,000.[10] These undocumented immigrants represent a mix of nations different from that of documented immigrants. Unlike documented immigrants, who tend to be heavily Dominican, and more recently Russian, the mix of undocumented immigrants tends to be more varied, with substantial numbers from Ecuador, Poland, the Dominican Republic, and Colombia.[11] These well-established flows are likely to continue since, as Andreas observes, they act as a safety valve for unemployment crises in many of the sending countries.

Immigration Flows and Population Growth: 1950–2000

Population change occurs through two basic processes: natural increase (the balance of births and deaths) and net migration (the balance of in-migrants and out-migrants). In-migrants may be either domestic migrants or immigrants. In the postwar era, most domestic in-migration to New York City has consisted of relatively small flows into Manhattan, primarily made up of young, upwardly mobile individuals seeking to establish careers. The postwar years have also seen a substantial out-migration from the city. There are a number of reasons for these moves, including life-cycle changes related to childbearing (for example, a desire for more living space in a suburban environment), retirement, employment opportunities outside the city, and a desire to return to one's place of origin.

Immigration affects both net migration and natural increase. The entry of immigrants directly offsets losses through out-migration. The effects of immigration flows are also felt indirectly, through natural increase. Immigrants are generally younger on average than the population as a whole and have higher-than-average fertility. Immigrants thus account for a disproportionately higher share of births, and being young, a lower share of deaths.

While immigration to New York City has increased since 1950, so has out-migration. The influx of immigrants has ameliorated what could have been catastrophic losses through out-migration. The components of change in New York's population between 1950 and 1990, and projections for the year 2000, are illustrated in Figure 6.5.

In the 1950s, large-scale suburbanization led to a net out-migration of 857,000 persons; yet because of the "baby boom," the city's population declined by only 110,000. Had it not been for the 471,000 arriving im-

Figure 6.5   Components of Population Change for New York City, 1950–2000

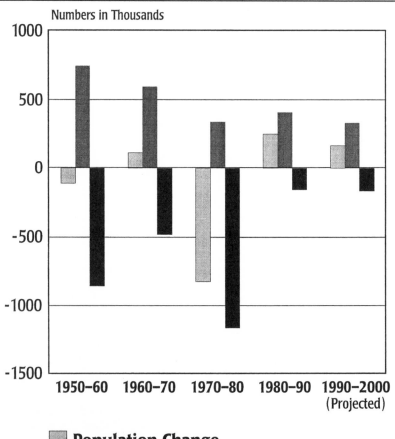

Population Change

Natural Increase

Net Migration

Sources: Vital Statistics, New York City Department of Health; decennial population censuses.

migrants, the decline would have been over five times greater. In the 1960s, losses through net out-migration were 482,000, but the city's population grew by 113,000, only as a result of natural increase. However, the city would have lost population but for the arrival of 576,000 immigrants during this period. In the 1970s, the city lost over 10 percent of its population, the result of a record net out-migration of nearly 1.2 million people. The decline in population would have been much greater had it not been for the 783,000 immigrants who arrived during the decade. The city's population increased 4 percent between 1980 and 1990, largely as a result of the 856,000 immigrants who entered during that decade.

Population Change in the Largest U.S. Cities

Not all American cities have been as fortunate as New York. In the early decades of this century, cities in the Northeast and the Midwest boomed as a result of domestic as well as international inflows. However, in the 1950s, 1960s, and 1970s, with the onset of massive suburbanization and the decline in manufacturing jobs, these cities lost substantial portions of their populations. Of the eighteen largest U.S. cities in 1950, five—St. Louis, Cleveland, Detroit, Buffalo, and Pittsburgh—experienced losses of 29 percent or more between 1970 and 1990. (See Figure 6.6.)

Each of these cities experienced declines in their foreign-born population, which indicates that they attracted few of the post–1965 immigrants. (See Figure 6.7.)

The marked increases in the percentage of foreign-born in Washington, D.C., and Chicago were accompanied in both instances by big losses in population. Evidently, immigration was insufficient to counter the effects of widespread suburbanization in these cities.

While many central cities in the Northeast and the Midwest were hollowed out, their suburbs boomed, giving rise to the peculiar doughnut-shaped urban areas that exist today. This population redistribution resulted in the dual problems of underutilized and decaying infrastructure in the central cities, coupled with urban sprawl. For those cities that experienced the biggest problems, immigrants were not available to fill the void created by the out-migration of the native-born population. In contrast, cities that lost proportionately fewer persons, or gained population—Boston, New York, San Francisco, and Los Angeles—all experienced substantial gains in their foreign-born populations. Moreover, these cities had substantial bases of foreign-born persons to begin with. New York City's foreign-born population rose from 18 percent in 1970 to 28 percent in 1990. The foreign-born population of San Francisco

Figure 6.6   Population Change of Major Cities, 1970–1990

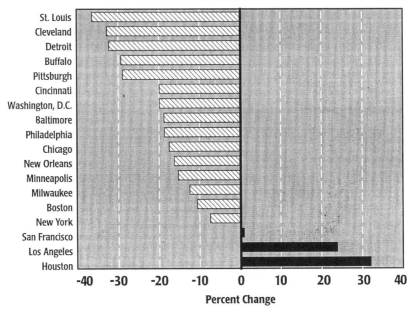

Note: Cities included had a population over 500,000 in 1950.
Source: Immigration and Naturalization Service.

increased from 22 percent to 34 percent during the same period, while that of Los Angeles rose from 15 percent to 38 percent. Although Boston lost 11 percent of its population between 1970 and 1990, this was modest compared to the losses experienced by other cities. Moreover, the loss would have been much greater had it not been for the rise in the percentage of foreign-born from 13 to 20 percent.

Net Outflows in New York City's Suburban Counties

New York City's suburban counties are also increasingly a destination for immigrants. In the early 1970s, 13 percent of all immigrants to the New York region settled in counties outside the city; the proportion rose to 37 percent in the early 1990s.[12] This has resulted in a large increase in the foreign-born population of many suburban counties, helping to offset substantial domestic out-migration. In the 1990–95 period, Bergen County, New Jersey, for example, experienced a net loss of 23,000 persons through domestic migration but posted a net gain of

Figure 6.7   Percentage Foreign-Born in Major Cities, 1970 and 1990

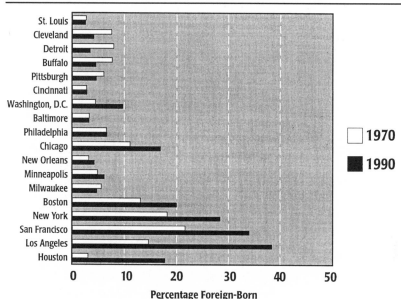

Note: Cities included had a population over 500,000 in 1950.
Source: Immigration and Naturalization Service.

28,000 international migrants. Other suburban counties are more similar to the city in that substantial immigration has not been able to offset the even greater losses from domestic migration. In Nassau County, a net loss of 47,000 through domestic migration was only partly offset by a net gain of 29,000 international migrants; Westchester's losses from domestic migration totaled 33,000, while net international migrants numbered 22,000; and in Hudson County, New Jersey, net domestic outflows totaled 58,000, while the county experienced a net gain of 35,000 international migrants.[13]

New York in the Year 2000

Between 1990 and the year 2000, New York City's population is projected to grow by 166,000 persons. Despite the expected arrival of over a million immigrants, a net out-migration of 166,000 is projected. This net outflow will be offset by a natural increase of 332,000. With foreign-for-native replacement continuing through the decade, one-third of the city's population is projected to be foreign-born by the year 2000. However, the percentage of foreign-born tells only part of the story. The relative youth of immigrants, combined with the high fertility of some groups, has led to substantial growth of the second generation. While it is routine for people to refer to the large number of immigrants from the Dominican Republic, for example, not commonly cited is the fact that fully one-third of the Dominicans enumerated in the 1990 census were second-generation and beyond. In 1990, foreign-born women accounted for 43 percent of all births to city residents, and this is expected to increase. As a result, by the year 2000, over 55 percent of all persons in the city will either be foreign-born or have at least one foreign-born parent.[14] However, this figure is still below the figure for 1920, when 78 percent of the city's population was either foreign-born or of foreign parentage.[15] Thus, both recent immigrants and their U.S.-born children have enabled New York to escape depopulation, which has been the fate of so many other older central cities.

Racial and Ethnic Diversity

The volume of the post-1965 immigration to New York tends to obscure a significant aspect of these flows—the unprecedented racial/ethnic diversity fostered. In 1970, New York City's non-Hispanic white population numbered nearly 5 million, or 63 percent of the total population; by the year 2000, this population is projected to decrease to 2.6 million, or 35 percent of the total. (See Figure 6.8.)

At the other end of the spectrum, the city's Hispanic population, which stood at 1.3 million in 1970, is expected to increase dramatically, to 2.2 million in the year 2000, or from 16 percent to 29 percent of the total population in the city. Asians numbered 118,000 in 1970, accounting for less than 2 percent of the population; by the year 2000, they are expected to number 762,000, or over 10 percent of the city's population. Non-Hispanic blacks, who made up 19 percent of the city's population in 1970, and 25 percent in 1990, are projected to experience a more modest increase, to 26 percent in the year 2000.

Not only is the city becoming more racially/ethnically diverse, there is growing diversity *within* groups. In each racial/ethnic group, entering immigrants are offsetting losses among the native-born population (either through death or migration). As a result, the composition of each of the city's major racial/ethnic groups is undergoing significant change. (See Figure 6.9.)

The Hispanic population is projected to grow by 400,000 between 1990 and the year 2000, through positive natural increase and positive net migration. However, the latter is expected to account for only one-

Figure 6.8   **Population by Race and Ethnicity, New York City, 1970–2000**

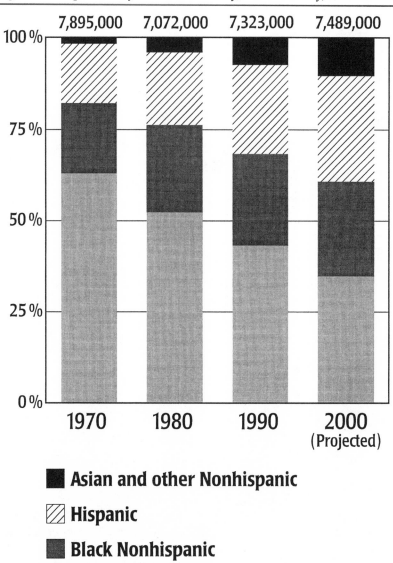

Sources: Decennial population censuses; New York City Department of City Planning, *Population Projections for the Year 2000*, Technical Report 1.

Figure 6.9   Projected Components of Change by Race and Ethnicity, New York City, 1990–2000

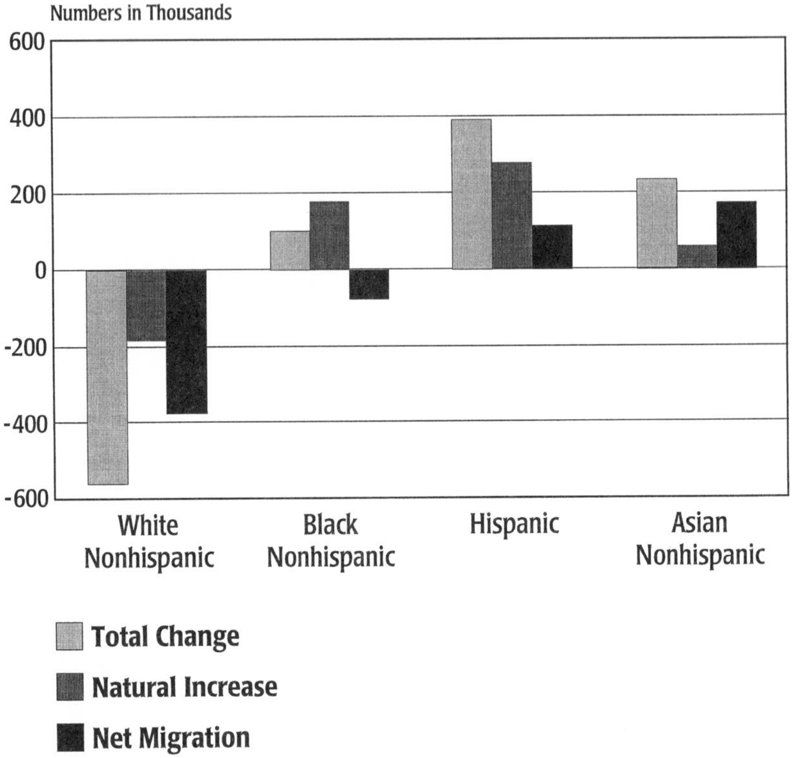

Source: New York City Department of City Planning, *Population Projections for the Year 2000*, Technical Report 1.

quarter of the increase: Hispanic immigrant flows from the Caribbean and South America will be offset by a net outflow of Puerto Ricans from the city. Births among Hispanics are expected to account for three-quarters of the projected growth. While the Puerto Rican population is expected to grow moderately through natural increase, non–Puerto Rican Hispanics will increase dramatically through both natural increase and net migration. In 1960, 75 percent of all Hispanics in the city were Puerto Rican; by 1990 only one-half were Puerto Rican.[16] By the year 2000, Puerto Ricans will constitute only a plurality among Hispanics.

The declining share of the Puerto Rican population among Hispanics is a result of the surge in immigration from the Dominican Republic,

Colombia, Ecuador, Peru, and Mexico as well as high immigrant fertility. The Dominican population, for example, increased from 125,000 in
1980, to nearly 333,000 in 1990, an increase of 165 percent.[17] Unpublished
estimates by the Population Division of the New York City Department
of City Planning indicate that the Dominican population crossed the
500,000 mark in 1995. If current trends hold, it is likely that Dominicans
will constitute the largest Hispanic subgroup in the city early in the next
century. Although other Hispanic groups are not nearly as large, they
too are increasing at a brisk pace. The Mexican population, for example,
increased from only 23,000 in 1980 to 62,000 in 1990. Mexicans are
unique in that their increased numbers are largely a function of the
IRCA provisions and domestic in-migration.

New York City's non-Hispanic black population is projected to grow
by only 101,000 in the 1990s. The surplus of births over deaths will be
responsible for all this growth. Gains resulting from West Indian immigration will be insufficient to offset net out-migration of native-born
blacks. The native-born, who tend to migrate to the southern states,
have displayed negative net migration for the past two decades. They
are being replaced by black immigrants from Jamaica, Guyana, and
Haiti. Between 1970 and 1990, decennial census data show that the
foreign-born share of the black population rose from 8 percent to almost
25 percent.

Non-Hispanic whites are the only group projected to decline in the
1990s, by over 500,000 persons, through both net out-migration and
negative natural increase. Immigration from the former Soviet Union,
Poland, and Ireland will not be sufficient to offset the outflow of native-
born whites. While the loss through migration is responsible for two-
thirds of the overall decline, this actually represents a lower toll than
in the prior two decades, when migration accounted for upwards of
80 percent of white losses. Whites, who have the highest median age,
are the only group experiencing negative natural increase, or more
deaths than births.

The Asian population of the city is projected to increase by 233,000
persons, maintaining a steep pattern of growth that has been evident
since 1960. Natural increase will account for only one-quarter of this
growth, testimony to the higher median age of Asians and their lower
aggregate fertility. Most of the growth in this population is expected to
occur through migration. Although some foreign-for-native replacement is occurring among Asians, it has not yet had a major impact.
Asians are overwhelmingly an immigrant group: the foreign-born accounted for 77 percent of the city's Asian population in 1980 and 80 percent in 1990. The Asian presence is dominated by the Chinese, who

accounted for approximately one-half of all Asians in the city in both 1980 and 1990. But increases in immigration from Bangladesh, along with the still small but marked growth in immigration from western Asia, may change this balance significantly in future years.

This racial and ethnic heterogeneity and the influx of immigrants have important implications for intergroup relations in the city. Immigrant groups are frequently held up as "model minorities," which can drive a wedge between them and native-born minorities. Very often, as Robert Smith observes in Chapter 7, immigrant groups see themselves as different from native-born minorities. To take one example, West Indian immigrants stress cultural and behavioral attributes they feel set them apart from native-born blacks. They see themselves as more disciplined and as harder workers than native-born blacks, who in turn often resent this attitude.[18] However, both groups have come together in racial solidarity on issues such as police brutality and discrimination.[19] In general, while there has been some friction between recent immigrants and previously established groups, there are also signs of cooperation.[20]

In a city where no one racial group dominates demographically, the need for coalitions, especially in politics, is obvious. Even when the city was overwhelmingly white, no single ethnic group dominated, and ethnic coalitions were the hallmark of city politics. The coalition between the Irish and Jews helped elect the city's first Irish mayor in 1880 and helped decide subsequent elections as well.[21] As the immigrant presence in the city increases, and as more new immigrants become eligible to vote, these new immigrant groups will form an important part of political coalitions, both with the native-born and with other immigrant groups. These coalitions will have to span both ethnic and racial boundaries. David Dinkins was elected mayor in 1989 by just such a coalition: the overwhelming support of West Indian immigrants, native-born blacks, and Manhattan Jewish voters helped ensure his victory. However, a low black turnout and tepid Jewish support cost Dinkins the 1993 election.[22] Hispanics, particularly Dominicans, will play an increasingly important role in future coalitions as their numbers in the city continue to increase.

A City Dependent on Immigrant Flows

Congress is considering various proposals that would once again curb immigration to the United States. Thus, it is important to consider the potential effects of any drop in immigration on the city's population base.

Immigrant flows to New York in the 1800s and early 1900s were primarily responsible for placing it into the ranks of the world's largest cities. In the years following the restrictionist immigration policies of the 1920s, however, the city continued to grow. This was partly a result of domestic in-migrants streaming in from other Middle Atlantic and northeastern states, from the rural South, and from the island of Puerto Rico, displaced by agricultural mechanization and endemic rural poverty. While there has always been a steady stream of out-migrants from the city, until recently this has been relatively small in comparison with the flows into the city.

The post–World War II years marked the advent of mass suburbanization, which resulted in large numbers leaving New York City for its suburbs. The magnitude of this out-migration has been so great that despite the entry of 2.7 million immigrants between 1950 and 1989, the city still registered a net outflow totalling 2.7 million over this period. Thus, international flows, combined with natural increase, have helped the city maintain its population base. In that respect, New York has been fortunate compared to other large cities of the northeast and midwest, which have hemorrhaged population in recent decades.

As with most older central cities, New York continues to lose population as a result of net domestic flows. In the 1985–90 period, for example, 389,000 people with origins in the 50 states and Puerto Rico migrated to New York City, but 1,024,000 people moved out, resulting in a net domestic loss of 635,000 people.[23] With losses through domestic migration continuing, New York's neighborhoods depend on immigrants to replenish the population that leaves. There are a substantial number of neighborhoods in the city where a majority of recent occupancy is associated with new immigrants.[24] If the city's current out-migration trends continue, restrictions on immigration would result in massive population losses, and many neighborhoods would experience increases in housing vacancies and the inevitable deterioration in housing stock that is associated with such underutilization.

Notes

1. See Frederick M. Binder and David M. Reimers, *All the Nations under Heaven: An Ethnic and Racial History of New York City* (New York: Columbia University Press, 1996).

2. See Ira Rosenwaike, *Population History of New York City* (Syracuse: Syracuse University Press, 1972).

3. See Kenneth T. Jackson, *Crabgrass Frontier: The Suburbanization of the United States* (New York: Oxford University Press, 1985).

4. See Pastora Cafferty et al., *Dilemma of American Immigration: Beyond the Golden Door* (New Brunswick, N.J.: Transaction Books, 1983).

5. See Saskia Sassen's chapter in this volume.

6. See Charles B. Keely, "An Immigration Policy for America in the 21st Century," in Mary G. Powers and John J. Macisco, eds., *The Immigration Experience in the United States: Policy Implications* (New York: Center for Migration Studies, 1994).

7. See Frank Bean et al., *Opening and Closing the Doors: Evaluating Immigration Reform and Control* (Washington, D.C.: The Urban Institute Press, 1989).

8. See Arun Peter Lobo and Joseph J. Salvo, *The Newest New Yorkers: 1990–1994* (New York City Department of City Planning, 1996).

9. Ibid.

10. See Robert Warren, *Estimates of the Unauthorized Immigrant Population Residing in the United States by Country of Origin and State of Residence* (Washington, D.C.: Immigration and Naturalization Service Statistics Division).

11. Ibid. Also see GAO Report 95-20, *Illegal Immigration: INS Overstay Estimation Methods Need Improvement* (Washington, D.C.: General Accounting Office). This report revised the initial INS estimates of undocumented immigrants from some countries.

12. See Ronald Ortiz-Flores and Joseph J. Salvo, "Immigrant Settlement Patterns in the New York Metropolitan Region" (paper presented at the Annual Meeting of the American Sociological Association, New York, August 1996).

13. See U.S. Bureau of the Census, "Estimates of Components of Change for the Population of Counties." Unpublished tabulations prepared by the New York State Department of Economic Development, State Data Center, and the New Jersey Department of Labor, Division of Labor Market and Demographic Research.

14. The estimate for persons of foreign birth or parentage was derived from data from the *1991* and *1993 New York City Housing and Vacancy Surveys (HVS)*, as well as from data from past decennial censuses. The 1970 census was the last census to include a question on the birthplace of parents.

15. See Walter Laidlaw, ed., *Statistical Sources for Demographic Studies of Greater New York* (New York: NYC 1920 Census Committee, 1922).

16. Joseph J. Salvo, Ronald Ortiz-Flores, and Arun Peter Lobo, *Puerto Rican New Yorkers in 1990* (New York City Department of City Planning, 1994), p. vi.

17. *Socioeconomic Profiles: A Portrait of New York City's Community Districts from the 1980 and 1990 Censuses of Population and Housing* (New York City Department of City Planning, 1993), p. 8.

18. Nancy Foner, "Race and Ethnic Relations in Immigrant New York," *Migration World* 23 (1995): 14–18.

19. See Philip Kasinitz, *Caribbean New York: Black Immigrants and the Politics of Race* (Ithaca, N.Y.: Cornell University Press, 1992).

20. Foner, "Race and Ethnic Relations in Immigrant New York," 14–18.

21. See Chris McNickel, *To Be Mayor of New York: Ethnic Politics in the City* (New York: Columbia University Press, 1992).

22. See John Mollenkopf, *A Phoenix in the Ashes: The Rise and Fall of the Koch Coalition in New York City Politics* (Princeton, N.J.: Princeton University Press, 1992).

23. Salvo, Ortiz-Flores, and Lobo, *Puerto Rican New Yorkers in 1990*, p. 120.

24. See Lobo and Salvo, *The Newest New Yorkers*.

Chapter 7

Transnational Migration, Assimilation, and Political Community

ROBERT C. SMITH

T HE HONORED guest at a dinner hosted by leaders of the Mexican community in New York City in 1993 was Dr. Roger Díaz de Cossio, the first director of the Program for Mexican Communities Abroad, which was created in 1990 by Mexico's president, Carlos Salinas de Gortari, to reach out to Mexicans living in the United States.[1] In conversations over the previous year and a half, Dr. Díaz de Cossio and I had discussed the program's mission, and on this occasion I gave him a copy of an article on a similar program Portugal had created some twenty years before.[2] Seeing the subtitle, "Creating the Portuguese Global Nation," he pounded his finger on the page and said with conviction, "This is exactly what I am trying to do. This is my job, to create the Mexican global nation."[3]

If this seems a farfetched goal, consider the following:

- The Dominican Republic and Colombia have both changed their constitutions in recent years to allow migrants living abroad to hold dual citizenship, including the right to vote in national elections. Colombia's constitutional changes even provide for the election of an official who will act as an advocate for Colombians living abroad. Enabling legislation for these constitutional changes has not yet been put into practice.[4]

- Portugal has not only allowed but has encouraged dual nationality for more than twenty years, but has also urged its emigrants to acquire citizenship in their host countries and thus "establish Portugal's presence in the world."[5]

- The Mexican government has recently shown itself to be more disposed toward the concept of dual nationality, which was considered anathema just a few years ago. In June 1996, the major political parties agreed to allow Mexicans residing outside Mexico to vote in Mexican presidential elections beginning in the year 2000.

- Politicians from the Dominican Republic, Colombia, the Anglophone Caribbean, Haiti, and Mexico all make regular campaign stops in New York in an attempt to gather support and to raise funds. Mexican and Portuguese politicians are similarly active in Los Angeles and Massachusetts, respectively.

- Leonel Fernandez, the recently elected president of the Dominican Republic, holds an American "green card" and attended New York City public schools.

- During the first part of his presidency, Jean Bertrand Aristide designated Haitians living abroad the "Tenth Department" of Haiti—thereby granting them, symbolically, at least, equal status with Haitians in the nine geographical departments (provinces) of the country.[6]

Assimilation, Transnational Migration, and Political Community

What do these developments mean? Do they signal or will they contribute to an unwillingness on the part of immigrants to become assimilated? Are they signs of an incipient irredentism? How do such practices change the meaning of membership in a political community, or, for that matter, the concept of citizenship? And, finally, how new is transnational life among immigrants? Did the immigrants of the past engage in similar transnational practices? The short answer is that these practices are not as new as scholars originally had thought, but they are quantitatively and qualitatively different from past practices because, in part, of differences in technology as well in the domestic and international politics of both sending and receiving countries. These differences may result in a changed and more durable ongoing relationship with the country of origin, as well as a different experience of assimilation in the United States.[7] Hence, emigrants from the Dominican Republic, Haiti, Mexico or elsewhere are increasingly seen to be and see themselves as part of a Dominican, Haitian, or

Mexican diaspora or global nation, even while they are becoming members of U.S. society and political community. As a result, New York is becoming an increasingly important center of transnational political activity. As a city with more than one-quarter of its population foreign-born (see the chapter by Joseph Salvo and Peter Lobo in this volume), and one that is deeply enmeshed in the global economy, New York will be more affected than most cities by such changes, and hence they merit the close examination this chapter attempts to provide.

There are two principal ways of looking at immigration, assimilation, and membership in a political community. The "classic model" equates membership in the nation with membership in the state, or citizenship.[8] There is a mutually exclusive relationship between an immigrant's membership in the home country's political community and the host country's political community. In this view, one leaves off membership in the old country when one emigrates and takes up a new membership in the new country. There is a "clean break," which Oscar Handlin described as an "uprooting."[9]

"Postnational membership" posits that the national state is being superseded by transnational processes. For example, sociologist Yasemin Soysal asserts that international legal regimes now guarantee the human rights of the "modern person" within a framework that supersedes citizenship and the national state. Hence, individuals do not depend exclusively on the states in which they reside for defense of their rights, and "the logic of personhood supersedes the logic of national citizenship."[10] Anthropologist Michael Kearney argues similarly in analyzing how Mixtec and Zapotec farmworkers from Oaxaca, Mexico, have organized panethnically and across borders in defense of their human rights and culture.[11] Others question whether the concept of sovereignty itself should be modified in attempting to understand emerging realities.[12]

A third way of viewing the current state of immigrant assimilation and membership in a political community focuses on the simultaneous memberships and identities that immigrants hold, and their simultaneous relationships with their home and host societies. It should be noted that "simultaneous" does not mean coequal memberships: especially in the second generation, local and national American identity are most likely to be primary and the diasporic identity, secondary. This condition emerges in response to several factors that differ in importance in varying cases: (1) advances in communications and travel technology; (2) the increased importance of immigrants in the economies of their home countries; (3) the sending states' attempts to legitimize themselves at home through their good works among "their" emigrants and emigrants' children abroad;[13] (4) the increasing importance of the United States in the economic and political futures of sending societies; and (5) the social marginalization of many immigrant groups within the United States. These developments can be understood significantly as the responses of immigrants and their home states to processes of globalization such as those described by Saskia Sassen and others in this volume. Moreover, the state, rather than being simply circumvented by it, is in fact often central to the creation and durability of transnational life.

Transnational practices and simultaneous memberships can have important democratizing effects, especially in empowering immigrants to participate in politics in their home and/or host societies.[14] One observer points to transnational practices as a "potentially potent counter" to the disenfranchising effects of economic globalization that are analyzed in this volume by Saskia Sassen, Carol O'Cléireacáin, and Rae Rosen and Reagan Murray.[15] Such practices may help ameliorate the apartheid-like divisions Jorge Castaneda sees emerging between "those who work" (mainly nonwhite undocumented or nonvoting immigrants) and "those who vote" (mainly white-skinned natives).[16] I believe that better understanding of simultaneous memberships could lead the United States and immigrant sending states to implement policies to increase the participation of immigrants in democratic processes in both countries or in one, thereby lessening the antidemocratic effects of the "limbo" in which many immigrants and their children dwell. Moreover, it might also ameliorate fears that irredentist or separatist sentiments among immigrants might eventually lead to an "American Québec." Hence, I am more optimistic than Jay Kaplan, in this volume, about the prospects for the democratic incorporation of immigrants into American society, though I share the concern expressed by Josh DeWind, also in this volume, about the negative impact that great and growing inequalities, especially the cities, may have on the process.

The next section of this chapter examines the broader context within which transnationalization of migrant life is occurring. The second compares Italian immigration to New York at the turn of the century[17] with that of Mexican and other immigrants to New York today, focusing on both macro- and micro-level processes in order to put a more human face on the analysis. The third section focuses on the largest current immigrant group in New York, analyzing the case of the political participation of Dominicans in New York and in the Dominican Republic.

The Context of Transnational Migration and Membership

The current transnationalization of migrant social, political, and economic life takes place within a particular context. Recent increases in immigration are part of an overall surge in international travel in recent years. This exponential increase is corollary to the more open legal and trade systems of industrialized nations meant to ensure the free movement of many classes of persons, and thus to foster trade and tourism between them within an increasingly integrated world economy.[18] Consistent with this, approximately half of the undocumented people in the United States each year enter on tourist or other visas and overstay, while the other half enter surreptitiously at the United States-Mexico border.[19]

A second aspect of this movement is that industrialized democratic states have a hard time restricting undocumented immigration as completely as they would like, although reports that undocumented immigration is "out of control" exaggerate the reality.[20] Family reunification provisions, the need to respect constitutional liberties, and the intolerance of democratic populations for "police state" enforcement of immigration laws make it difficult to stop chain migration from occurring, wherein family and friendship networks facilitate the entrance of newcomers.[21] Given these conditions, a steady and relatively high level of immigration from the south seems likely in the foreseeable future. Moreover, once here, immigrants are more likely today to settle in more highly segregated neighborhoods than they were in the prior waves of migration, in part due to discrimination, and this slows down the assimilation process, the attenuation of links to the home country, and the learning of English. When combined with the effects of racism, it may also have negative effects on group mobility.[22] Such conditions have changed all aspects of assimilation and may facilitate transnational life.

Another factor facilitating the formation of transnational life is that the United States has recently experienced the second largest influx of immigrants in its history. Indeed, 9.9 million immigrants entered the United States legally between 1983 and 1993 (including more then 3 million admitted under the Immigration Reform and Control Act of 1986), while 10.1 million were admitted during the all time high of the 1905–15 decade, though the number of immigrants per thousand United States residents was lower in the more recent period (3.7 versus 11.1, respectively), as pointed out by Joseph Salvo and Peter Lobo in this volume. As we will see in greater detail later, these immigrants do not simply break off their connections with their home countries but rather maintain a regular flow of immigrants, remittances, goods, and ideas between the United States and those home countries.

The magnitude and importance of these flows of people and money is impressive. Studies estimate that Mexicans in the United States remit approximately $2 billion to Mexico annually, an amount nearly equivalent to Mexico's 1990 earnings from export agriculture and equal to 78 percent of direct foreign investment, 59 percent of tourist revenues, and 56 percent of earnings from *maquiladora* (in-bond, border assembly plant) production.[23] The flow of people between the two countries is two-way and extensive. Lately, more than a million undocumented immigrants a year are apprehended trying to cross the United States-Mexico border. Yet, for each 100 undocumented Mexican immigrants who enter the United States, 86 will go back to Mexico in the same year.[24] Most immigrants, whether legal or undocumented, travel back to their home country at some point.

In the Dominican Republic, tourism is the country's greatest source of foreign exchange, outstripping its earnings from sugarcane or other sources. According to official estimates, almost a third of total revenues from tourism in 1985 came from Dominicans living abroad, making them in all likelihood the single biggest contributor to foreign-exchange earnings.[25] In El Salvador, remittances have become so important to the economy—accounting for 15 to 25 percent of GDP by some measures[26]—that the Salvadoran government has sent consular personnel to the United States to help Salvadorans fill out asylum and extended voluntary departure applications, so that they do not have to leave the country.[27] Also, in April 1987, a dying President Duarte appealed in the *New York Times* to the United States not to deport Salvadorans, in large part because their remittances were needed to rebuild his war-torn nation. On a more macro scale, another study estimated that Caribbean immigrants as a group remitted $2.5 billion in 1990, or $1,163 per migrant on average; and that Central American immigrants as a group remitted $1.1 billion, or $739 per migrant on average. If the estimate of Mexican remittances of $2 billion is correct, this would yield an average of $522 per migrant.[28]

Such remittances make the emigrant populations increasingly important to sending states, both as sources of foreign exchange and economic development, and as potentially autonomous political actors. The reality is that large segments of the population of the Dominican Republic, Mexico, Central America, and other sending countries depend more directly on what happens with their relatives in the United States for their livelihoods than on what happens in their home countries.

Hence, not only do these population segments have more economic power at home, but their potential political influence at home makes the opinion of these emigrant populations more and more important for domestic politics. Hence, sending-state politicians increasingly campaign in New York and elsewhere in the United States.[29]

Moreover, it is not just the remittances and importance of the remitters at home that has led to closer and more durable ties between sending states and their diasporas, but also the fact that the economic and political futures of many of the major sending areas depend to a great extent on their relationship with the United States. This has led Latin American and Caribbean immigrants and their countries to pursue mutual interests. The model for these ties are those between Israel and American Jews, where American Jews are full members of American society yet also maintain ties of affection toward Israel that often influences their political stances. In the Mexican case, two important reasons for creating the Program for Mexican Communities Abroad were to mobilize support among Mexican Americans for the North American Free Trade Agreement (NAFTA) and to foster a diasporic Mexican cultural identity among the second generation in the United States.[30]

Similarly, Colombian immigrants in New York have used Colombia's interest in improving its image in the United States as leverage in pressing their demands for three things: (1) changes in the Colombian constitution that would allow unilateral dual citizenship, (2) the election of a representative of Colombians abroad to the country's Congress, and (3) help in changing the image of Colombian immigrants in the United States as closely linked to drug trafficking.[31] Colombia has made these constitutional changes, and Colombians in the United States and the Colombian government are working together to change the image of Colombia and Colombian immigrants. The end result is that the Colombian Consulate in New York has facilitated community-organization efforts in New York among Colombian immigrants—including naturalization and involvement in local politics—at the same time it promoted stronger ties between itself and the community. Concern for the image of Colombia in the United States was clearly one cause of the increased transnational links between Colombian immigrants and Colombia today.

The point here is that sending states are attempting to institutionalize diasporas both because of the influence of the United States in the region and its importance as a trading partner, and because of the increasing importance of remittances and political support from their diasporas. This is somewhat different from the last wave of migration in the 19th and early 20th centuries. The economies and development strategies of Italy, Germany, Ireland and other European sending states were not so closely intertwined with the United States, nor was U.S. influence so preponderant, as is the case for Caribbean and Central American states and Mexico today.

In considering these developments, we will do well to remember Saskia Sassen's insight in this volume and elsewhere that processes such as globalization take place in specific sites and are carried out by particular actors. With this in mind, we will examine how transnationalization was different in the past and how it can have democratizing effects.

Comparing Italian Transnational Practices in New York during the Last Great Wave of Migration with Contemporary Practices of Mexican and Other Immigrants

Comparing the actions of Italian immigrants and the Italian state in the period between 1880 and 1930 with Mexican and other immigration to New York today can yield interesting findings because the many similarities make differences into potential sources of insight. Mexicans are one of New York City's newest and fastest growing ethnic groups, currently numbering about 150,000.[32] A first similarity is that there was a great deal of back-and-forth movement between New York and Italy during the last wave of immigration. Contemporary observers estimated that 50 percent or more of Italian migrants who came to the United States went back to Italy and that at least a third of these then returned to the United States.[33] Moreover, then as today, technology played an important role in facilitating visits. Ocean liners made travel fast and inexpensive, including the $30 Christmas-time fares to Italy advertised in an Italian language newspaper in New York in the 1920s.[34]

Second, the Italian state promoted immigration and then return migration as part of its strategy of national development and nation building.[35] Indeed, temporary immigration and return were seen as developmental engines generating remittances and as integral parts of the Italian view of citizenship. When Italian immigrants demanded dual citizenship, the Italian state broached the topic to the United States and other Western Hemisphere nations, but it was rejected. However, Italy did set up institutions designed to facilitate the return of its emigrants and their savings and to maintain links with emigrants while settled abroad. The Banco di Napoli was empowered by the Italian state to open branches overseas to receive emigrant savings and remittances to be used for Italian development, ultimately remitting about 25 percent of the total flow to Italy.

Also, many in the Italian Congress urged that Italy's official policy encourage Italians abroad to become citizens of their adopted countries, even while retaining a link with Italy. One congressman argued that: "If I may say so, we ought to at one and the same time develop in them the national culture and love of Italy, and to confer on them the political power [in the adopted lands] they now lack [by becoming citizens]."[36] Such sentiments, voiced before 1920, came to seem more quixotic during the 1920s and 1930s, as the United States passed legislation based on eugenic theories positing the racial inferiority of southern and eastern Europeans, and as fascism, the Depression, and looming war ended emigration from Italy until the postwar period. This history is important because it shows that the idea of a global nation, although perhaps not conceived this way, and of simultaneous memberships among immigrants are not completely new.

Still, there are some things that are new and different about today's immigrant experience. These include changed technology, a different domestic political atmosphere regarding ethnicity, and the identity of the second generation. These differences are illustrated by comparing the histories of Mexican and Italian village-level religious and civic associations in New York, which organized both immigrant communities and were often devoted to a home village's patron saint. Such village-level associations underwent precipitous decline after World War I, as pressures to Americanize mounted in a context where eugenic theories underpinned the immigration law reforms. According to Ware's 1935 study of Italians in Greenwich Village, 50 percent of Italian men belonged to such societies before World War I, but only 10 to 15 percent did in the 1920s. Moreover, Ware reports that by the 1930s, a typical second-generation immigrant man associated such organizations with "the 'backwardness' of his parents" and did not participate in them.[37] And by the 1930s, few second-generation Italians made return trips to Italy.[38]

Contemporary Mexican immigrants and their civic and religious village associations in New York receive a very different reception from the Italians. The prevailing ethos is of ethnic pluralism, not Americanization, and hence institutions from the Catholic Church to the City of New York encourage the maintenance of such organizations and view them as completely compatible with full membership in American society. Moreover, many, though not all, in the second generation view such hometown or religious associations as positive forces in organizing their communities in New York.

Technology makes it possible for both the first and second generation to have significant and ongoing lived experiences in the home village from which they or their parents came. For example, immigrants from a village I call Ticuani in the state of Puebla, which has sent immigrants to New York City since the 1940s, have for the last thirty years funded many of their major public works projects through a committee that collects donations from Ticuanenses in New York. In fact, this committee has regularly sent delegations back to Ticuani to disburse payments and check on a public work's progress: they leave New York on Friday after work, spend the weekend in Ticuani, and fly back to New York on Monday for work. They often coordinate their activities by conference calls involving groups of leaders in Brooklyn and in Ticuani. Most recently, with the help of the Program for Mexican Communities Abroad mentioned at the outset of the chapter, they brought the municipal president of Ticuani to visit "his" Ticuanense constituency in New York. Hence, Ticuanenses are simultaneously living their lives in New York and are politically influential leaders in their towns and villages of origin.

Moreover, the second generation actively and increasingly participates in Ticuani's annual feasts in January and return during the summer to spend their vacations in a safe, inexpensive place. Indeed, several of the young women chosen as Ticuani's queen of the mass—an honored position awarded to someone embodying the best of Ticuani's youth—have been New York–born and New York–raised college students on vacation. The point is that instantaneous communications and rapid travel makes it possible for today's immigrants and their second-generation children simultaneously to maintain significant lives or at least to have significant lived experience in their communities of origin and destination. This in turn enables some social forms "imported" from the old country to persist and be adapted to the new one, and for Ticuanenses in New York to influence life there. While Italians may have had such inclinations, the fact that they could not go home for the weekend or negotiate with their counterparts in the village via speaker phone as do the Ticuanenses today makes the quality and quantity of relations on the micro level quite different from those of the past. We must also keep in mind that such transnational practices are engaged in by most other immigrant groups in New York, including Dominican "tropical capitalists," Haitian activists, West Indian politicians, and others.[39]

There are two other significant differences. The first is that while the Program for Mexican Communities Abroad today and the Italian state's outreach at the turn of the century had many similar objectives, the anti-immigrant tenor and international political context of the previous era blocked the extent to which such links could be institutionalized. While there is an anti-immigrant tone in today's politics, it is not as powerful as it was in the 1920s. Furthermore, the clearest expression of this senti-ment—Proposition 187 in California—is a California state measure that Governor Pete Wilson was not able to export successfully to the rest of the country in his bid for the Republican Party presidential nomination. Moreover, Proposition 187 had the unintended consequence of mobi-lizing many previously "nonpolitical" immigrants and contributed to the defeat of such anti-immigrant politicians as Republican Robert Dor-nan in Orange County, California. This anti-immigrant measure does not compare to the anti-immigrant sentiment translated into law in the 1921 and 1924 immigration laws, which codified racial theories of in-feriority in an attempt to stop immigration from southern and eastern Europe. And the United States cannot stop immigration as easily as it did in the 1920s, by simply shutting its ports of entry.

A second difference lies in the broader relationship between sending states and the United States, a point discussed above but which bears repeating. The relationship of most sending states with the United States—in terms of trade relations, political influence, and in others—is the most important for most Latin American sending countries. This was not true in the Italian case, at least not to the same extent. Moreover, the current political climate of ethnic pluralism makes it more likely that diasporic relations with the home country will resonate with domestic ethnic identities.[40] In the following section, we focus on one such case, "los Dominicanyorks" in New York and in the Dominican Republic.

"Los Dominicanyorks," Dual Nationality, and the Election of Guillermo Linares

Dominicans are the single largest nationality group among current im-migrants in New York, accounting for 17 percent of all legal interna-tional migration to the city.[41] According to the 1990 census, there were an estimated 225,000 Dominicans living in the city, while New York City Planning Department officials estimate more than 500,000 Dominicans were in the city in 1990. The recent history of Dominicans in New York provides a very clear instance of the development of simultaneous memberships in more than one political community, via their direct in-volvement in New York City politics and their increased importance in Dominican national politics. Two events demonstrate the mutually re-inforcing nature of these forms of participation. The first was the pas-sage of an amendment to the Dominican constitution providing for unilateral dual citizenship for Dominican immigrants abroad. The sec-ond was the creation of a Dominican-dominated electoral district in the Washington Heights section of New York City and the subsequent election of Guillermo Linares to the City Council. These events are analyzed here drawing on the work of sociologist Luis Guarnizo and political scientist Pamela Graham.

To understand how these two events are related, it is necessary to explore the emergence of Dominican immigrants as a distinct social group in New York and in the Dominican Republic. In New York, Dominicans are largely concentrated in Washington Heights and a few other neighborhoods, and see themselves as a nonnative minority largely excluded from political and economic power. In the Dominican Republic, they are known as "Los Dominicanyorks," a term employed by the Dominican elite to disparage them, but which also aptly captures their in-between status—they are of both places but are seen to be native to neither.[42]

Part of the story of constitutional reform relating to nationality in the Dominican Republic begins with the economic success and periodic or semipermanent return of many migrants, combined with their political and social marginalization by the traditional Dominican elite. These *retornados* or *ausentes* (returned or absent migrants) are said to "possess the economic power to belong to the upper classes but lack the social status to legitimize such power."[43] For example, these absent and returned migrants have purchased 60 percent or more of the country's housing industry. Indeed, there are entire housing developments created exclusively for them. According to one estimate, if migrant remittances are added to the value of migrant participation in the housing industry and in export-processing zones, Dominican migrants must be considered the "single most important social group contributing to the Dominican economy."[44]

Such economic power has been translated into political power. Dominican candidates make campaign stops and raise money—by some estimates up to 15 percent of the total funds for a given election—in New York. Presidential candidate José Francisco Peña Gomez made seven trips to New York, Florida, and Massachusetts in the year or so before the 1994 elections.[45] Dominican political parties have long organized social and political activities in the Dominican community in New York, and throughout the 1980s the pressure mounted for a change in the Dominican constitution to allow dual citizenship. The Committee on the Affairs of Dominicans Living Abroad was formed in the Dominican Senate in the early 1990s, and delegations of leaders from the Dominican Republic visited New York, while leaders from New York visited the republic. Although some Dominicans on the island opposed extending dual citizenship to migrants who had "deserted" their country, the constitutional change that came about in 1994 reflected the widely held view expressed by one activist: "Today the Dominican nation is composed of nationals in the territory, and those [in] Dominican communities abroad—a concept that must be reflected undoubtfully in the laws that give legal unity and integrity to the Dominican nation."[46] The economic role that Dominicans abroad play in the country's economy and politics was widely cited as a reason for supporting the constitutional change.

At the same time that Dominicans abroad were pushing for a dual citizenship amendment, their leaders were incorporating themselves into political structures in New York City. During the 1980s a generation of Dominican political leaders who had come to the United States when they were quite young came of age. These young leaders began to focus not only on Dominican politics but on New York politics as well. In the beginning, they got themselves elected to local school and community boards. Then a historic opportunity presented itself in the 1990s when the U.S. Supreme Court invalidated New York City's governing Board of Estimate system as violating the one-person, one-vote rule. The city's electoral districts were redrawn, in part, with the goal of increasing Latino and Asian representation. The end result was the election of the first Dominican, Guillermo Linares, to the City Council. During his campaign, Linares returned to the Dominican Republic to deliver an ambulance to his hometown and meet with the Dominican president, leading opposition candidates, and the archbishops of two major sending areas to New York.[47]

What is important about this is that the simultaneous memberships of Dominican immigrants in New York and in the Dominican Republic are not mutually exclusive but, in fact, appear to be mutually reinforcing. Many of the same political activists in New York who pushed for dual citizenship mobilized support for Guillermo Linares and, before that, helped Dominicans win seats on local school and community boards. Moreover, both outcomes are the products of the same economic and social processes operating between the United States and the Dominican Republic: Dominicans in Washington Heights are identifiable as a distinct social group just as Los Dominicanyorks are in the republic.

The Dominican nation is clearly no longer limited to those living in territory controlled by the Dominican state. It has instead been redefined as a "global nation" in the sense that it is possible for a Dominican to live abroad and still be counted as a member—if not a full member—of the national political community. Moreover, the organization and empowerment of local Dominican leaders in New York politics and within Dominican national politics are mutually reinforcing. Dominicans in New York are increasingly able to press for changes in the Dominican Republic, especially as New York has become a more important place for the practice of Dominican national politics. Thus, a global nation and a locally empowered ethnic group are being created at the same time.

Conclusion: Theoretical and Policy Implications

What do these developments tell us about our theories of immigrant assimilation, political community, and transnationalization? And what are the implications for policymakers? First, they tell us that we have not been asking the right questions if we wish to reach a greater understanding of the transnationalization of political and social life.[48] One lesson to be learned from these examples is that the creation of political community need not be wedded to territory as completely as some would have it, nor divorced from territory in the new global environment as others insist. They also point to a growing disjuncture between classical theories of immigrant assimilation and political community and the practices of contemporary migrants and their sending states. Such practices include unilateral dual nationality or citizenship and other sending-state links with immigrants or with the second generation, and the increasing frequency of lived experience in, or more intense identification with, the home country among the second generation. Another lesson is that the classical models do not fit history so well either. The Italian case shows that the "global nation" is not a new idea, although the conditions of globalization, changed technology, and changed domestic and international politics make current transnational links more intense, important, and probably more durable.

But just what is the importance and nature of the relationship between these simultaneous memberships and identities? Some have expressed concern that unilateral dual citizenship or "global nation" initiatives including the second generation will endanger the assimilation process and contribute to America's disuniting.[49] Such fears and the analysis that underlie them are misplaced for several reasons. First, "assimilation" is still proceeding. Mexican immigrants and their children are indeed becoming Mexican Americans or Chicanos or Latinos, learning English, and adopting U.S. political attitudes.[50] Second-generation Dominican activists in New York place increasing emphasis on empowerment in New York as the key to their futures, even while wanting to maintain links with the Dominican Republic. The difference is that immigrants today do not undergo the same kind of all-encompassing Americanizing experience that was supposed to have happened in the past.[51]

What seems to be emerging are weakly institutionalized diasporas, in which secondary political communities (such as global nations) transcend primary political communities (the national state) but remain just that—secondary.[52] And while it is unlikely for a variety of reasons that an ethnic lobby as powerful as American Jews for Israel will develop,[53] it is possible that there will be increasing coordination between sending states and "their" expatriate communities in the United States. Moreover, the Dominican and Colombian cases suggest that simultaneous memberships can promote participation in American political life. Moreover, the main effect of increased transnational life among migrants seems to be an increased ability of those in the diaspora—emigrants and their children—to influence *sending*-country politics and society, and the subsequent efforts, often successful, of sending states to capture and control this influence. This may explain why sending states have addressed the issue while the United States has not.

A second reason why the fear that transnationalization will disunite America is misplaced is that there are far greater dangers to immigrant assimilation and American unity than the diasporic memberships analyzed here. Chief among these dangers is growing inequality and its dangerous coincidence with race and ethnicity among some immigrants and native minorities, especially African Americans. These inequalities are indeed related to the transformations that many cities have undergone as a result of trends of globalization and industrial restructuring as analyzed in this volume and elsewhere.[54] Moreover, these transformations can have profoundly disintegrative effects on public life, on our sense of community, and on the life chances of the poor, including immigrants. Indeed, it is possible to envision a future (which bears a striking resemblance to the present) in which the rich do not really inhabit the same communities as the poor, even while living in the same municipality, region, or state. The increasing disparities of income, educational opportunity, and general life chances place greater and greater strains on the social fabric.[55]

Yet the problem with regard to immigrants in this scenario is not that they are disloyal or do not feel "American" because of the actions of their parents' home country. As with native minorities, the risk lies rather in their feeling their "American-ness" all too fully, because for many in the second generation this means confronting a future of limited horizons where they expect opportunity.

One response to this situation has been to build more prisons, hire more police, and stigmatize the poor and immigrants. A better response might be to acknowledge that assimilation, or incorporation, is a two-way process. Immigrants exploit opportunities and adapt themselves to the norms of the new society in which they find themselves, but it is the host society that sets the conditions of incorporation. If immigrants attend underfunded schools, live in dangerous neighborhoods, and are afforded little chance for upward mobility, we can expect frustrated aspirations. This negative result will be intensified by the fact that most current immigrants are nonwhite, and it has been demonstrated that blacks and other groups with African features experience more severe and longer-lasting discrimination than do other immigrants.[56] Hence, an important step in preventing the fragmentation of community would be for the United States to face up to the extent to which the cumulative effects of racism determine the outcomes for which individuals or groups are blamed.

A second step would be to declare and implement an immigrant policy. We have an immigration policy that decides how many immigrants are admitted to the United States each year, but we have few policies designed to help immigrants incorporate into our institutions, as do many of our European neighbors. Readier access to English as a second language or citizenship classes would be a start. For immigrants and natives alike, at the very least, we would be wise to reverse our pattern of disinvestment in public institutions, especially in urban schools and housing.

Notes

Research for this chapter was made possible by the William and Flora Hewlett Foundation, the Institute for Latin American and Iberian Studies at Columbia University, Barnard College, the Social Science Research Council, the Rockefeller Foundation, El Colegio de la Frontera del Norte, the Tinker Foundation, and the International Center for Immigration, Ethnicity, and Citizenship at the New School for Social Research.

1. There are about 150,000 people of Mexican origin living in New York, including immigrants and their U.S.-born children. During the 1980s, Mexican immigration to a number of nontraditional destinations—including cities like Portland, Seattle, Washington, Atlanta, and those parts of the states of New York, New Jersey, and Connecticut that make up the New York metropolitan region—increased dramatically. The author has conducted field research with Mexicans in the northeastern United States as well as in Mexico and California for the past ten years.

2. Bela Feldman Bianco, "Multiple Layers of Time and Space: The Construction of Class, Race, Ethnicity, and Nationalism among Portuguese Immigrants" in Linda Basch, Nina Glick-Schiller, and Cristina Blanc-Stanton, eds., *Towards a Transnational Perspective on Migration; Race, Class, Ethnicity,*

and Nationalism Reconsidered (New York: Annals of the New York Academy of Sciences, vol. 645, 1992).

3. This interpretation of the program's mission seems to have been institutionalized. Mexico's National Development Plan for 1995–2000 proposed an initiative called "Mexican Nation" to "strengthen cultural links with Mexicans abroad and with people with Mexican roots in other countries, in part to recognize that the Mexican nation extends beyond its physical borders" (p. 8), *Plan Nacional de Desarrollo, 1995–2000* (Mexico: Poder Ejecutivo Federal, Gobierno de Mexico, 1995).

4. See Luis Guarnizo, "Comparing Dominican and Mexican Transnationalism" (paper presented at the American Ethnological Association Annual Meeting, San Juan, Puerto Rico, April 1996), and "Los Dominicanyorks: The Making of a Binational Society," *Annals of the American Academy of Political and Social Science* 536 (November 1994); Pamela Graham, "Nationality and Political Participation in the Transnational Context of Dominican Migration" (paper presented at the Conference on Caribbean Circuits: Transnational Approaches to Migration, Yale University 1995); and Arturo Ignacio Sanchez, "Transnational Political Agency and Identity Formation Among Colombian Immigrants" (paper presented at the Conference on Transnational Communities and the Political Economy of New York, New School for Social Research, February 1997).

5. Bela Feldman Bianco, "Multiple Layers." Dual citizenship is different from dual nationality; the latter does not include voting rights in the country of origin but normally enables an immigrant to hold two passports, the advantages of which are related to the holding of property and freer movement in and out of both host country and country of origin.

6. See Linda Basch, Nina Glick-Schiller, and Cristina Szanton Blanc, *Nations Unbound: Transnational Projects, Postcolonial Predicaments, and Deterritorialized Nation States* (New York: Gordon and Breach, 1994).

7. For a more detailed analysis, see Robert C. Smith, "Los Ausentes Siempre Presentes: The Imagining, Making, and Politics of a Transnational Community between Ticuani, Puebla, Mexico and New York City" (Ph.D. dissertation in political science, Columbia University, 1995). A brief note regarding definitions: As used here, a "nation" refers to a community of people who share a common culture, and usually a common language, and who understand themselves to be part of a nation or national political community. In order to exist, nations must be "imagined," to use Benedict Anderson's word, in that people must think themselves related to all others in that national political community. *A nation is normally territorially bound but increasingly may not be so.* The "state" refers to the bureaucratic apparatus of a country. Following Max Weber, a key element of the state is that it holds a monopoly on the legitimate use of violence within a given territory. The state is also territorially defined, but its relationship to territory

may be ambiguous in certain situations. Finally, "government" refers to the people in control of the state, including its administrators and/or elected officials.

8. Rogers Brubaker, *Immigration and the Politics of Citizenship in Europe and North America* (Washington D.C.: German Marshall Fund of the United States and University Press of America, 1989).

9. Oscar Handlin, *The Uprooted* (New York: Grosset's Universal Library, 1951).

10. Yasemin Soysal, *Limits to Citizenship: Migrants and Postnational Membership in Europe* (Chicago: University of Chicago Press, 1994) p. 164.

11. Michael Kearney, "Borders and Boundaries of State and Self at the End of Empire" *Journal of Historical Sociology* 4 (1991).

12. See Joseph A. Camilleri and Jim Falk, *The End of Sovereignty? The Politics of a Shrinking and Fragmented World* (Aldershot, England: Edward Elgar Publishing, 1992); Saskia Sassen, *Losing Control? Sovereignty in an Age of Globalization*, the 1995 Columbia University Leonard Hastings Schoff Memorial Lectures (New York: Columbia University Press, 1996); Tom Farer, *Beyond Sovereignty: Collectively Defending Democracy in the Americas* (Baltimore: Johns Hopkins University Press, 1996); Kathryn Sikkink, "Human Rights, Principled Issue Networks, and Sovereignty in Latin America," *International Organization* 47 (1993): 411–41.

13. See Basch et al., 1994; Alejandro Portes, "Global Villagers; The Rise of Transnational Communities," in *American Prospect* (March-April 1996), and "Transnational Communities: Their Emergence and Significance in the Contemporary World System" (paper presented at the Annual Conference on Political Economy of the World System: Latin America in the World Economy, North-South Center, University of Miami, 1995); Guarnizo "Los Dominicanyorks"; Michael Kearney,"The Local and the Global," *Annual Review of Anthropology* (1995); Smith, "Deterritorialized Nation Building: Transnational Migration and the Re-imagination of Political Community by Sending States" (Occasional Paper Center for Caribbean and Latin American Studies, New York University, originally presented to NYU-Columbia Consortium as part of the project "Migration, the State, and International Relations," April 1993); Robert Smith and Luin Goldring, "Transnational Migration and Social Citizenship" (proposal to the National Science Foundation, January 1994); Luin Goldring, "Diversity and Community in Transnational Migration: A Comparative Study of Two Mexico US Migrant Communities" (Ph.D. dissertation in rural sociology, Cornell University, 1992); and "Blurring Borders: Migration, Social Movement, and the Construction of Transnational Community," in D. Chekki, ed., *Research in Community Sociology* (forthcoming). For an interesting analysis of colonial migration and how this status affects incorporation into the host society, see Ramon Grosfoguel, "Colonial Caribbean Migra-

tions to France, the Netherlands, Great Britain, and the United States," *Ethnic and Racial Studies* 20, no. 3 (forthcoming 1997).

14. See Guarnizo, "Comparing Dominican and Mexican Transnationalism"; and Portes, "Transnational Communities."

15. Portes, "Transnational Communities," p. 2.

16. Jorge Castaneda, "The Paradox of Tolerance and Dedemocratization" in A. Lowenthal and K. Burgess Stanford, eds., *The California-Mexico Connection* (Stanford, Calif.: Stanford University Press, 1993), p. 35. He makes this observation with respect to southern California, although some but not all of the same dynamics can be perceived in New York.

17. See Nancy Foner, "What's New About Transnationalism? New York Immigrants Today and at the Turn of the Century" (paper presented at the Conference on Transnational Communities and the Political Economy of New York in the 1990s, New School for Social Research, February 1997); and Robert Smith, "Reflections on Migration, the State, and the Construction, Durability and Newness of Transnational Life," Ludger Pries, ed., *Soziale Welt* (forthcoming). Foner's analysis and my own are similar in many ways, although I discuss the importance of changes in international politics and national development strategies, and she does not.

18. Saskia Sassen, *The Mobility of Capital and Labor* (New York and London: Oxford University Press, 1988), and *The Global City: New York, Tokyo and London* (Princeton, N.J.: Princeton University Press, 1991). That the migration of labor has been excluded under most international trade regimes is a point made insightfully by Aristide Zolberg in "International Migration and International Economic Regimes: Bretton Woods and After" (paper presented at the International Union for the Scientific Study of Population, Malaysia, September, 1988). See also Aristide Zolberg and Robert Smith, "Migration Systems in Comparative Perspective: An Analysis of the Inter-American Migration System with Comparative Reference to the Mediterrean-European System" (report prepared for the U.S. Department of State, Bureau of Population, Refugees and Migration by the International Center for Migration, Ethnicity and Citizenship at the New School for Social Research, May 1996).

19. *Immigration and Naturalization Service Yearbook*, 1992 and 1993.

20. Rogers Brubaker, "Are Immigration Control Efforts Really Failing?" in W. Cornelius, P. Martin, and James Hollifield, eds., *Controlling Immigration: A Global Perspective* (Stanford, Calif.: Stanford University Press, 1994).

21. James Hollifield, *Immigrants, Markets, and States: The Political Economy of Immigrants in Postwar Europe* (Cambridge: Harvard University Press, 1992); Peter Schuck and Rogers Smith, *Citizenship without Consent: Illegal Aliens and the American Polity* (New Haven: Yale University Press, 1985).

22. Douglas Massey, "The New Immigrants and Ethnicity in the United States," *Population and Development Review* (forthcoming).

23. Jorge Durand, Emilio Parrado, and Douglas Massey, "Migradollars and Development: A Reconsideration of the Mexican Case," *International Migration Review* 30, no. 114 (1996): p.1.

24. Douglas Massey and Audrey Singer, "New Estimates of Undocumented Mexican Migration and the Probability of Apprehension," *Demography* 32, no. 2 (May 1995).

25. Guarnizo, "Los Dominicanyorks," p. 79.

26. Nora Hamilton and Norma Stoltz Chinchilla, "Social and Economic Aspects of Central American Migration and Return" (Monograph 1, Center for Multicultural and Transnational Studies, University of Southern California, 1995); Michael P. Smith, "Transnational Salvadoran Migration" (paper presented at the American Ethnological Association Annual Meeting, San Juan, Puerto Rico, April 1996).

27. Sarah Mahler, "Transnationalism among Salvadorans on Long Island, New York: Empirical and Theoretical Considerations" (paper presented at the Conference on Transnational Communities and the Political Economy of New York City in the 1990s, New School for Social Research, February 1997).

28. Raul Hinojosa Ojeda and Sherman Robinson, "Regional Integration in a Greater North America: NAFTA, Central American and the Caribbean" (paper presented at the International Studies Association Annual Meeting, March 1994); and "Labor Issues in a North American Free Trade Area," in N. Lustig, B. Bosworth, and R. Lawrence, eds., *North American Free Trade: Assessing the Impact* (Washington D.C.: Brookings Institution, 1992); Hinojosa Ojeda et al., 1992, p. 17.

29. See Smith, "Deterritorialized Nations," and "Domestic Politics Abroad, Diasporic Politics at Home: The Mexican Global Nation, Neoliberalism, and the Program for Mexican Communities Abroad" (paper presented to the Annual Meeting of the American Sociological Association, New York, August 1993, and to the Annual Meeting of the American Political Science Association, San Francisco, August 1996). For an excellent analysis of this aspect of Chicano-Mexican relations, see Maria Rosa García Acevedo, "Return to Aztlan: Mexico's Policies towards Chicanas/os," in D. Maciel and I. Ortiz, eds., *Chicanas/Chicanos at the Crossroads: Social, Economic, and Political Change* (Tucson: University of Arizona Press, 1996) and "Contemporary Mexico's Policy toward the Mexican Diaspora in the United States" (Ph.D. dissertation in political science, University of Arizona, 1996).

30. Smith, "Domestic Politics Abroad," and Maria Rosa García Acevedo "Return to Aztlan."

31. This paragraph summarizes the analysis of Arturo Ignacio Sanchez, "Transnational Political Agency and Identity Formation."

32. This estimate was made using a Census Bureau report on the undercount of Mexicans in New York City and adjusting some of its assumptions about housing types and other factors: S. Mahler and B. Dominguez, "Undercount of Mexicans in New York," unpublished report commissioned by the Bureau of the Census, 1990. Also, though there were approximately 62,000 Mexican-origin people estimated in the official census, the New York City Planning Department estimated that there were approximately 100,000 such people in the city in 1990, which was my estimate as well at that time. In making the current estimate, I am assuming a slower rate of growth in the Mexican population than there was during the 1980s (when the population almost tripled from approximately 23,000 in 1980) because much of that surge came from the facilitating effect of the "amnesty" under the 1986 Immigration Reform and Control Act. Despite their relatively small number, Mexicans in New York accounted for the second largest number of applications for amnesty in New York, with about 9,000, compared with first-ranked Dominicans, with approximately 11,000.

33. Robert Foerster, *The Italian Emigration of Our Times* (Cambridge: Harvard University Press, 1919).

34. Virginia Yans-McLaughlin, *Family and Community: Italian Immigrants in Buffalo, 1880–1930* (Ithaca, N.Y.: Cornell University Press, 1977), pp. 76–77.

35. This paragraph draws on Dino Cinel, *The National Integration of Italian Return Migration, 1870–1929* (New York: Cambridge University Press, 1991); Francesco Cordasco, *Italian Mass Emigration* (Totowa, N.J.: Roman and Littlefield, 1980); and Barbara Schmitter Heisler, "Sending States and Immigrant Minorities—the Case of Italy," *Comparative Studies of Society and History* 26 no. 2 (April 1984).

36. Foerster, p. 488; brackets added.

37. Carolyn F. Ware, *Greenwich Village, 1920–1930: A Comment on American Civilization in the Postwar Years* (Boston: Houghton Mifflin Co., 1935), p. 158.

38. Irvin Child's classic *Italian or American? The Second Generation in Conflict* (New Haven: Yale University Press, 1943), the research for which was done in the 1930s, makes only one mention of a second-generation Italian wanting to return to visit Italy.

39. See Alejandro Portes and Luis Guarnizo, "Capitalistas del trópico: la inmigración en los Estados Unidos y el desarollo de la pequeña empresa en la república Dominicana" (Santo Domingo: Facultad Latinoamericana de Ciencias Sociales, 1991); Basch et al., *Nations Unbound*; Nancy Foner, "West Indians in New York City and London: A Comparative Analysis," in Constance Sutton and Elsa Chancey, eds., *Caribbbean Immigrants in New York*

(New York: Center for Migration Studies, 1987); Constance Sutton "The Caribbeanization of New York City and Emergence of a Transnational Socio-Cultural System," also in Sutton and Chaney eds., *Caribbbean Immigrants.*

40. See Michael Jones-Correa, "Becoming 'Hispanic': Secondary Panethnic Identification among Latin American–Origin Population in the United States," *Hispanic Journal of Behavioral Sciences* 18, no 2 (May 1996): 214–54.

41. This section draws extensively on Guarnizo (1994) and Graham (1995).

42. "Los Dominicanyorks" is a cousin to the Mexican term "pocho," used to describe U.S.-born children of Mexican immigrants.

43. Guarnizo "Los Dominicanyorks," p. 76.

44. Ibid., p. 79.

45. Graham (1995).

46. Graham (1995), p. 23.

47. Ibid., p. 36.

48. For an intriguing discussion of this issue, see Basch et al., *Nations Unbound.*

49. Arthur Schlesinger, Jr., *The Disuniting of America* (New York: Norton 1992); David Ayon, "Democratization Imperils U.S. Latino Empowerment," *Los Angeles Times*, May 26, 1996.

50. Rodolfo de la Garza, "Mexican Americans, Mexican Immigrants, and Immigration reform," in Nathan Glazer, ed., *Clamor at the Gates* (San Francisco: Institute for Contemporary Studies, 1985), and "Mobilizing the Mexican Immigrant: The Role of Mexican American Organizations," *Western Political Quarterly* 38:4 (1985); and Rodolfo de la Garza and Claudio Vargas, "The Mexican Origin Population of the United States as a Political Force in the Borderlands: From Paisanos to Pochos to Potential Political Allies," in L. Herzog, ed., *Changing Boundaries in the Americas* (La Jolla, Calif.: Center for US-Mexico Studies, 1992).

51. Some evidence suggests that such was not always the case in the past. For example, visitors to Pennsylvania in the 1830s and 1840s found German-speaking communities educating their children in German-speaking schools, with German-speaking policemen, judges, and German-language newspapers.

52. See Smith (1995); Graham (1995); Basch et al. (1994); and Jones-Correa (1996).

53. See de la Garza, "Mexican Americans."

54. Sassen (1988) and (1991); Roger Waldinger, *Still the Promised City? Blacks and Immigrants in Postindustrial New York* (Cambridge: Harvard University Press, 1996).

55. See Basch et al. (1994); Sanchez (1996); Guarnizo (1996); Smith (1996) and (1995); Graham (1995); Smith and Goldring (1994); and Goldring (1996).

56. Douglas Massey and Nancy Denton, *American Apartheid* (Cambridge: Harvard University Press, 1994); and Douglas Massey and Brooks Bitterman, "Puerto Ricans and Segregation" *Social Forces*, 64, no. 2 (December 1985).

Chapter 8

Educating the Children of Immigrants in New York's Restructured Economy

Josh DeWind

N EW YORK'S role as a world city has long been reflected not only in its economic reach but also in the numbers of immigrants who have come to it from every nation on earth in search of economic advancement. Today, the numbers of immigrants living in New York City are approaching the peaks reached earlier in the century, and their cultural diversity is greater than ever.[1] But the city's economy has changed dramatically over the past few decades—a transformation that has diminished the prospects for labor-market mobility for newer immigrants and, more important in the long-term, for their children.[2]

One of the challenges facing the offspring of recent immigrants is to obtain the skills necessary to compete for decent jobs within New York's restructured "hour-glass" labor market. New York's deindustrialization, which has accompanied its growing dependency on external domestic and foreign markets, has contributed to increasing disparities in employment opportunities and earned income. The number of middle-level manufacturing jobs, which served past immigrants as a ladder of mobility, has been steadily shrinking since the 1950s. Recently, employment opportunities have expanded at the top, where relatively well-paid jobs are available for highly educated workers, especially in finance, insurance, and real estate, as well as information-based enterprises,[3] and at the bottom, where service and retail jobs offering little chance for promotion or advancement are available at close to the minimum wage for workers with a high school education or less.

The challenge facing New York City's leaders is not only to educate immigrant children from vastly different cultures, providing them with the skills they will need to advance into better jobs, but also to assure the children of native-born Americans who are trapped at the bottom of the labor market—most of whom are from minority racial and ethnic backgrounds—of such an education. Social scientists are already predicting a difficult and bleak future for new immigrants, not only because the middle rungs of the labor market ladder are missing, but also because racial and ethnic prejudice and discrimination continue to be directed against the children of non-European immigrants. This is also the case for native-born minority groups with whom they often are identified and with whom they are linked in the minds of employers.[4]

While the task of providing the educational skills to meet the economic aspirations of the children of immigrants in New York City appears daunting, there are some promising programs in place. Ultimately, the educational and political success of such efforts may lie in tying them to similar efforts to help poor native-born children of minority backgrounds, while recognizing the differences between the circumstances and needs of the two groups.

The Challenge of Educating Immigrant Children

The large numbers and sociocultural diversity of immigrant students have challenged the educational capacity of urban school systems not only in New York but also in California, Texas, Florida, Illinois, New Jersey, and other states with high concentrations of immigrants. In New York City alone over one-third of the students are immigrants from nearly 190 different nations. Some school systems have created special programs to help immigrants cope with the language, cultural, and educational challenges they face, but the majority of immigrant students, even in California, the state with the most extensive and elaborate efforts, do not have access to such programs.[5]

Most school systems lack the resources necessary to tailor educational programs to the needs of U.S.-born students from diverse ethnic and racial backgrounds, much less create new programs for immigrants. As a result, immigrant students needing help are generally thrown into existing special language programs and other programs created for U.S.-born students. In these circumstances, school officials and teachers do not expect most new immigrants to be successful academically. Moreover, the persistence of many educational problems, including increasingly irregular patterns of attendance, declining grades, and high drop-out rates, is often attributed to the growing number of immigrants.

A preliminary look at the achievement test scores of immigrants in the New York City public school system suggests that, contrary to these low expectations and perceptions, the educational achievements of most recent immigrant groups are generally quite high, often higher than those of U.S.-born students of both majority and minority backgrounds. The best explanations for this unexpected phenomenon have been offered by anthropologists on the basis of recent ethnographic case studies in the United States and abroad. Their findings suggest that the programs designed to support new immigrant students could also benefit many disadvantaged native-born minority students.

Many recent studies on educating immigrants have focused on the "challenges" that immigrants, with their diverse cultural, social, and educational backgrounds, present to schools and the urgent need for new policies and programs suited to their special needs.[6] While many immigrant students do require specially tailored programs, the success of a substantial portion of these students and the implications of this success for designing new programs for both immigrants and native minority groups have generally been overlooked.

One factor behind the low expectations regarding recent immigrant students may be the assumption that they face even greater hurdles to academic success than do native-born students of minority background. Because of the language, cultural, and academic hurdles facing immigrants, one researcher in a project examining Los Angeles high schools doubted the preliminary finding that Mexican immigrant students were enrolling in college preparatory courses at a higher rate than native-born Mexican-American students. Not only were the unexpected findings confirmed in a subsequently published report, but it also became apparent that by eleventh grade a significantly higher percentage of immigrant Mexican students were enrolling in an important college "gatekeeper" algebra course than were all other native-born students.[7]

Similarly low academic expectations of immigrant students were expressed by teachers and administrators in the New York City public schools during conversations held in preparation for a 1992 conference on immigrant students.[8] Many school personnel attributed the low achievement test scores in many school districts to the influx of large numbers of inadequately prepared immigrant students. Of the 995,465 New York City public school students enrolled in the spring of 1993, 13.8 percent were immigrants who had entered the system during the previous three years. According to a high-ranking school official, the high proportion of immigrants underscored the need to increase funding for special education programs, which were originally designed to assist students with severe academic or emotional handicaps.[9]

The Performance of Immigrants in Achievement Tests

While little research has been conducted to determine the actual educational accomplishments of immigrant students, a preliminary analysis of standardized tests of recent immigrants in New York City public schools suggests that their achievements compare favorably with those of other students in two respects: in the improvement in their test scores from one year to the next and in the demonstration of unexpectedly high levels of proficiency. Although immigrant students entering the city's public schools face as many or more academic difficulties as native-born students, their test scores indicate that their language and academic skills improve relatively quickly. Between the 1989–90 and 1990–91 academic years, recent immigrants in grades three through twelve improved their median reading, math, and English test scores at a higher rate than did all other students. (See Table 8.1.)

Despite this apparently remarkable improvement in the skills of immigrant students, their median level of proficiency remains somewhat lower than that of all other students. But when these immigrants are divided according to national origin, the median test scores of half of the nationality groups are similar to or better than those of all other students. Of the twelve largest immigrant groups in New York public schools, students from China, Guyana, India, Korea, the Soviet Union, and Trinidad and Tobago performed better than all other students in one, two, or all three tests. However, students from Colombia, the Dominican Republic, Ecuador, Haiti, Jamaica, and Mexico had lower median scores than all other students in all three tests.

Even the six groups with the lowest median test scores showed substantially greater gains in the level of their scores from one year to the next than did all other students (the only two exceptions being the relatively slower increase in English scores on the part of Haitian and Jamaican students). How various immigrant groups would compare with students separated into native-born racial and ethnic categories cannot be determined from the available data; but, clearly, recent immigrant students as a group are not far behind all other students. Moreover, given the rapid rate of improvement among these immigrant groups, it may be reasonable to expect that the younger students just beginning

Table 8.1   Test Scores of Recent Immigrants and Other Students, New York City Public Schools, Grades 3–12, 1991

	Test Scores[a]					
	Reading		Math		English	
Nationality	Mean	Gain	Mean	Gain	Mean	Gain
China	46.9	4.4	72.1	4.9	23.9	12.9
India	57.1	3.8	74.9	3.5	36.2	16.1
Guyana	46.8	4.5	55.9	4.5	37.9	11.0
Korea	56.8	5.3	81.5	3.5	32.8	19.6
Trinidad-Tobago	50.8	3.8	60.2	4.0	42.6	10.9
Soviet Union	61.5	5.8	80.8	4.6	29.3	20.8
Colombia	48.8	3.7	54.5	3.0	28.5	15.5
Dominican Republic	40.6	3.9	44.4	3.8	22.1	11.2
Ecuador	43.7	2.3	51.4	3.2	24.6	13.3
Haiti	40.5	4.2	46.7	3.5	22.3	9.9
Jamaica	46.7	4.6	52.9	4.7	28.3	7.8
Mexico	40.3	3.9	46.8	2.6	18.7	11.2
All Recent Immigrants	47.7	4.1	54.7	3.7	26.1	13.9
All Other Students	51.9	2.4	59.2	1.3	33.2	10.7

Note: "Recent Immigrants" refers to foreign-born students who first enrolled in the public schools within the previous 36 months. "Other Students" refers to all native-born students (including Puerto Ricans) and foreign-born students enrolled in the schools longer than 36 months.
[a] Scores measure normal curve equivalents ranging from 1 to 99 where 50 is the national mean score. The "gain" is the mean increase in score over the previous year.
Source: Based on data provided by the New York City Public Schools, Office of Research, Evaluation and Assessment.

their schooling will raise their scores to or above the level of all other students within a few years.

The variations in test results between recent immigrant nationality groups are not easily explained, especially since some of the higher scoring groups face the same difficulties—a non-English-speaking background, limited family education, and poverty—as the lower scoring groups. But the results for the six higher scoring recent immigrant nationality groups undercut the widely held assumption that immigrants do not do well in school. That these students come from similar racial and ethnic backgrounds to some U.S.-born minority students who are experiencing greater difficulty attaining success in school makes their attainments striking.

Why Do the Test Scores of Immigrants Surpass Expectations?

What accounts for the unexpected success of so large a portion of immigrant students in the New York City public schools? Anthropologists Margaret Gibson and John Ogbu offer a compelling hypothesis based upon a comparison of the strategies that immigrant and native-born minority students adopt toward their schooling.[10]

Gibson and Ogbu suggest that the greater success of the Sikh, Korean, Mexican, and West Indian immigrants they studied compared with that of African-American, Mexican-American, and Native American students derives from the accommodative approach that the former frequently adopt toward their schooling in contrast to a more resistant stance adopted by many native-born minority students. According to the researchers, the different approaches of the two groups of students are the result of their different expectations regarding the long-term benefits of education.

The key factor shaping the educational strategy of native-born minority students, according to Gibson and Ogbu, is their involuntary incorporation into American society through enslavement, conquest, or colonization. That racial discrimination, ethnic prejudice, and class barriers have kept so many members of these "involuntary" minority groups from improving their economic and social standing, despite their individual and collective efforts, has resulted in the devaluation of education. Learning from their families, friends, and neighbors to expect that education is unlikely to enable them to alter their subordinate status, involuntary minority students tend to resist schooling. Those who do not and who try to accommodate themselves to the requirements of getting an education are pejoratively identified as "acting white," behavior that is rejected by many as self-abnegating and humiliating because it is not expected to lead to future social acceptance or success. Resistance or opposition to education is seen as being based on realistic expectations and may be seen as an attempt to at least preserve the group's cultural integrity.

Immigrant students, in contrast, tend to have more positive expectations and so embrace their schooling. Like their parents who abandoned their homelands and came to the United States with the expectation of finding new opportunities to improve their economic and social well-being, immigrant students see the schools as offering skills they need to "make it" in American society. Even when they experience discriminatory treatment or social barriers, they tend to expect that with persistence and hard work they can still have better lives than they would have had in their home countries.

Although both immigrant and involuntary minority students begin with backgrounds quite different from the dominant American school culture, their adaptive strategies may diverge because they experience the pressures for acculturation differently. Margaret Gibson finds that immigrant students experience the demands of the schools as "additive" acculturation, while involuntary minority students feel it to be "subtractive" acculturation.[11] In accommodating themselves to the schools, immigrant students learn new cultural traits that they believe will be of benefit to them later on without losing the cultural identities they bring with them to the United States. They can accommodate the demands of U.S. schools without assimilating into American culture. In contrast, because of their subordinate status within U.S. society, many involuntary minority students feel that accommodating themselves to the demands of the schools requires total assimilation, that is, it requires them to abandon their group characteristics and become more like the majority population.

Programs to Bridge Cultural and Educational Gaps

Virtually all immigrant students face educational, language, and social gaps that they must bridge in order to participate fully in U.S. schools. While a surprising percentage of immigrant students seem to bridge these gaps successfully and attain educational success, the test score data in Table 8.1 suggest that a substantial percentage, perhaps the majority, have more difficulty.

In some parts of the United States, public schools have created special programs for immigrant students who need help adjusting to American education. Most of these programs are consistent with the notion of "additive acculturation" in that they are designed to promote respect for the newcomers' cultural backgrounds while providing them with the skills they need to succeed in American schools. Such additive acculturation programs might also benefit American minority students. Treating the cultures of native minority groups as an asset would represent a notable departure from approaches that set out to compensate minority students for their supposed lack of cultural resources compared to white, middle-class students.

The Education Gap

Many immigrant students arriving in the United States are ill-prepared to enroll in American schools. A substantial portion of foreign-born students do not speak, read, or write at their grade level in their native language, much less in English. Immigrants who are used to learning by rote, or who have been raised to accept the teacher's word as law, or who have learned to subordinate individual achievement to the success of the group may find it difficult to adapt to the American emphasis on critical thinking, speaking up in class, and competitive and independent learning. Moreover, immigrant students often enter U.S. schools at midyear, rather than at the beginning of the academic calendar, and must struggle to catch up.

Some school systems have created special bridge programs or even separate schools to make the transition easier. Typically, bridge programs orient students to school life and provide them with intensive language instruction and social studies classes that focus on the nature of both other cultures and American society. Some of these programs are also designed to provide sheltered emotional environments for students who have been traumatized by the circumstances that forced them to flee their homelands or by the dislocations of international migration.[12]

The beneficial impact of these programs is difficult to assess as they usually last for only from a few weeks to a year. Nevertheless, the students' high rates of successful completion of these programs and their transfer to regular public schools (for example, 95 percent from the Newcomer High School in San Francisco and the Liberty High School in New York City) suggest that special school programs have a positive impact. The benefits that can result from extending such programs are suggested by the extraordinary 95 percent college attendance rate of graduates from New York City's International High School, which educates immigrants exclusively with a full four-year program.[13]

Immigrant students are not alone in their need for a general introduction to schooling, sheltered environments, intensive instruction, and an orientation to mainstream culture. Native-born minority students raised outside the mainstream culture have similarly distinctive social practices, languages or dialects, and learning styles and could also benefit from the type of programs created for immigrant students, which is the conclusion reached in a RAND study of newcomer programs: "The insularity of poor urban neighborhoods means that many native-born students are, in effect, immigrants as they cross into mainstream jobs and post-secondary education. Schools that address the acculturation needs of immigrant students may be pioneering a new and important element of education for all disadvantaged urban students."[14] How an additive approach to immigrant education can benefit both immigrant and native-born minority students may be most clearly seen with respect to language instruction.

The Language Gap

Many immigrants arriving in the United States do not speak, read, or write English, and schools find that by the time immigrant students become proficient in English they have fallen behind in other subjects and catch up only with great difficulty if at all. Since the Supreme Court ruled in *Lau v. Nichols* (1974) that, in order to provide equal access to education, schools must provide special language instruction to students with limited English proficiency (LEP), most schools with heavy immigrant enrollment complied by offering such students instruction in English as a second language. In addition, some schools set up bilingual math, social studies, and science programs in which instruction in the students' native language is gradually replaced by instruction in English until the students are ready to join regular classes taught in English. Critics of these transitional classes say that they invalidate immigrant students' native languages and cultures.

An alternative approach to bilingual education, and one that is more consistent with the additive acculturation approach, bilingual/bicultural education, was designed to maintain or develop immigrant students' native language skills as well as teach them English. Bilingual/bicultural programs are intended not only to help students develop dual language skills but also to help them become comfortable in both their native and American cultural contexts. Two-way bilingual classes combine LEP and native English speakers so that both groups can learn the other's language. Such programs encourage immigrant students to learn the skills necessary for full participation in U.S. society without demanding total assimilation.

Bilingual education programs, on the other hand, were developed primarily with native-born LEP students in mind, particularly Mexican Americans and Puerto Ricans who, as members of involuntary minorities, have some of the lowest rates of academic achievement and the highest school dropout rates. One reason special language programs have not helped to overcome the persistent educational difficulties for these groups is that because of scarce resources, many entitled students do not have programs in which to enroll. However, the fact that the majority of special language classes for LEP students are limited to instruction in English as a second language means that, during the four to six years it takes most LEP students to attain fluency in English, they are not fully comprehending their other courses taught in English. If the additive acculturation approach toward immigrant students is a useful guide, native-born LEP students would also benefit from bilingual/bicultural programs.

The Culture and Identity Gap

One of the most complex and difficult problems immigrants face is the establishment of a social identity within U.S. society. This is often complicated by the disparity between how immigrants identify themselves based on their social status in their home countries and how Americans, whose views are often derived from or influenced by stereotypes of American racial and ethnic minority groups, see them.

Upon their arrival in the United States, immigrants from non-European countries often find that the identities that provided them with their roles and social status within their home cultures do not have similar effects in the context of American society. When, because of their race, language, or culture, immigrants are identified as part of an American minority group they experience what feels like "downward mobility." Upper- and middle-class mulatto families from Haiti are frequently shocked at the prejudice and discrimination they experience in the United States because they are identified as being black.[15] Similarly, some Colombian and Argentinean immigrants feel uncomfortable being identified as "Latino" or "Hispanic" because this does not recognize the differences between themselves and Chicanos, Puerto Ricans, Cuban Americans, or other Spanish-speaking minority groups. For immigrant students, discovering that Americans have assigned them racial or ethnic identities that make them the targets of the same prejudice and hostility that is often aimed at American minority groups can be disconcerting, if not traumatic.

Multicultural education programs that help American students to recognize the diversity and legitimacy of immigrants' unique cultural backgrounds can not only help immigrants avoid becoming trapped in U.S. racial and ethnic identities but also reinforce efforts by American minority groups to escape an oppressive hierarchy of racial labeling by redefining the basis of their social identities. In New York City, immigrants from the British West Indies refer to themselves and, increasingly, are being referred to by native-born New Yorkers on the basis of national or regional names—such as "Jamaicans" or "Caribbean Americans"—rather than in terms of race. Similarly, many native-born New Yorkers who once embraced a racial label as "blacks" have adopted the immigrant tradition of hyphenated geographic identity and begun calling themselves "African Americans." This term is often intended not only to reaffirm the validity of African cultural traditions weakened by slavery but also to undermine the logic of discrimination based on race. The underlying persistence of race in spite of the changing names, of course, was illustrated by the insistence of African-

American and immigrant New York City high school students in a classroom discussion of social identity that the term "African American" could not apply to Americans of white South African or Arabian African ancestry. Nevertheless, an "African-American" identity provides "blacks" with the same logical possibility of escaping racial categorization that "Caribbean-American" immigrants are pursuing. An educational perspective that promotes the recognition of immigrants' cultural and national identities, and not just their race, can contribute to the broader process of social redefinition.

The Next Steps

The children of many non-European and nonwhite immigrants who have come to the United States since 1965 are attaining unexpected educational success. If Gibson and Ogbu's hypothesis—that immigrants' voluntary incorporation into U.S. society enables them to accommodate themselves to the demands of the schools as part of an additive approach of acculturation—is correct, educational programs that sustain or validate involuntary minority students' cultural origins might also enable them to accommodate themselves to, rather than resist, the demands of schooling.

Additional research would be useful both to refine and apply the additive acculturation approach to the development of education programs. To attain a clearer understanding of immigrant students' accommodation strategies, it would be useful to know more about the sources of differences in the achievements of immigrants within their own nationality groups as well as between immigrant nationality groups and native racial and ethnic minority groups. Other researchers have proposed that such differences might be explained by factors not fully considered in Gibson and Ogbu's hypothesis, such as the strong educational backgrounds that some immigrant parents and students bring from their home countries, different levels of class or socioeconomic resources, and the extent of ethnic solidarity within immigrant communities.[16] It has been suggested that the successful strategy of some Chinese students is related not only to their favorable perception of opportunities in the United States, as opposed to those in China, but also to the stage they have reached in adapting to American life, their relative social insulation from American society, and the expectations of the schools.[17]

Ethnographic research among students is needed to understand more fully the dynamics and interrelations in the evolution of immigrant and native-born minority social identification. It is not clear, for example, how long immigrant students and their children continue to maintain an additive approach to acculturation. Some recent findings suggest that immigrant students' high levels of achievement decline as they become more Americanized.[18] To what extent and at what point do immigrants begin to identify themselves as native minorities, and do they then begin to resist mainstream education even though they were not incorporated into American society involuntarily? Similarly, to what extent do the distinct social identities insisted upon by immigrants provide American minority students with possibilities for alternative identities and school strategies?

It has been argued persuasively that because the resources available for designing and implementing educational reforms for American-born, much less for foreign-born students, are shrinking throughout the nation, the most practical approach to educational reform is to address the needs of both groups at once.[19] The additive acculturation approach can serve as a guide to formulating school orientation, bilingual classes, and multicultural curricula to benefit both groups. However, the extent to which a successful immigrant strategy can become a model for American minority students should not be exaggerated.

If immigrants' success in education is based on their adopting an approach of accommodation without assimilation, policies that reinforce respect for cultural backgrounds of all groups in the schools may create a more friendly and encouraging learning environment, but such reforms will not directly reduce the discrimination and social inequality that have led involuntary minorities to view education with skepticism and resistance. Ultimately, the lesson to be learned from the educational success of immigrants is that the likelihood of native involuntary minority students' adopting a similarly accommodative strategy toward their schooling will depend upon the elimination of discriminatory racial, ethnic, and class barriers to social, economic, and political equality in the society at large.

Notes

1. This demographic trend toward greater racial and ethnic diversity is amply documented in this volume's chapter by Joseph J. Salvo and Arun Peter Lobo.

2. The growing dependency of the New York City economy on external markets and its accompanying transformation of the labor market are described in Carol O'Cléireaćáin's chapter in this volume.

3. Underpinning the growth of high-level employment in New York's information-based financial, publishing, television, and radio enterprises is the expanding computer and telecommunications sector. Despite the optimism and glossy coverage of the "new media," Edward Mozely Roche in his chapter in this volume presents a skeptical view of the "dangerous myth that New York can rely on this sector to fuel its growth into the next century." He describes employment conditions for the industry's "intellectual migrant labor force" as "neo-medieval" with regard to low wages, lack of job security, and minimal social benefits. The extent to which "imported" or native-born workers are attracted to these new media jobs is not clear, nor is it clear that local educational institutions, including public schools and colleges, will soon provide appropriately skilled graduates.

4. See Herbert J. Gans, "Second Generation Decline: Scenarios for the Economic and Ethnic Futures of the Post-1965 American Immigrants," *Ethnic and Racial Studies* 15 (1992): 173–92.

5. Lorraine McDonnell and Paul T. Hill, *Newcomers in American Schools: Meeting the Educational Needs of Immigrant Youth* (Santa Monica, Calif.: RAND, 1993), pp. 55–84; Hedy Nai-Lin Chang, *Newcomer Programs: Innovative Efforts to Meet the Educational Challenges of Immigrant Students* (San Francisco: California Tomorrow, Immigrant Studies Project, 1990); Laurie Olsen and Carol Dowell, *Bridges: Promising Programs for the Education of Immigrant Children* (San Francisco: California Tomorrow, Immigrant Students Project, 1989).

6. See George M. Szabad and Gary E. Rubin, *Educating the Newest Americas: Report of the Task Force on New Immigrants and American Education* (New York: American Jewish Committee, 1989); Joan McCarty First and John W. Carrera, *New Voices: Immigrant Students in U.S. Public Schools* (Boston: National Coalition of Advocates for Students, 1988); Laurie Olsen, *Crossing the Schoolhouse Border: Immigrant Students and California Public Schools* (San Francisco: California Tomorrow, Immigrant Students Project, 1988); and McDonnell and Hill, *Newcomers in American Schools.*

7. McDonnell and Hill, *Newcomers in American Schools*, pp. 71–72.

8. Conference on Immigration and Public Education in New York City, May 6, 1992, sponsored by the New York City Public Schools Committee on Immigrant Affairs, Association of the Bar of the City of New York, and Latin American and Caribbean Studies Program, Hunter College, City University of New York.

9. Thomas J. Lueck, "Immigrant Enrollment Rises in New York City Schools," *New York Times*, April 16, 1993.

10. Margaret A. Gibson and John Ogbu, eds., *Minority Status and Schooling: A Comparative Study of Immigrant and Involuntary Minorities* (New York: Garland Publishing, 1991).

11. Margaret A. Gibson, "Minorities and Schooling: Some Implications," in Gibson and Ogbu, *Minority Status and Schooling*; and also Margaret A. Gibson, *Accommodation without Assimilation: Sikh Immigrants in an American High School* (Ithaca, N.Y.: Cornell University Press, 1991).

12. See Chang, *Newcomer Programs*, pp. 9–19; First and Carrera, *New Voices*, pp. 84–115; and McDonnell and Hill, *Newcomers in American Schools*, pp. 74–75, 92–97.

13. See Chang, *Newcomer Programs*, pp. 22–23; First and Carrera, *New Voices*, pp. 84–115; Olsen and Dowell, *Bridges*, pp. 37–47, 72–83; and *Directory of the Public High Schools* (New York: N.Y. Board of Education, 1991), pp. 390, 395.

14. McDonnell and Hill, *Newcomers in American Schools*, p. 79.

15. See Nina Glick-Schiller, Josh DeWind, Marie Lucie-Brutus, Carolle Charles, Georges Fouron, and Antoine Thomas, "All in the Same Boat? Unity and Diversity in Haitian Organizing in New York," in C. Sutton and E. Chaney, eds., *Caribbean Life in New York City* (Staten Island, N.Y.: Center for Migration Studies, 1988), pp. 182–201.

16. José Macias, "Forgotten History: Educational and Social Antecedents of High Achievement among Asian Immigrants in the United States" (unpublished manuscript, 1993); Alejandro Portes and Ruben Rumbaut, *Immigrant America: A Portrait* (Berkeley: University of California Press, 1991), pp. 180–221.

17. Betty Lee Sung, *The Adjustment Experience of Chinese Immigrant Children in New York City* (Staten Island, N.Y.: Center for Migration Studies, 1987), pp. 91–95.

18. Ruben Rumbaut, "Paradoxes (and Orthodoxies) of Assimilation," (paper presented at the Conference on Becoming American/America Becoming: International Migration to the United States, Social Science Research Council, January 1996).

19. McDonnell and Hill, *Newcomers in American Schools*, pp. 101–11.

Chapter 9

Building A New Public Realm: Moral Responsibility and Religious Commitment in the City

ANTHONY M. STEVENS-ARROYO

M AJOR religions and major cities have always been linked. Thus, any analysis of life in New York City would be lacking completeness if its religious aspects were omitted. Just as surely as church spires, synagogue domes, and mosque minarets dot the city's skyline, religion stands prominently alongside other important elements of life in New York.

Although it is fashionable in some quarters to view the Big Apple as "Sin City," reliable survey data show that characterization to be erroneous. In terms of church attendance, and of the importance people ascribe to religion, the population of New York appears to be as religious as that of any city in the American heartland, the main difference being that New York has proportionally more Roman Catholics than the nation as a whole. With 43 percent of the city's population, Catholics outnumber all Protestant denominations combined (32 percent).[1] There are about as many Protestants who are African American or Asian as there are white Protestants. There are more African-American Catholics than black Muslims, and more Asian Christians than Buddhists. Jews make up 10 percent of the population; in fact, more than a quarter of all Jews in the United States live in the city. (See Figure 9.1.)

What makes New York special in religious terms is the variety of faiths, denominations, and national traditions that coexist within its

Figure 9.1 Denominational Membership in New York City

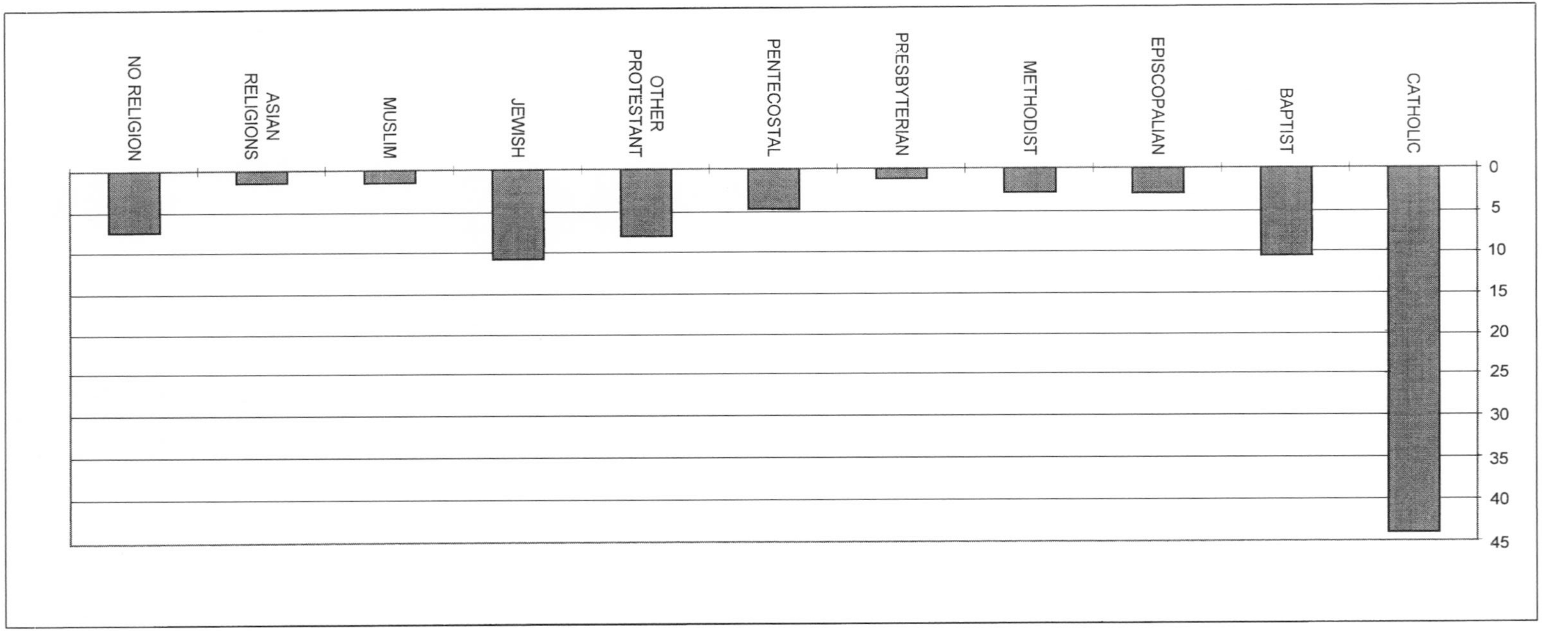

boundaries. It is truly a cosmopolitan city, with few rivals in the world in its diversity. For the price of a subway token, an observer can rub shoulders in the subway with turbaned Indian Sikhs, becurled Hasidic Jews, Haitian practitioners of Vodun wearing multicolored beads, Muslim women with veils over their faces, Bible-bearing Chinese Evangelicals, Puerto Rican Jehovah's Witnesses with pamphlets in hand, Italian Catholic widows dressed in black, and—perhaps—an Anglo-Saxon Protestant.

This concentration of so much diversity in such a small geographic area may be called "cultural compression." Like a pressure cooker that makes for faster meals, New York City promotes religious change more rapidly than many other settings. There is probably greater religious tolerance in New York than in many other parts of the United States, simply because of the proximity and number of coexisting groups. Moreover, the different religions tend to adopt what they see of value in other denominations, so that syncretism large and small is always at work.

While it is certainly true that such social factors as immigration, the global economy, and the information explosion all affect the practice of religion, the latter can also influence the public realm. The rise of religious observance is a worldwide phenomenon that has caught most social observers by surprise. Religion today is often the organizer of collective action and a pillar of cultural identity. These roles are especially pronounced in many of the nations sending immigrants to New York City. But religion is not limited in its appeal only to immigrant peoples: its influence has also increased among more established sectors of the population. In fact, many religious institutions in New York effectively act like bridges between them, "taking from the rich and giving to the poor," as they distribute donations from more wealthy congregants to those in need. According to one estimate, religious institutions in New York City provide $3 billion a year in services.[2] Through networks of hospitals, AIDS clinics, day-care and senior-citizen centers, social-welfare agencies, immigration services, housing-advocacy groups, and myriad volunteer programs, religion provides many of the services government is expected to offer.

In discussing "religion" it is important to look beyond the official institutions of church, synagogue, or mosque. These are the places where religious people meet and worship—but without people, they are only empty buildings. Likewise, the clergy and ecclesiastical administrators may control institutional services and policies, but they can be effective leaders only if they have followers, and their programs can flourish only with contributors. All three—people, places, and leaders—combine to shape religious experience, making it at once intensely personal, communitarian, and institutionally powerful.

In this sense, "religion" is sometimes hard to distinguish from "culture." In actual experience, cultural values are often inseparable from moral and religious ones. It was only with the Enlightenment that culture was divorced from religion: prior to that, virtually all expressions of human culture came from within the context of religion. When we speak of Egyptian or Greco-Roman culture, for instance, we are speaking mostly of Egyptian and Greco-Roman religion. The peculiar Western approach to reason as antagonistic to religion is a product of the Enlightenment and its heirs: rationalism, secularism, and positivism.

The divorce of religion and culture introduced what Mahandas Gandhi called the "seven social sins": politics without principle, wealth without work, commerce without morality, pleasure without conscience, education without character, science without humanity, and worship without sacrifice. The compartmentalization of values into separate "cultural," "religious," or "civic" categories is not a necessary condition of human society and, in fact, is a tendency in retreat throughout most of the world. Together with sociologist José Casanova, author of *Public Religions in the Modern World*, I would argue that life in New York would not be livable without the efforts of the religiously committed.[3]

Many of the religiously active in New York are people with high levels of altruistic motivation and a sharp focus upon self-improvement who belong to communities closely identified with local neighborhoods. While in our skeptical age many people have lost faith in public institutions, including political parties and public schools, religious institutions are among the most trusted by New Yorkers, especially the poor. Religious communities offer a fictive kinship to their members, often with a sense of continuity with life in their countries of origin. Newcomers to the city quickly learn that the religious community is a place where they can be called "brother/sister," speak their native language, and celebrate the traditions of their homeland. Religion provides a public space in which immigrants can begin to discover their place in society in the new country. Studies of assimilation have long emphasized this function of religion.[4] For example, there is evidence that most Latin Americans are not assimilated to white, middle-class Euro-America but to Latino groups that have been established in the United States for several generations. In other words, second-generation Latin Americans from Mexico, Central America, or the Dominican Republic become more like Puerto Ricans than like Italians or Jews.[5]

In a climate in which Americanization is no longer as important as in the past, churches and synagogues are slowly turning away from their historical function as Americanizers.[6] Parishes and congregations in New York have become agents for preserving the immigrants' languages, promoting ethnic traditions through esthetically satisfying public celebrations, organizing neighborhoods for material survival, and reinforcing a transnational identity.[7] Moreover, religion provides a context for interactions between those born in the United States and the newly arriving. Exchanges occur not only between the "Dominiyorks" and their Dominican-born parents, or between "Niuricans" with their Puerto Rican island-born families, or between the Dominiyorks and Niuricans growing up together in New York, but also the Dominiyorks and Niuricans returning to the Dominican Republic and Puerto Rico who join parishes and congregations there. These contacts, which religion legitimates, contribute to increasingly transnational religious identities.

Religion and Multiple Citizenships

The Jesuit sociologist, John Coleman suggests that loyalty and participation revolve around four different poles: the world community or humanity; the national state; civil society; and the partisan political party.[8] I would add a fifth, a cultural one that complements rather than impedes immigrant participation in the larger society. It is cultural citizenship, through which people can feel loyalty to multiple languages, religious customs, and family traditions.[9] The components of ethnicity—culture, language, and traditions—are often reimaged as solutions to current problems.[10]

There are two areas in particular in which religion in New York helps maintain multiple identities that transcend the usual concept of citizenship as a function of the national state. They are religious communities that often overlap with organizations concerned with material aspects of the common good and religiously influenced education. The sociologist Sidney Verba and his associates have recently provided us with considerable information about local community organizing groups, primarily nonprofit agencies, many of which are funded through private-public partnerships.[11] Most of these groups depend on coalitions of churches for their basic membership, and they have assumed an increasingly important role in city life throughout the United States, performing a mobilizing function that previously was expected from such groups as labor unions and political parties. It has been suggested that these "paradenominational organizations" are the most viable of present-day social movements. Through services as varied as refurbishing houses or delivering meals to the elderly or to AIDS victims, they establish networks for civil activity, confirm a sense of loyalty to a local setting, provide training in transferable skills, and educate people about politics. Given evidence that secular alternatives such as neighborhood poverty organizations and civil rights and labor advocacy groups are apparently on the wane, it appears that religiously based organizations may be a more likely route for community mobilization in the next century.[12]

Father Coleman, citing the *Nation* magazine, reported that two-thirds of those active in social movements in the United States "draw principally on religious motivation for their involvement. From soup kitchens to nonprofit, low-cost housing alternatives, from AIDS hospices to shelters for the homeless and services to immigrants, the religious sector takes up the slack where government programs fall down."[13] Sociologist Robert Wuthnow thinks that these paradenominational groups are "the ones that increasingly define the public role of American religion."[14] The paradenominationals are a principal source of "social capital"—to borrow a concept elaborated by political scientist Robert Putnam—in New York today because contemporary religion encourages believers to participate actively in different organizations that address the needs not only of the church but also of society.[15] Furthermore, in helping believers survive, religion emphasizes personal and communitarian responsibility in ways that government and public programs can seldom replicate.

Many paradenominationals employ thoroughly modern strategies and frequently rely on sophisticated training techniques to achieve their goals. These groups are not secularizing, however. While they operate effectively in the public sphere, they are rooted in ritual and fictive kinship relations that engender symbolic capital. These roles for religion are enhanced in the New York City of today by conditions of poverty and exploitation, so that the most intense religious experiences often take place among people in the lower income categories. Simply put, with fewer reliable alternatives for effective public action or individual achievement, religion is of greater importance to the poor in decaying neighborhoods of the city than to Euro-Americans in suburbia.

Religious institutions in the United States are also becoming more active in calling for social justice, even though some causes are not politically popular with some sectors of their membership. Thus, for instance, the Catholic Church in California opposed Proposition 187, intended to deny services to immigrants. Citing papal encyclicals, the bishops argued that Gospel values impelled Catholics to oppose this measure. As a national body, the Catholic bishops have also taken a firm stance against provisions in the Republicans' Contract with America because so much of the proposed legislation would disproportionately affect the poor. Jewish philanthropies in New York, feeling their responsibility toward Russian Jewish immigrants, have acted similarly, while Protestant denominations have also spoken out on poverty issues.

Religion and Education

A similar dynamic is at work in education, another means by which religion has considerable impact upon life in the city. Religious people in New York approach education in four manners: they demonstrate strong family support for education; emphasize religious values in education; are suspicious of secular education; and expect the educated individual to assist the community. High levels of aspiration and educational achievement, as well as an emphasis on value-laden education, can be found among people who are *not* religious, but in New York's poorer neighborhoods they are found most frequently among those who *are* religious.[16]

Participation in Academic Education

The moral training imparted by religious schools, combined with discipline and parental involvement at every level, underpin their success— as evidenced by student scores on standardized tests. New York's Catholic high schools have a particularly remarkable record. While the national drop-out rate for Latinos, for example, fluctuates between 40 and 50 percent, the retention rate of Catholic schools is over 90 percent.[17] A 1993 study by the state Department of Education for the governor's blue ribbon panel on Catholic schools found that Hispanics who attended Catholic schools demonstrated significantly higher proficiency than public school Hispanic students in every academic category.[18] Correspondingly, the rates of graduation from high school and entrance into four-year colleges were significantly higher. In fact, nearly 95 percent of Catholic high school graduates obtain a college degree, while only about 20 percent of public high school graduates do so. Since 40 percent of Latinos drop out of New York's public high schools, this suggests that about half of all Latinos educated in New York State who obtain university degrees have attended Catholic school at some time.

The success rate of Catholic schools is sometimes attributed solely to selective admissions policies. Catholic schools can throw students out, it is argued, while public schools must accept and keep all comers.

However, the governor's blue ribbon panel found that in New York City there was less than a 5-point variance in the percentage of students at risk in Catholic schools and in public schools. In the rest of the state, there were proportionally *more* students at risk in Catholic schools than in public schools. These findings suggest that Latinos of religious conviction are among the most likely to succeed in higher education. Religious observance is also a predictor of attainment in higher education among all women. With the exception of Pentecostals and Southern Baptists, the tested denominations showed higher rates of educational participation for observant women than the general population.[19]

It is from the pool of college graduates that the leaders of the immigrant and minority communities come. Doctors, lawyers, and successful business and community leaders are necessarily influenced by the value systems that infused their educations. Some would say that educational achievement reflects a desire for assimilation, not distance from the values of the larger society. It is not educational achievement alone, but the purposes to which it is put, however, that define its appeal to religious believers. Thus, while religion may promote assimilation through professional achievement, it also stimulates resistance to the adoption of purely secular values.

The Emphasis on Education in Religious Values

There are clear indications that religiously active parents want their children to receive an education in moral values and for this reason prefer religious over secular schools. This also explains the popularity of Bible institutes, leadership formation programs, catechetical, and other continuing education programs for youths and adults sponsored by churches and synagogues. Public school educators are also groping for ways to make their institutions more effective. Faced with draconian cuts in funding due to a declining tax base, urban public schools increasingly seek private donations and involve parents in fund-raising activities, much as religious schools do. In these circumstances, support for school choice, including a voucher system that would help finance a parochial education, is growing among the poorer segments of New York's population. Many people view the issue not in the traditional terms of the separation of church and state, but as a question of how best to provide their children with a high-quality education in the face of a deteriorating public school system. Without taking sides in what is a complicated political debate, it should be emphasized that among the children it serves, religious schooling is highly successful. Meanwhile, the problem of how to teach moral responsibility and show respect for religious commitment without violating the principle of the separation of church and state will be a vital issue for public educational reform in the twenty-first century.

Suspicion of Secular Education

Believers want an education, and if possible, a college degree; but they are suspicious that secular institutions ignore or even disparage the moral responsibility and religious commitment that are at the core of their educational aspirations. This explains why many Latinos seek college degrees from church-affiliated institutions. Public universities, such as the City University of New York, often fail to attract the most talented Latino Catholic or Protestant high school graduates because there is a suspicion that the city and state university systems lack or are hostile to cherished values and beliefs. As a result, many religious people suspect that the systems of public education are not designed for their purposes. Steps must be taken to win back their trust if the energies of the religiously committed are to be harnessed to improve public schools.

The Responsibility of the Educated Individual

Religion predisposes its adherents to see community service as a moral responsibility. Analysts argue that to the degree that religion makes believers more conscious of social inequalities and of racial and ethnic prejudice, it can stimulate those with educational and professional achievements to act to combat social ills. Because ecumenical or para-denominational organizations tend to resolve such political tensions internally, they have certain advantages in contrast to community service organizations that are merely serving their own constituencies. Religious groups also enjoy more flexibility and closer community identification than do government programs.

A Less Secular Future

The New York City of the twenty-first century may very well be a less secular city than the one of today. As José Casanova has convincingly argued, religion is no longer in retreat from public life or on the way to becoming "invisible"[20] or merely a "canopy."[21] Nor is it likely that religion will become so privatized in the future that it will become largely irrelevant.[22] Casanova does not dispute that society is moving toward functional differentiation, but, he argues, institutional religion is capable of strategies to minimize the negative impact of such a trend. Among his examples is the adaptive capacity of Catholicism in religious and social movements such as Solidarity in Poland and Liberation Theology in Brazil. He sees religion reclaiming functions that supposedly had been conceded to secular institutions. "In this respect, both concepts, that of civil society and that of 'the people' were not so much principles of mediation between state and society as principles of self-organization of society without mediation and without the state, principles of direct communitarian democracy. . . ."[23]

Casanova's concepts have relevance for the New York experience. Via religious institutions and movements, "the people" can become a moral force that is more effective than government in accomplishing collective tasks conducive to the common good. Efforts by religious groups to promote more locally based community activities in response to social problems are not necessarily contrary to increasing globalization. Indeed, the multiple impacts of this phenomenon on cities such as New York, including job displacement, increased unequal distribution of income, declines in real wages, and pressures on the city's tax base and hence on city services, are requiring more nongovernmental responses. It is not surprising that religious institutions, communities, and individuals are organizing to deal with current problems. In so doing, they are demonstrating a creative dynamism that may transform the face of New York and the role of religion within it in the twenty-first century.

Notes

1. Barry A. Kosmin and Seymore P. Lachman, *One Nation under God: Religion in Contemporary American Society* (New York: Harmony Books, 1993), p. 110.

2. Barry A. Kosmin, "Religion in New York Today" (speech given at the Union Theological Seminary, New York, March 1996).

3. See José Casanova, *Public Religions in the Modern World* (Chicago: University of Chicago Press, 1994).

4. See Milton Gordon, *Assimilation in American Life: The Role of Race, Religion and National Origins* (New York: Oxford University Press, 1974).

5. See Anthony Stevens-Arroyo with Segundo Pantoja, *Discovering Latino Religion: A Comprehensive Social Science Bibliography* (New York: Bildner Center Books, 1995).

6. Ibid., pp. 35–37.

7. Ana María Díaz-Stevens, *Oxcart Catholicism on Fifth Avenue* (Notre Dame, Ind.: University of Notre Dame Press, 1993).

8. John A. Coleman, SJ, "Under the Cross and Flag," John Courtney Murray Lecture, Fordham University, *America*, May 11, 1996, pp. 6–14.

9. See Rina Benmayor, Rosa M. Torruela, Ana L. Jurabe, "Responses to Poverty among Puerto Rican Women: Identity, Community, and Cultural Citizenship," Centro de Estudios Puertorriqueños, Hunter College, New York, 1992.

10. See Anthony Stevens-Arroyo, "The Emergence of a Social Identity among Latino Catholics: An Appraisal," in Jay Dolan and Alan Figueroa Deck, SJ, eds., *Hispanic Catholicism in the U.S.*, vol. 3 (Notre Dame, Ind.: University of Notre Dame Press, 1994), pp. 77–130.

11. See Sidney Verba, Kay Schlozman, and Henry Brady, *Voice and Equality* (Urbana, Ill.: University of Illinois Press, 1994).

12. See Marilyn Gittell et al., *Limits to Citizen Participation: The Decline of Community Organizations* (Beverly Hills, Calif.: Sage Publications, 1981).

13. Coleman, "Under the Cross and Flag," p. 8.

14. As cited in Coleman, "Under the Cross and Flag," p. 8.

15. Robert D. Putnam, "Turning In, Tuning Out: The Strange Disappearance of Social Capital in America" (Ithiel de Sola Pool Lecture, American Political Science Association, Cambridge, Mass., September 1995).

16. See Anthony M. Stevens-Arroyo and Ana María Díaz-Stevens, "Latino Church and Schools as Urban Battlegrounds," in Stanley Rothstein, ed., *Urban Schooling in America* (Westport, Conn.: Greenwood Press, 1993) pp. 245–70.

17. For the national rates see Joan Moore and Henry Pachon, *Hispanics in the United States* (Englewood Cliffs, N.J.: Prentice-Hall, 1985), pp. 68–69; and Suzanne Hall and Carleen Reck, eds, *Integral Education: A Response to the Hispanic Presence* (Washington, D.C.: National Catholic Education Association, 1987). For a discussion of the Catholic school experience among Latinos in New York, see Ruth Doyle et al., *Church Related Hispanic Youth in New York: An Exploratory Study* (New York: Office of Pastoral Research, Archdiocese of New York, 1983), pp. 3–4.

18. State Education Department, "Roman Catholic Schools in New York State," report of the Office for Planning, Research and Support Services (Albany, 1993).

19. See Barry A. Kosmin and Ariela Keysar, "The Impact of Religious Identification on Differences in Educational Attainment among American

Women in 1990," *Journal for the Scientific Study of Religion* 34 (March 1995), pp. 49–62.

20. See Thomas Luckmann, *The Invisible Religion* (New York: Macmillan, 1967).

21. See Peter Berger, *The Sacred Canopy* (Garden City, N.Y.: Doubleday, 1967).

22. See Niklas Luhmann, *Religious Dogmatics and the Evolution of Societies* (New York: Edward Mellen Press, 1984).

23. Casanova, *Public Religions*, p. 131.

Chapter 10

Rooting for a Logo: Culture, Identity, and Civic Experience in the Global City

JAY KAPLAN

NEW YORK CITY enjoyed uncontested primacy among America's cultural centers from the end of the nineteenth century to the middle of the twentieth. In almost every area of artistic and public intellectual life, it played a central, dominant, or exclusive role. Following the Second World War, New York City grew into a position of global leadership, so that today it has arguably become first among the world's cultural centers. Along the way, though, something changed.

While forces internal to the cultural sector have contributed to its evolution, its transformation largely reflects the economic and demographic changes described elsewhere in this volume. As one of the twentieth century's largest and most important urban centers, New York City has been particularly affected by the globalization of the economy, the worldwide activities and structures of the largest corporations, the ongoing concentration of corporate financial power, the greater differentiation of corporate management, information control, and financial services from production, and the new patterns of spatial dispersal of all these various functions. These forces have left their marks on the physical city, its economy, and its residents.

Since 1965, moreover, changes in the nation's immigration laws have contributed to a drastic recomposition of the city's population. As Joseph J. Salvo and Arun Peter Lobo point out in Chapter 6, New York in the 1990s more closely resembles New York in the 1920s than New

York in the 1950s. The new New Yorkers have revitalized the city in many ways, but they have also brought and posed problems. Unfortunately, the prevailing patterns of human and economic change clash in important respects. What they have in common is their increasingly transnational, as opposed to international, dimensions, the ways in which they reflect direct flows between societies rather than exchanges subject to governmental regulation, as Robert Smith's chapter in this volume aptly describes.

Gotham built its cultural dominion upon its historic role as the most important port connecting the North American continent to Europe, and as a transshipment center between Europe and the Caribbean. Through the Narrows passed not just commerce, but, also, people and ideas. The city was an entry point for what was new and exciting, a place of interaction and hybridity.[1] From the late eighteenth to the early twentieth century, the vernacular culture of New York's inhabitants—their ideas, values, and creativity—gradually found expression in market-oriented cultural production as well as in noncommercial, but public, venues such as clubs, lyceums, and cafés.[2] New York's cultural products reflected the connections between people, place, and time. They owed their popularity and commercial success to the vibrancy of these relationships. It was but a natural step for the nation's premier center of ideas, popular entertainment, and high culture to develop both cultural tourism and a cultural "export" economy. The vaudeville circuit, for example, had long been taking the city's cultural ferment on the road for profit, only to be improved upon by the theatrical empire staked out by the Shubert brothers, which filled vacant theaters around the country with traveling road companies performing Broadway shows.[3]

In other words, New York's national market position in cultural products was built upon the foundation of a solid local relationship between cultural production and consumption. The local market produced cultural products for local consumers and tourists, reflecting local values and conditions. In vaudeville and the theater, for example, cultural producers and consumers encountered one another face-to-face, on the same site, at the same time, with a give-and-take that allowed for interplay and even some modest blurring of roles between performers and audiences.

From the end of the nineteenth century through the first half of the twentieth, local cultural attractions offered New Yorkers not only recreation and stimulation but also established the basis for a shared public discourse, thereby helping to build a common civic culture. They provided New Yorkers with meeting places, shared experiences, and opportunities to interact with one another. Of course, some of these cultural experiences such as the philharmonic or opera were accessible virtually only to the upper sectors of society, but even these helped to mold a *bourgeois* sensibility in the literal sense, one in which class consciousness combined with urban civic pride. Other cultural experiences, from vaudeville to Anton Seidl's Coney Island concerts of strikingly contemporary classical music, brought together a remarkable range of New Yorkers from virtually every station of society and every immigrant group, although restrictions were imposed on African Americans.[4] New Yorkers saw their separate identities reflected in popular entertainments and, through the solvent of their collective engagement, acquired a new sense of themselves as New Yorkers.

When, for example, they went to the ball park to cheer for the Dodgers, the Giants, or the Yankees, they participated in a civic ritual that affirmed their hometown connection and transcended their differences in an epiphany of shared emotion. Demonstrating what today seems a touching innocence, New Yorkers at that time did not regard their teams as mobile corporate franchises. They saw them, rather, as consisting of players who were fellow New Yorkers, perhaps not by origin but, at least, by adoption. Their skills and idiosyncrasies were familiar, and, in most cases, they could be expected to be around for a long time. They were not traded with aplomb and moved about the leagues like anonymous units of production, nor did they yet have the opportunity to place themselves upon the market as free agents available to the highest bidder. New Yorkers' deep and lingering sense of betrayal at the way the Dodgers and Giants abandoned the city provides eloquent testimony to the familial sense of attachment, the sense of social contract, that had bound fans to players. Today, in a less innocent time, when it has become commonplace for baseball owners to threaten to move their clubs, fans still go to the ballpark for recreation, but it is a lot harder for them to muster quite the same enthusiasm for teams identified more by a familiar corporate logo than by the constantly changing roster of their players.

As the twentieth century progressed, technological developments worked to undermine the significance of local cultural geography relative to national market demographics. Films and recordings, for example, severed the temporal and spatial links that made producers and consumers collaborators in a common, evanescent experience. The new communications media allowed for the separation of cultural production and consumption. If these new technologies thus transformed the occasions they hoped to replicate faithfully, they *were* able to "capture" their visual and aural traces once and for all time so that they could be endlessly reproduced and sold as physical products. During the second half of the twentieth century, the culture industries increasingly wedged their concentrated financial power and commercial expertise between actors and audiences, writers and readers, artists and viewers, musicians and listeners, attenuating the basic interactions of a vital local cultural life.

Today, New York City's cultural preeminence no longer rests on a virtual monopoly. On the contrary, its postwar ascendancy has been achieved against a backdrop of broad cultural diffusion, fostered in no small measure by New York City–based philanthropies and cultural institutions. In fact, some observers sympathetic to the city have fretted over the proliferation of competitors, warning that insofar as cultural superiority encourages emulation, it reduces its own margin of supremacy.[5] But such a view is essentially static. Cultural expansion is not a zero-sum game. It is a growth industry. Far from undermining the role of dance in New York City, for example, the Ford Foundation's support for regional dance programs enhanced esteem for the art, democratized access to it, and multiplied the audiences who could appreciate the achievements of New York City's great classical, modern, and avant-garde companies.

While New York City remains powerful as a cultural producer and a locus of cultural consumption, its paramountcy ultimately inheres in its ability to determine "what is good." New York City gives *direction* to cultural enterprise in two ways. First, it establishes aesthetic standards, offers serious criticism and consumer advice, launches styles and trends, and arbitrates matters of taste. Journalism, advertising, marketing, the media, and a good part of cultural activity itself promote cultural consumption by assisting consumers to identify and discriminate among the products of the culture industries. Second, those who make financial decisions on behalf of the city's vast concentrations of wealth exercise cultural control through the clout they bring to bear both in market-oriented decisions, such as which books, magazines, films, or Broadway productions to back, or which cable systems and film libraries to invest in, as well as in their charitable giving to nonprofit cultural activities.

As a major center of cultural decision making, production, assembly, financing, marketing, and consumption, the city retains a still-sizable, albeit diminished and somewhat atavistic, sector of locally oriented cultural production and consumption. A large part of this sector could not survive economically without subsidy, and it has long received state and city support as well as foundation, corporate, and individual gifts.[6] However, in this time of diminished public revenue, competing charitable priorities, and uncertain demographic prospects (particularly for "high-culture" performing arts activities other than dance), the justifications for contributions have increasingly been offered in economic terms, rather than through appeals to civic conscience. One government study, for example, underlines the importance of the city's cultural attractions to its tourist sector, in particular its hotels and restaurants.[7]

Cultural philanthropy, more highly developed in New York City than perhaps anywhere else, serves four vital purposes: it supports protected staging areas for, ultimately, more commercial forms of creative activity and nurtures new talent; it validates "what is good" or, at least, promising; it helps inculcate cultural literacy by educating prospective audiences; and, in what amounts both to a summary and a separate point, it sustains the infrastructure that contributes to cultural productivity. Here and there a lone painter, writer, or composer might successfully work in virtual isolation, but far more seem to thrive on the confluence of other artists, libraries, concerts, museums, universities, bookstores, and cafés, not to mention the artists' service organizations, fellowships, internships, part-time work opportunities, revolving loan programs, agents, intellectual property lawyers, studio and rehearsal spaces, laboratories, specialized shops, and artisanal services that can only be found in a place such as New York. As in many other areas of metropolitan dominance, advantages accrue to the already privileged: the existence of such an infrastructure exerts a powerful attraction upon would-be artists, intellectuals, artisans, and cultural entrepreneurs.

New York City's cultural hegemony derives in significant measure from the city's economic transformation. One of the central features of what we term globalization is an ever-increasing economic concentration and differentiation between strategic planning, financial control, and information management on the one hand, and manufacturing or service delivery on the other. As America's and the world's corporations have gobbled up one another in an acquisitive orgy, and dismembered one another and dispersed the pieces to wherever cost and profit projections dictated, New York City has fared far better in retaining corporate heads than corporate body parts. And the city's culture industry has profited from its association with corporate management—through commissions and employment opportunities, through the patronage of wealthy and, often, sophisticated high-income employees, and through corporate contributions designed to demonstrate good citizenship or to embellish the corporate name with untaxed dollars. What is more, many of the giants of the culture industry itself are located in New York City, where they number among the city's largest corporations. Even the movie industry, economically the most important segment of the culture industry not based in New York, depends on New York City to help finance its productions.

Speedy, cheap, and prolific channels of transportation and communication have transformed the cultural sector, creating audiences on several continents for productions conceived, assembled, financed, and marketed globally. In the world of opera, for example, highly engineered, digital studio recordings—more perfect than it is possible for any individual live performance ever to be—have made the consummate talent of a handful of genuine superstars familiar throughout the world and stimulated a voracious demand for live appearances. Established singers of the caliber of Pavarotti, Domingo, Krauss, Hampson, Ramey, Freni, Rysanek, Battle, Gruberova, Te Kanawa, Norman, and von Stade, or emerging talents such as Alagna, Heppner, Bartoli, or Larmore will, often in one season, appear in houses in Europe and the United States as well as in South America, Japan, and Australia. Whole productions will sometimes travel intercontinentally, as did—to cite just two examples from recent years—those of the Kirov Opera or William Christie's *Les Arts Florissants*.

As opera lovers the world over will testify, much has been gained through improved technology and increased mobility. But something has also been lost. Increased uniformity has been the cost of opera's commodification. The superstars have set performance criteria and audience expectations very high, but a significant measure of national or regional diversity—and downright quirkiness—of style has been sacrificed. Today, for example, as young French singers are being trained in the same international style prevailing elsewhere, the aficionado rarely finds true exemplars of the French lyric tradition. Artistic standardization has also beset the operas themselves: the blocking of entrances, stage movements, and exits is increasingly governed by convention, the better to whisk superstars through productions with a minimum of expensive rehearsal time. Ironically, as the educator and musician Leon Botstein has written, recordings have made performances of unparalleled technical sophistication available to audiences that are more geographically far flung and numerically larger, but far less musically literate, than those of the past.[8] In these circumstances, showmanship—not to say vulgar exhibitionism—has sometimes blossomed where musicianship and dramatic values have wilted.

Elsewhere in the field of classical music a similar phenomenon prevails. A recent article in the *Economist* on "Why Orchestras Are Too Alike" notes that:

Fine orchestras once sounded as distinctive as the cultures which bred them. French ones, with their light, thin horns and bassoons, used to have a sound as strong and airy as the Eiffel Tower. Strings in Central Europe had the colour and touch of Hapsburg-plush. German orchestras with their granite discipline got burgomasterly weight from the double-basses. American ones had a brassy directness, in New York, an aggressiveness even.[9]

But, "that was then." The magazine quotes pianist Andras Schiff to the effect that today only the Vienna Philharmonic has a recognizable sound. It identifies four factors as contributing to increased uniformity: national distinctions in the instruments themselves have largely disappeared; local teaching traditions have been disrupted by international travel, sabbaticals, and guest conductorships; recordings have disseminated an international style; and conductors have made shorter-term commitments to their orchestras and perform with them less frequently than in the past, with consequently less opportunity to mold a unique orchestral voice.

The homogenization of popular culture has far outstripped anything that has occurred in the world of classical music. Movies, television, radio, print journalism, and book publishing have made major contributions to cultural uniformity, not to say cultural leveling. Despite the highly vaunted possibilities of narrow casting—the definition and service of distinct audience segments—market pressures favoring mass audiences have proven virtually inexorable, and not just in the United States. One indicator from 1991 shows that all of the top ten grossing motion pictures in Argentina, Austria, Brazil, Egypt, Greece, Hungary (only eight listed), the Netherlands, Poland, Switzerland, and the United Kingdom were imported, usually from the United States. In Chile, Denmark, Germany, Iceland, Spain, and Sweden, nine of the top ten were imports, while, even in France, for all the importance of its historic contributions to the art of film, eight of the top ten were imports.[10] Other examples prove the same point. Reruns of "I Love Lucy," "Bonanza," and "Dynasty" play to audiences worldwide, while African audiences tune in to CNN and Chechen rebels proudly point to pictures of themselves in *Newsweek*.[11]

Ironically, multiculturalism has emerged as an ideal or a cause at precisely the moment when the global marketing of largely American, popular culture threatens local cultural expression virtually everywhere. Even more ironically, it often employs a sales strategy emphasizing a spurious "diversity."[12] As one sardonic observer has commented: "when we talk about the dominance of one culture, or even, less agonistically, of the globalization of culture, it is important to keep in mind that what is really at issue is the victory of culture that makes money over all other forms, and particularly, over both folk culture and elite culture."[13]

Cultural globalization has, of course, not proceeded without counterpoint. With increasing frequency in recent years, militantly rejectionist forms of ethnic, nationalist, and religious chauvinism have offered sometimes violent resistance to the insidious integrationism of the marketplace.[14] On a commercial level, the neglect of certain relatively affluent audiences with specialized interests has allowed boutique publishers and a few successful low-cost, independent movie producers to enter fields dominated by corporate giants lacking the suppleness or incentive to pick these crumbs up off the floor. Nor has cultural diffusion been entirely unidirectional. Building upon an extensive literature in ethnomusicology, for example, Orlando Patterson has shown how, in drawing upon indigenous Jamaican musical traditions, reggae evolved from an imitative response to American rhythm-and-blues, cowboy, and bluegrass music to a distinctively original form, one which in the dance-hall versions brought to New York by underclass Kingston immigrants stimulated in turn the development of African American rap.[15] But, while his documentation of what he terms "periphery to center cultural flows" offers a useful corrective to a more simplistic model of cultural exchange, Patterson's neglect of the significance of economic disparities casts doubt on his more far-reaching claim that "it is simply not true that the diffusion of Western culture, especially at the popular level, leads to the homogenization of the culture of the world. Indeed, . . . just the opposite is the case."[16] The originality of Patterson's analysis lies in its grassroots focus. Rather than examining cultural decision making at the level of recording industry executives, Patterson, adopting Saskia Sassen's term, traces cultural transmission to the Jamaicans living in the "transnational space" of what he calls "multicultural America."[17] With a majority of their adult working population living abroad, many Caribbean societies, according to Patterson, no longer find political and social boundaries meaningful. Their expatriates in the United States "are not ethnic groups in the traditional American sense." Instead, quoting Jamaican folk poet Louise Bennett, Patterson describes their enclaves as "colonization in reverse," as a physical migration involving "no traumatic transfer of national loyalty from the home country to the host polity," since "home is readily accessible and national loyalty is a waning sentiment in what is increasingly a postnational world." As far as he is concerned, such a multicultural America—consisting, in addition to this "West Atlantic Regional Cosmos," of the "Tex-Mex cosmos of the Southwest," the "Southern California cosmos," and the "Pacific Rim cosmos"—is a fact; it coexists with a "traditional America" and an "ecumenical America," which synthesizes the divergent values and practices of the other two sectors. In an assertion that bears further examination, Patterson warns that: "Any cultural policymaker must begin by recognizing the fundamentally tripartite nature of America."[18]

The eclipse of place, optimists will note, has not progressed as far in New York City as elsewhere, thanks to the city's genuine cosmopolitanism, the centrality of its role in directing cultural globalization, its enormous enclave of only partially assimilated foreign-born residents, and its mall-resistant geography, zoning, and tax policies. Two recent theatrical examples give expression to the vitality and commercial potential of artistic productions drawing on the traditions and lives of New Yorkers. George C. Wolf's successful production at the Public Theatre of *Bring In Da Noise, Bring In Da Funk*, with tap dance phenomenon Savion Glover, moved from its nonprofit venue to a Broadway run, and *Rent*, a low-budget, off-off-Broadway musical depicting the life of the community surrounding the hole-in-the-wall East Village theater where it premiered to rave reviews, also opened on Broadway. Encouragement comes, too, from the creativity the city's post–World War II migrants and immigrants have brought to New York. In a spectrum of traditional and novel forms—including, among others far too numerous to cite, the poetry of the Nuyorican Café; the photography of Charles Biasiny-Rivera's En Foco workshop; the costumes designed by Brooklyn's Caribbean community for the annual Labor Day Parade; the impeccable instrumental skills being acquired at Juilliard, Manhattan School of Music, and Mannes by young Asian Americans; the popular and commercial success of jazz and salsa artists in the Afro-Caribbean tradition; or the emergence of writers such as Edwige Danticat or filmmakers such as Mira Nair—the bounteous talents of newcomers and their children are manifesting themselves in the city's daily life and enriching all its inhabitants.

Pessimists, however, can point to several inauspicious portents. The Broadway success of *Beauty and the Beast* has led its owner and producer, the Disney Company, to acquire and refurbish one of the theater district's landmarks, the New Amsterdam Theatre. While few who actually have to cross 42nd Street will regret this encroachment upon a stronghold of the pornography industry, and many will rejoice at the rehabilitation of a dilapidated movie house to a state of architectural grandeur, the importation from Hollywood of corporately imagineered entertainment, even more so than the recent reign of insipid Andrew Lloyd Weber musicals and their imitators, sadly seems to mark a reversal of the natural order, a slippage moving New York City one step closer to ordinariness.

Even more troubling, however, is the growing disjunction among the major components of New York City's population. One of the most detrimental effects of cultural globalization is the way it erodes meaningful local discourse, opportunities for civic engagement, and, even more basically, occasions to share public space and experiences as equals with one's fellow city residents. While it may be convenient to sit at home and watch the Mets on television or listen to a Dvorak quartet on CD, it does not build a sense of community. Over and over we hear how, over vast distances, the Internet brings people of common intellectual (and class-based) interests together in "virtual" groups whose members have more in common with one another than with their geographical neighbors, but not enough attention is paid to how this diminishes the capacity for participatory democracy in the place where we actually live. The erosion of the public sector, including local cultural institutions such as libraries and museums, has, as Christopher Lasch has pointed out, distended the linkage between the insularity and particularism of the ethnic neighborhood and the cosmopolitanism of the city as a whole.[19] It has done so, moreover, at a time when an influx of immigrants of varied cultural and linguistic backgrounds severely strains the civic culture. Seen in conjunction with the out-migration from the city of the descendants of earlier generations of immigrants, those who have patronized and sustained many of the city's most important cultural institutions, this bodes ill for the future of New York City's cultural sector.[20]

It is in this context that Patterson's views take on an ominous aspect. While it is not at all clear that New York City's newest immigrants have any less desire to assimilate than their predecessors, it is true that in certain respects they experience somewhat less pressure to do so. Modern transportation and communications technologies permit them to remain in regular touch with their homeland.[21] Distinct "colonies" or neighborhood enclaves, combined with a two-tier economy, mean that many do not undergo some of the socializing experiences of earlier immigrants who shared schools, neighborhoods, and jobs with other immigrants and native-born Americans.[22] Current immigration policies, moreover, permit a continuous influx of newcomers to refresh their community's linguistic, cultural, and political ties to the country of origin. The danger, of course, is one of entrapment by choice or circumstance in "transnational space," involving political disenfranchisement for the immigrants and a concomitant loss of public services, as well as increased civic polarization and xenophobia. To the extent that Patterson is correct in his description of such a multinational America, the prospects for democracy are dim.

All that ultimately holds America together is a shared belief in democracy and the responsibilities of civic participation. To the extent that America opens its doors to immigrants (and there are a host of reasons rooted in liberal and humane values, as well as a concern for tolerance, to suggest the wisdom of regulating the flow to match society's resources and absorptive capacity), it must guarantee them full access to civic life, provide them with a full panoply of government services, and expect them to fulfill their civic duties. The alternative of doing as Patterson suggests and accepting "the fundamentally tripartite nature of America" is to sanction an even more divided society in which increasingly overt means of social control replace the bonds of shared civic and cultural values.

Notes

1. See the contribution to this volume by Joseph J. Salvo and Arun Peter Lobo.

2. See Thomas Bender, *New York Intellect: A History of Intellectual Life in New York City, from 1750 to the Beginnings of Our Own Time* (Baltimore: Johns Hopkins University Press, 1987).

3. See Brooks McNamara, *The Shuberts of Broadway, A History Drawn from the Collections of the Shubert Archive* (New York: Oxford University Press, 1990).

4. On Seidl, see Joseph Horowitz, *Wagner Nights: An American History* (Berkeley: University of California Press, 1994). David Nasaw suggests that the enforcement of the color barrier helped to mute differences among whites. See his *Going Out: The Rise and Fall of Public Amusements* (New York: Basic Books, 1993), p. 2.

5. See Paul Di Maggio's discussion of cognitive entropy in "On Metropolitan Dominance: New York in the Urban Network," in Martin Shefter, ed., *Capital of the American Century: The National and International Influence of New York City* (New York: Russell Sage Foundation, 1993), especially pp. 204–7. Martin Shefter offers the concept of a "dialectic of domination and diffusion" in "New York's National and International Influence," in ibid., pp. 1–25.

6. See, however, the pessimistic outlook presented in Nina Kressner Cobb's report for the president's Committee on the Arts and the Humanities, *Looking Ahead: Private Sector Giving to the Arts and the Humanities* (Washington, D.C., 1996).

7. Port Authority of New York and New Jersey, the Alliance for the Arts, the New York City Partnership, the Partnership for New Jersey, *The Arts as an*

Industry: Their Economic Significance to the New York–New Jersey Metropolitan Region: Part I of Tourism and the Arts in the New York–New Jersey Region, 1993.

8. Leon Botstein, "Making Classics: 'I Know What I Like' vs. 'I Like What I Know,'" *culturefront* 2, no.1, (winter 1993): 28.

9. March 2, 1996, pp. 77–78.

10. Quoted from *Variety International Film Guide,* 1993, in Benjamin R. Barber, *Jihad vs. McWorld* (New York: Random House, 1995), pp. 299–301.

11. Jean Herskovits, "CNN and Africa," *culturefront* 3, no. 2 (summer 1994): 21; and Michael Specter, *New York Times,* February 6, 1996, p. A12.

12. Benetton's magazine, for example, is entitled *Colours.* According to David Rieff, "multiculturalism helps to legitimize whole new areas of consumerism." See, "Multiculturalism's Silent Partner," *Harpers* 287, no. 1719 (August 1993): 64. More bitingly, Christopher Lasch has written of the "tourist's view of the world" proffered by multiculturalism "in a global bazaar in which exotic cuisines, exotic styles of dress, exotic music, exotic tribal customs can be savored indiscriminately, with no questions asked and no commitments required." See *Revolt of the Elites and the Betrayal of Democracy* (New York: Norton, 1996), p. 6.

13. David Rieff, "A Global Culture?" *World Policy Journal* 10, no. 4 (winter 1993–94): 76.

14. See, for example, Mark Juergensmeyer, *The New Cold War? Religious Nationalism Confronts the Secular State* (Berkeley: University of California Press, 1993); Hans Magnus Enzensberger, *Civil Wars: From L.A. to Bosnia* (New York: The New Press, 1994); and Benjamin R. Barber, *Jihad vs. McWorld.*

15. Orlando Patterson, "Ecumenical America: Global Culture and the American Cosmos," *World Policy Journal* 11, no. 2 (summer) 1994: 103–17.

16. Ibid., pp. 104, 109.

17. For an introduction to Saskia Sassen's views on the denationalization of certain urban institutional arenas, see her chapter in this volume.

18. Ibid., pp. 111–18.

19. Lasch, *Revolt of the Elites,* pp. 130–32.

20. See Salvo and Lobo on the out-migration of earlier European immigrants.

21. See Robert Smith's discussion of simultaneous memberships among Mexicans and Dominicans in Chapter 7.

22. Salvo and Lobo outline the local impact of recent immigration on specific New York City neighborhoods in their contribution to this volume.

Chapter 11

Cities, Foreign Policy, and the Global Economy

Saskia Sassen

A NY ANALYSIS of how global processes play out in New York City and how these might be linked to a more responsive formulation of foreign policy needs to consider at least three major issues.

The first is the relationship between the global economy and subnational units, particularly major cities that are international business and financial centers. This means understanding how and to what extent global processes are embedded in strategic concentrations of resources and infrastructure, such as financial districts. It also means understanding the importance of what is often referred to as world-class culture, typically found in large international cities.

The second issue is the extent to which deregulation, privatization, and the declining role of the national state in the economy in general—all key elements in the current phase of globalization—may change the traditional national state/global economy relationship by adding a third component, namely subnational units, particularly global cities. This would clearly have major implications for foreign policy, particularly since the content of foreign policy today has shifted more toward economic issues to such an extent that a greater component of what we call foreign policy is now international economic policy.

The third issue is the impact of economic globalization on the overall social, political, and economic structure of the city. This requires expanding the analytic terrain within which we understand global processes in order to include activities typically regarded as local, backward, or unconnected to globalization. Also, it means expanding the notion of globalization to include processes such as immigration, which have potentially significant cross-border political implications. The fact that Dominican residents in New York City can now vote in elections in the Dominican Republic or that Colombian politicians campaign in Jackson Heights, Queens, is evidence of a new form of international politics that is being conducted outside the formal confines of intergovernmental relations.

The challenge in exploring these issues is that there has been little cross communication between two distinct fields of scholarship: cities and the global economy on the one hand, and foreign policy and globalization, on the other. My research, largely centered on the first, is now leading me to the second field as well. This is in good part due to an understanding of globalization that regards global cities as key elements of the global economy and hence as sites where governance of the global corporate economy and foreign policy are linked.

In this chapter, I will try to address both of these broad subjects, the relation between the city and the global economy and the relation between governance of the global corporate economy and foreign policy, using the concrete geographic and policy setting of New York City.[1] The first step in this effort is to understand why and how cities matter in today's global economy. Is there something different about their role today from twenty or thirty years ago? Is New York City's role unique or does the city share a number of traits with other major cities in the world in terms of the kind of functions it fulfills in the new global corporate economy? Finally, this chapter will illuminate how the concentration of global processes—internationalized markets and foreign firms—in cities such as New York, in the context of deregulation and the growing importance of economic factors, affects the traditional concept of state sovereignty and, more specifically, affects foreign policy.

A More Encompassing Account of Globalization

Globalization has transformed the meaning of and the sites for the governance of economies.[2] The current phase of the world economy is marked by the ascendance of information technologies, an associated increase in the mobility and liquidity of capital, and a resulting decline in the regulatory capacities of national states over key sectors of their economies—particularly the leading information industries, finance, and advanced corporate services, which tend to have transnational markets and are partly embedded in electronic spaces that override conventional jurisdictions and boundaries.[3]

Yet, the global economy requires strategic sites with vast concentrations of resources and infrastructure, sites that are located in national territories and are far less mobile than much of the general commentary on the global economy suggests. The impact of globalization, therefore, cannot simply be reduced to the notion of the declining significance of the national state, as is so often asserted. Rather the strategic relationship now encompasses the national state, the global economy, and strategic localities—typically major international financial and business centers.

Indeed, one of the primary characteristics of the world economy is the reassertion of the importance of such subnational units as global cities and strategic regions like Silicon Valley in California.[4] The chapters by O'Cléireacáin and Rosen and Murray in this volume document the ongoing concentration of key financial activities in New York City in spite of the enormous pressures for deconcentration and dispersal to other areas of the country and the region. Similarly, though on a different front, the chapters by Kaplan and Roche show the ongoing concentration of key cultural institutions and of the new, supposedly hypermobile, electronic media in the city.

Moreover, the excessive emphasis on the hypermobility and liquidity of capital tends to obscure the relationship among foreign policy, local policy, and the global economy. It excludes the possibility of a de facto participation of global cities in the creation of international economic policy and practice, and hence in the formulation of foreign policy *insofar* as economic policy has gained added weight. And it ignores the effects of global processes that are really about the *re-territorializing* of people, economic practices, and cultures, of which the immigrant communities and the neighborhood subeconomies they often form are an example. The chapters by Salvo and Lobo, Smith, and Stevens-Arroyo in this volume address these subjects.[5]

What is the actual role of cities in a global economy? Two propositions underpin the analysis that follows. The first is that to a large extent the global economy materializes in concrete processes situated in specific places, and that this holds even for the most advanced information industries. We need to distinguish between the capacity for global transmission/communications and the material conditions that make this possible; between the globalization of the financial industry and the array of resources—from buildings to labor inputs—that makes this possible.

The second proposition is that the geographic dispersal of economic activity made possible by telematics[6] actually contributes to an expansion of centralized functions in an economic system characterized by concentration of control, ownership, and profit appropriation. More conceptually, we can ask whether an economic system with strong tendencies toward such concentration can have a space economy that lacks points of physical agglomeration of strategic components and what it takes to service these. In other words, can the global economy do without centers of power? New York City has historically been such a center of power. Beginning with the Reagan administration, we see the decline in influence of the eastern seaboard foreign-policy "establishment," many of whose institutions, such as the Council on Foreign Relations and the *New York Times*, are located in New York. It is easy to assume, then, that New York City is less significant when it comes to international relations than it was in the past. But globalization and telecommunications have reconfigured the meaning of centers of power, and there is evidence to suggest that what New York City has lost in terms of influence through a foreign-policy "establishment," it may have gained in terms of globally oriented corporate power, including strategic concentrations of the telecommunications infrastructure necessary for the operation of the global marketplace—particularly given the growing importance of economic policy in international relations. This is illustrated by the work done on Wall Street and the crucial role of the Department of the Treasury in solving the Mexican financial crisis at the end of 1994.[7]

Place and Work Process in the Global Economy Today

The specific forms assumed by globalization over the last decade have created particular organizational requirements. The emergence of global markets for finance and specialized services, as well as the growth of international investment transactions, have contributed to the expansion in central managerial and coordination functions and in the demand by firms for specialized services. Transnational corporations and banks are major sites for international management functions and major consumers of specialized services. Yet much global economic activity is not encompassed by the organizational form of the transnational corporation or bank. Nor is much of this activity simply a function of the power of such firms, a power often invoked to explain the fact itself of economic globalization. Much of this activity involves work and places that do not form part of such organizations. The spatial and organizational forms assumed by globalization, and the actual work of running transnational operations, have made cities one type of strategic place in the global economy and made the advanced corporate services a strategic input for the implementation of global economic systems.

The combination of the geographic dispersal of economic activities and system integration that characterizes the current economic era has contributed to new or expanded central functions, and the complexity of transactions has raised the demand by firms for highly specialized services. Rather than becoming obsolete due to the dispersal made possible by information technologies, cities: (1) concentrate command functions in the global economy; (2) are postindustrial production sites for leading industries, particularly finance and specialized services for firms; and (3) are transnational marketplaces where firms and governments can buy financial instruments and specialized services.[8]

The Intersection of Globalization and Service Intensity

The new or sharply expanded role of a particular kind of city in the world economy since the early 1980s results from the intersection of two major developments. One of these is the sharp growth in the globalization of economic activity. This has raised the scale and complexity of economic transactions, thereby feeding the growth of top-level multinational headquarters functions and the demand for services by firms, particularly advanced corporate services.[9]

It is important to note that while globalization raises the scale and complexity of these operations, these operations are also evident in firms that operate regionally. Thus, while such regionally oriented firms need not negotiate the complexities of international borders and the regulations of foreign countries, they are still faced with a regionally dispersed network of operations that requires centralized control and servicing, or with central functions sufficiently complicated to lead them to buy specialized services rather than producing them in-house. These services range from financial and insurance to computer programming and telecommunications network services. Some of the data presented by Rosen in this volume showing New York City losing share in a range of service industries are partly a function of those services' growth throughout the urban system (rather than simply a loss of share for New York City), as firms in all industries are buying more of such service inputs.

The second development is that the growing demand for services by firms in all industries, from mining and manufacturing to finance and consumer services, has had a significant growth effect on cities, large and small, beginning in the 1980s.[10] These services include financial, advertising, accounting, legal, telecommunications, and consulting services. Cities are key sites for the production of such services. It is important to recognize that this growth in the production of services for firms takes different forms from one city to another. Some cities cater to regional or subnational markets, others to national markets, and yet others to global markets. Again, the data in Rosen's chapter reveal that cities throughout the urban system have become production sites for such services, which is different from saying that New York City has lost firms and jobs to other cities, although this has also happened.

In the context of this growing service intensity in the organization of the economy, the distinctive trait of globalization is that it adds scale and complexity to functions shared by both national and globally oriented firms. While it is true that firms operating only nationally do not have to negotiate different legal or accounting systems, the point from the perspective of the urban economy is that there is growing demand for services by firms in *all* industries, and cities are the preferred, although not exclusive, production sites for such services.

As a result, we see in cities the formation of new types of banking and service activities less oriented toward manufacturing and trade. The urban economy of today is not so much about headquarters offices as about services for firms (and households). For cities that are major international business centers, the scale, power, and profit levels of this new service core are such as to suggest that we are seeing the formation of a new urban economy. This is so in at least two respects. While these cities have long been centers for business and finance, since the late 1970s there have been sharp changes in the structure of the business and financial sectors, and sharp increases in the overall magnitude of these sectors and their weight in the urban economy. The ascendance of the new finance and services complex, particularly international finance, engenders a new economic regime. That is, while this sector may account for only a fraction of the economy of a city, it imposes itself on the larger urban economy. Thus, in 1993 the FIRE—finance, insurance, and real estate—sector accounted for 15 percent of employment in New York City, but 27 percent of the wages, and the securities industry for only 4 percent of employment but 14 percent of the wages (see the O'Cléireacáin chapter in this volume). Most notably, the possibility for superprofits in finance and in specialized services has the effect of devalorizing manufacturing insofar as the latter cannot generate the same level of profits.

This is not to say that everything in the economy of cities has changed. On the contrary, there is a great deal of continuity and similarity among cities that are not global nodes. It is rather that the implantation of global processes and markets has meant that the internationalized sector of the economy has expanded sharply and has imposed a new valorization dynamic, often with devastating effects on large sectors of the urban economy. High prices and profit levels in the internationalized sector and its ancillary activities (such as restaurants and hotels) made it increasingly difficult in the 1980s for firms in other sectors to compete for space and capital. Many of the latter experienced considerable downgrading and/or displacement, or lost economic vigor to the point of not being able to retake their economic space when recession weakened the dominant sectors. To take just one example, neighborhood shops catering to local needs gave way to upscale boutiques and restaurants catering to new high-income urban elites. The sharpness of the rise in profit levels in the international finance and service sector in the 1980s also contributed to the severity of the ensuing crisis of the early 1990s. These trends were evident in many cities of the highly developed world, although rarely as clearly as in major U.S. cities.[11]

These trends—although at a different order of magnitude—also became evident toward the late 1980s in a number of major cities in the developing world that were becoming integrated into various world markets, including São Paulo, Buenos Aires, Bangkok, Taipei, and Mexico City, among others.[12] Central to the development of this new service core in these cities were the (albeit partial) deregulation of their financial markets, privatization and the associated foreign investment, and, generally, the integration of these economies into the world markets. This has contributed to the ascendance of finance and specialized services, real estate speculation, and high-income commercial and residential gentrification. Given the vast size of some of these cities, however, the impact of this new economic core has not always been as evident as in central London or Frankfurt, but the transformation has nonetheless occurred.

Accompanying these sharp growth rates in producer services in the 1980s was an increase in the level of employment specialization in business and financial services in major cities. There is today a general trend toward high concentrations of finance and certain producer services in the downtowns of major international financial centers around the world, from Toronto and Sydney to Frankfurt and Zürich. Those cities that have emerged as important producers of services for export tend toward specialization. For example, New York and London are leading producers and exporters of financial services, accounting, advertising, management consulting, international legal services, and other business services. More generally, out of a total private sector of 2.8 million jobs in New York City in December 1995, almost 1.3 million were export-oriented (both national and international). Cities like New York are among the most important international markets for these services, and New York leads the world in the export of services.

There are also tendencies toward specialization among different cities within countries.[13] In the United States, New York leads in banking, securities, manufacturing administration, accounting, and advertising. Washington leads in legal services, computing and data processing, management and public relations, research and development, and membership organizations. New York is more narrowly specialized than Washington as a financial, business, and cultural center. Some of the legal activity concentrated in Washington, for example, serves New York City businesses in their dealings with government regulatory agencies and in lobbying activities. Such services are bound to be in the nation's capital.[14]

It is important to recognize that manufacturing remains a crucial economic sector in all of these urban economies, even when it may have ceased to be so in some cities. Manufacturing in New York City today ranges from apparel production for the fashion industry to woodworking and metalmaking for the design industries.[15]

Furthermore, the new service economy benefits from manufacturing. Indeed, manufacturing feeds the growth of the producer services sector, but it does so whether it is located in the same place, in another region, or overseas. *Where* manufacturing—or mining and agriculture for that matter—are located is of secondary or no importance to globally oriented service firms, which can sell their services anywhere. Moreover, the territorial dispersal of plants, especially internationally, actually raises the demand for producer services because of the increased complexity of transactions. Thus globalization has contributed to the growth of producer service firms headquartered in major cities. It is worth remembering that as General Motors was moving production jobs offshore and devastating Detroit's employment base, its financial and public relations headquarters in New York City remained as dynamic as ever, indeed became even busier. A good part of the producer services sector is fed by financial and business transactions that either have nothing to do with manufacturing, as in many of the global financial markets, or to which manufacturing is incidental, as in mergers and acquisitions activity in which manufacturing firms are bought and sold as commodities. The examples of New York and London, two cities that have seen heavy losses in manufacturing and sharp gains in producer services, illustrate this point. New York lost 34 percent of its manufacturing jobs between 1969 and 1989, compared with the nation as a whole, which lost only 2 percent during that period, and in contrast with many areas that experienced growth in manufacturing employment. The British economy lost 32 percent of its manufacturing jobs from 1971 to 1989; the London region lost 47 percent of such jobs. Yet both cities experienced sharp growth in producer services. Here it is also worth noting the different conditions in each city's metropolitan region: the London metropolitan area experienced an overall 2 percent job decline compared with a 22 percent job growth rate in the New York metropolitan area.[16] This points up the fact that the finance and producer services complex in each city rests on a growth dynamic that is somewhat independent from the broader regional economy—a sharp change from the past, when a city's economy was presumed to be deeply entwined with the economy of its hinterland.

The Formation of a New Production Complex

According to standard conceptions about information industries, their rapid growth and disproportionate concentration in central cities should not have happened. This is well illustrated by the case of many of the advanced corporate services. Embedded in the most advanced information technologies, these services might have been expected to bypass the high costs and congestion typical of major cities. But cities offer economic benefits associated with agglomeration as well as highly innovative environments. Firms produce some of these services in-house, but they more frequently turn to specialized service firms. The growing complexity, diversity, and specialization of the services that businesses require make it more efficient for them to operate this way.

Moreover, producers of these services benefit from proximity to other producers of specialized services. This is especially the case in the most innovative sectors. Complexity and innovation often require multiple highly specialized inputs from several industries. For example, the production of a financial instrument requires inputs from accountants, advertising experts, lawyers, economic consultants, public-relations specialists, designers, and printers. Time replaces weight in these sectors as a force for agglomeration. That is to say, if speed were not a consideration, firms could call on a geographically dispersed array of specialized firms to fill their needs. This is often the case in routine operations. But when time is of the essence, as it is today in many of the leading sectors of advanced service industries, the benefits of agglomeration are so high as to be indispensable.

It is this combination of constraints that has promoted the formation of a corporate services complex in all major cities. This complex is intimately connected to the world of corporate headquarters—so much so that they are often thought of as forming a joint headquarters–corporate services complex. But we need to distinguish the two. While it is true that headquarters still tend to be disproportionately concentrated in cities, many have moved out of the cities over the last two decades. Even so, they need a corporate services complex somewhere in order to buy needed specialized services or obtain financing. Moreover, the headquarters that move tend to have more routinized lines of activity, aimed at predominantly regional or national markets. Headquarters of firms in highly competitive, innovative lines of activity and those with a strong world-market orientation appear to benefit from being located in major international business centers, no matter how high the costs. The point is that both types of headquarters need a corporate services complex to be located somewhere. Where such a complex is located is probably increasingly unimportant from the perspective of many, though not all, headquarters as long as the location provides a density of specialized firms and top know-how—the three or four law firms, and two or three accounting and financial services firms, needed for many of the most complex national and international operations.

Corporate Headquarters and Cities

Headquarters concentration is generally seen as an indication of a city's status as an international business center, and any significant loss of headquarters is usually interpreted to mean that a city is declining. However, headquarters concentration is a problematic measure.

First, how we measure or simply count headquarters makes a difference in how we view this issue. Frequently, the key measure is the size of firms in terms of employment and overall revenue. But some of the largest firms in the world are manufacturing firms and many of these have their main headquarters in proximity to their major factory complex, which is unlikely to be in a large city. (However, such firms are likely to have secondary headquarters for highly specialized financial and communications functions in major cities.) Nor do manufacturing firms oriented toward a national market need to be located in a major city. The much-publicized departure of major headquarters from New York City in the 1960s and 1970s involved these types of firms, and, indeed, many of the largest firms in the United States have left New York and other large cities. But if we look beyond size, we get a different picture. For example, 40 percent of U.S. firms with half their revenue from international sales have their headquarters in New York City. (See also Tables 11.1 and 11.2 for other highly specialized measures of firm location.)

Second, the nature of a country's urban system is a factor. Sharp urban primacy will tend to entail a disproportionate concentration of head-quarters in cities, no matter what measure one uses. Third, different economic histories and business traditions may combine to produce different headquarters location patterns in different countries. Furthermore, headquarters concentration may be linked with a specific phase in a country's economic history. For instance, while New York has been losing the headquarters of Fortune 500 companies, Tokyo has been gaining headquarters of the largest Japanese firms over the last ten years. Osaka and Nagoya, the two other major economic centers in Japan, are losing headquarters to Tokyo. This trend is linked to the increasing internationalization of the Japanese economy and the corresponding increase in central command and servicing functions in Tokyo. Extensive government regulation of the economy in Japan is another factor contributing to the movement of headquarters to Tokyo, insofar as international business transactions are subject to government approval.

The State and the City in the New Geography of Power

As we have seen, the strategic spaces in which many global processes are embedded are often subnational spaces. The infrastructure that makes possible the hypermobility of global financial capital is also em-

Table 11.1   Assets of the 50 Largest Diversified Financial Companies by Region (in US$ Millions), 1992

City	Assets	Percentage of U.S. Top 100
Total, Top 100 U.S. Firms	1,630,258.1	——
New York	835,461.8	51.24
Chicago	23,052.6	——
Metro Chicago Area	45,900.9	2.82
San Francisco	38,203.0	2.34
Los Angeles	1,913.8	.12
Total of Above Areas	944,532.1	57.94

Source: Sassen, *Cities in a World Economy,* 1994, p. 62.

Table 11.2   Assets of the 100 Largest Commercial Banking Companies
by Region (in US$ Millions), 1992

City	Assets	Percentage of U.S. Top 100
Total, Top 100 U.S. Firms	2,500,314.8	——
New York	715,064.9	28.60
San Francisco	263,507.7	10.54
Chicago	109,760.9	4.39
Los Angeles	58,163.1	2.33
Total of Above Areas	1,146,496.6	45.85

Source: Sassen, *Cities in a World Economy,* 1994, p. 62.

bedded in various national territories. This raises a question about the impact of the global economy on the form of sovereignty associated with the modern state, which was constituted in terms of mutually exclusive territories and the concentration of sovereignty in the national state. There can be little doubt that economic globalization signals a major transformation in the territorial organization of economic activity and politico-economic power.

We can begin to address this question by examining major aspects of economic globalization that contribute to what I think of as a new geography of power. One is the much-noted fact that firms can now operate across borders with ease. For many, this is what globalization is about. However, I see at least two other components of the new geography of power that confronts national states today.

The first of these components concerns the actual territories where globalization materializes in specific institutions and processes, the subject of the preceding section of this chapter. The question here is: what kind of territoriality is represented by a major international financial and business center such as New York City, where firms from around the world can do business with each other in deregulated markets and industries?

The second component of the new geography of power has arisen out of the innovations in the legal structure that have accompanied globalization. We are seeing the ascendance of a new legal regime to govern cross-border economic transactions, a trend not sufficiently recognized in terms of its implications for national states, as well as local governments. Indeed, there is a rather peculiar passion for legality (and for lawyers) at work in the globalization of the corporate economy. These legal innovations include the growth of private legal systems. Notable among these are the system of international commercial arbitration for settling transnational business disputes and the credit-rating agencies that have emerged as the arbiters of the global financial markets.[17] To this we could add the growing role of the global capital market in disciplining national governments when it comes to economic policy.[18]

This privatization and innovation in legal practice makes cities like New York and London key sites for the governance of global economic processes. Thus, a large share of international business transactions invoke New York law, the major credit-rating agencies are located in New York City, and the city boasts one of the major concentrations of corporate lawyers active in international commercial arbitration. This brings to the fore the issue of the role of such cities in the making of foreign policy. The fact that this governance role is partly privatized obscures the displacement of parts of the foreign-policy apparatus, hitherto seen as attached to the national state, onto the corporate world. This is a subject that deserves more research and discussion if government, at all levels, is going to be better equipped to deal with this reality.

We are used to thinking that what the global economy gains, the national economy or the national state loses. But instead of this traditional dualism, we are seeing a series of triangulations whereby subnational units, such as global cities, and supranational units, such as the World Trade Organization, emerge as players on the global scene. To these developments we need to add the formation of transnational communities through immigration, as described by Smith in this volume, which also displaces certain political functions—moving them away from the area of relations between national states and into the private spheres of individuals, households, and communities.[19]

In brief, globalization over the last ten to fifteen years has brought about a reconfiguration of territoriality and sovereignty. This reconfiguration is partial, selective, and above all strategic. The transformations in key aspects of the modern state and interstate system signal both a conceptual and a practical opening for the inclusion of global cities such as New York in what was once a partnership of two, the national state and the international economy.

Notes

1. See Saskia Sassen, *Cities in a World Economy* (Thousand Oaks, Calif.: Pine Forge/Sage Publications, 1994), and *Losing Control? Sovereignty in an Age of Globalization*, the 1995 Columbia University Leonard Hastings Schoff Memorial Lectures (New York: Columbia University Press, 1996).

2. See James Mittelmann, ed., *Globalization: Critical Reflections, International Political Economy Yearbook*, vol. 9 (Boulder, Colo.: Lynne Rienner Publishers, 1996), and, generally, *Competition and Change: The Journal of Global Business and Political Economy*, vol. 1 (Hardwood Academic Publishers, 1995).

3. There is a pronounced and relentless pressure toward deregulation in the financial and many advanced service markets of any country that wants to become integrated into the global economy. Japan, for example, was forced to begin deregulating its financial markets in the mid-1980s. In order to attract foreign capital, Mexico, Brazil, and Argentina had to deregulate their financial markets, reversing decades of protective policies. We can see this pressure to reduce the role of the state most recently in the move toward the privatization of the large French and German government-owned telecommunications companies. Globalization of the telecommunications industries requires fluid access into and exit from hitherto closed "national" sectors.

4. Global integration of markets and deregulation have not necessarily had the effect of dispersing firms and holdings to the point of eliminating their concentration in particular localities. In 1992, for example, New York City still accounted for 51 percent of assets (valued at $835,000 million) of the top 100 U.S. diversified financial companies; the second largest concentration was in Chicago with a far distant 4 percent ($232,000 million), followed by San Francisco with 2 percent ("The Service 500," *Fortune*, May 31, 1993; pp. 199–230).

5. See also Linda Basch, Nina Glick-Schiller, and Cristina Szanton-Blanc, *Nations Unbound: Transnationalized Projects and the Deterritorialized Nation-State* (New York: Gordon and Breach, 1994), and "Global Crisis, Local Struggles," *Social Justice*, vol. 20 (fall/winter 1993).

6. The term refers to advanced integrated communications and computer network technologies.

7. See Sassen, *Losing Control?* for a more detailed explanation of this event and, more generally, the growing importance of economic factors in international relations.

8. See John Friedman, "Where We Stand: A Decade of World City Research," and Janet Lippman Abu-Lughod, "Comparing Chicago, New York, and Los Angeles: Testing Some World Cities Hypotheses," in Paul L. Knox and Peter J. Taylor, eds., *World Cities in a World System* (Cambridge, England: Cambridge University Press, 1995).

9. Firms that operate many plants, offices, and service outlets must coordinate planning, internal administration and distribution, marketing, and other central headquarters activities. For instance, as large corporations moved into the production and sale of final consumer services, a wide range of ac-

tivities, previously performed by freestanding consumer service firms, were shifted to the central headquarters of the new corporate owners. Regional, national, or global chains of motels, food outlets, and flower shops, require vast centralized administrative and servicing structures. A parallel pattern of expansion of central high-level planning and control operations has taken place in governments, brought about partly by the technical developments that make this possible and partly by the growing complexity of regulatory and administrative tasks. Generally, diversification of product lines, mergers, and the transnationalization of economic activities all require highly specialized services. The territorial dispersal entailed by transnational operations of large enterprises illustrates some of the points raised here. For instance, in the early 1990s, U.S. and German transnationals had over 19,000 affiliates in foreign countries. These required a considerable quantity of managerial and coordination tasks. Moreover, the top transnationals have very high shares of foreign operations: the top ten largest transnational corporations in the world made 61 percent of their sales abroad. The average for the hundred largest corporations was almost 50 percent. (See United Nations Conference on Trade and Development, Programme on Transnational Corporations, *World Investment Report 1993: Transnational Corporations and Integrated International Production,* for detailed data on these and other variables for the hundred largest nonfinancial transnational corporations ranked by foreign assets. For a condensed table and description, see Sassen, *Cities in a World Economy,* pp. 70–72, tables 4.4 and 4.5.)

10.   In New York City in 1987, at the height of that decade's economic boom, producer services—that is, services largely for firms—accounted for 38 percent of private-sector jobs, up from 30 percent in 1977. Many of the producer services showed high growth rates during the period of economic restructuring in New York City from 1977 to 1985. Employment in legal services grew by 62 percent, in business services by 42 percent, and in banking by 23 percent; in contrast, employment fell by 22 percent in manufacturing and by 20 percent in transport. Saskia Sassen, *The Global City: New York, London, Tokyo* (Princeton, N.J.: Princeton University Press, 1991).

11.   See, for example, "Le Nouveau Paris," *Le Debat* (summer 1994) and Graham Todd, "'Going Global' in the Semi-Periphery: World Cities as Political Projects. The Case of Toronto," in Knox and Taylor eds., *World Cities in a World System,* pp. 192–214.

12.   See Sassen, *Cities in a World Economy,* and Knox and Taylor, *World Cities in a World System.*

13.   All the major economies in the developed world display a similar pattern of sharp concentration of financial activity in a single center: Paris in France, Milan in Italy, Zürich in Switzerland, Frankfurt in Germany,

Toronto in Canada, Tokyo in Japan, Amsterdam in the Netherlands, and Sydney in Australia. The concentration of financial activity in these leading centers has actually increased over the last decade. Thus, in Switzerland, Basel used to be a more important financial center, but has now been completely overshadowed by Zürich. Montreal, which was a major center in Canada two decades ago, has now been overtaken by Toronto. Similarly, Osaka was once a far more powerful competitor to Tokyo in Japan's financial markets than it had become by the late 1980s.

14. The data on producer services is creating a certain amount of confusion in the United States. For instance, faster growth at the national level and in medium-sized cities is often interpreted as indicating a loss of share and declining position among leading centers such as New York or Chicago as a result of the decentralization of producer services. But it is not a zero-sum situation in which growth in a new location necessarily means loss in an older center. I see these patterns pointing to a growing service intensity in the organization of the economy nationwide.

15. See, for example, Matt Mitchell "Design-Oriented Wood Manufacturing in New York City" in *Proceedings. Conference on Manufacturing Today in Major Cities* (Harvard University, Graduate School of Design, February 1996); Peter Rowe, ed., *Manufacturing in New York City* (Princeton, N.J.: Princeton Architectural Press, forthcoming); and Linda Cox, "Project Manufacturing in New York City," transcript of panel discussions (New York: Municipal Arts Society, Planning Center, 1996).

16. M. Frost and Nigel Spence, "Global City Characteristics and Central London's Employment," *Urban Studies* 30 (1993): 547–58.

17. See, for example, Jeswald Salacuse, *Making Global Deals: Negotiating in the International Marketplace* (Boston: Houghton Mifflin, 1991); and Gerald Aksen, "Arbitration and Other Means of Dispute Settlement," in D. Goldsweig and R. Cummings, eds., *International Joint Ventures: A Practical Approach to Working with Foreign Investors in the U.S. and Abroad* (Chicago: Chicago Bar Association, 1990).

18. For a detailed discussion of this issue see Sassen, *Losing Control?* There is a third component in the new geography of power: it is the fact that a growing number of economic activities are taking place in electronic space. This growing virtualization of economic activity, particularly in the leading information industries such as finance and specialized corporate services, may be contributing to a crisis in control that transcends the capacities of both the state and the institutional apparatus of the economy. The speed of transactions made possible by the new technologies is creating orders of magnitude in the foreign currency markets, for example, that escape the governing capacities of private and government

overseers. It may be remembered that it was the ungoverned manipulations of electronic markets by a 28-year-old trader that brought down England's Barings Bank.

19. See also James Holston, ed., "Cities and Citizenship," *Public Culture* (special issue, 1996); and Basch et al., *Nations Unbound*.

Further Reading

Printed Sources

Andreas, Peter, "U.S.-Mexico: Open Markets, Closed Border," *Foreign Policy*, no. 103 (summer 1996).

Barber, Benjamin R., *Jihad vs. McWorld* (New York: Random House, 1995).

Barry, Tom, with Harry Browne and Beth Sims, *Crossing the Line: Immigrants, Economic Integration, and Drug Enforcement on the U.S.-Mexico Border* (Albuquerque: Resource Center Press, 1994).

Basch, Linda, Nina Glick-Schiller, and Cristina Szanton Blanc, *Nations Unbound: Transnational Projects, Postcolonial Predicaments, and Deterritorialized Nation States* (New York: Gordon and Breach, 1994).

Basch, Linda, Nina Glick-Schiller, and Cristina Szanton Blanc, eds., *Towards a Transnational Perspective on Migration; Race, Class, Ethnicity, and Nationalism Reconsidered* (New York: Annals of the New York Academy of Sciences, vol. 645, 1992).

Bender, Thomas, *New York Intellect: A History of Intellectual Life in New York City, from 1750 to the Beginnings of Our Own Time* (Baltimore: the Johns Hopkins University Press, 1987).

Binder, Frederick M., and David M. Reimers, *All the Nations under Heaven: An Ethnic and Racial History of New York City* (New York: Columbia University Press, 1996).

Camilleri, Joseph A., and Jim Falk, *The End of Sovereignty? The Politics of a Shrinking and Fragmented World* (Aldershot, England: Edward Elgar Publishing, 1992).

Casanova, José, *Public Religions in the Modern World* (Chicago: University of Chicago Press, 1994).

Cornelius, Wayne, Philip L. Martin, and James F. Hollifield, eds., *Controlling Immigration: A Global Perspective* (Stanford, Calif.: Stanford University Press, 1994).

Díaz-Stevens, Ana María, *Oxcart Catholicism on Fifth Avenue* (Notre Dame, Ind.: University of Notre Dame Press, 1993).

Dolan, Jay, and Alan Figueroa Deck, SJ, eds., *Hispanic Catholicism in the U.S.*, vol. 3 (Notre Dame, Ind.: University of Notre Dame Press, 1994).

Edel, Matthew, and Ronald G. Hellman, eds., *Cities in Crisis: The Urban Challenge in the Americas* (New York: Bildner Center for Western Hemisphere Studies, Graduate School and University Center of the City University of New York, 1989).

Farer, Tom, *Beyond Sovereignty: Collectively Defending Democracy in the Americas* (Baltimore: Johns Hopkins University Press, 1996).

Garreau, Joel, *Edge City* (New York: Doubleday, 1991).

Gibson, Margaret A., and John Ogbu, eds., *Minority Status and Schooling: A Comparative Study of Immigrant and Involuntary Minorities* (New York: Garland Publishing, 1991).

Greider, William, *One World, Ready or Not: The Manic Logic of Global Capitalism* (New York: Simon & Schuster, 1996).

Guarnizo, Luis, "Los Dominicanyorks: The Making of a Binational Society," *Annals of the American Academy of Political and Social Science* 536 (November 1994).

Hägstrom, Peter, *The "Wired" MNC: The Role of Information Systems for Structural Change in Complex Organizations* (Stockholm: Institute of International Business, Stockholm School of Economics, 1991).

Hall, Peter Geoffrey, *Cities of Tomorrow: An Intellectual History of Planning and Design in the Twentieth Century* (Cambridge, Mass.: Blackwell Publishers, 1996).

Herzog, Lawrence A., ed., *Changing Boundaries in the Americas*, U.S.-Mexican Contemporary Perspective Series, 3 (San Diego, Calif.: Center for U.S.-Mexican Studies, 1992).

Jackson, Kenneth T., *Crabgrass Frontier: The Suburbanization of the United States* (New York: Oxford University Press, 1985).

Jackson, Kenneth T., ed., *The Encyclopedia of New York City* (New Haven: Yale University Press, 1995).

Jacobs, Jane, *The Death and Life of Great American Cities* (New York: Random House, 1961).

Kasinitz, Philip, *Caribbean New York: Black Immigrants and the Politics of Race* (Ithaca, N.Y.: Cornell University Press, 1992).

Kasinitz, Philip, ed., *Metropolis: Centre and Symbol of Our Times* (Basingstoke: Macmillan, 1995).

Knox, Paul L., and Peter J. Taylor, eds., *World Cities in a World System* (Cambridge, England: Cambridge University Press, 1995).

Kosmin, Barry A., and Seymore P. Lachman, *One Nation under God: Religion in Contemporary American Society* (New York: Harmony Books, 1993).

Krugman, Paul, *Geography and Trade* (Cambridge: MIT Press, 1991).

Lasch, Christopher, *Revolt of the Elites and the Betrayal of Democracy* (New York: Norton, 1996).

Lobo, Arun Peter, and Joseph J. Salvo, *The Newest New Yorkers: 1990–1994* (New York City Department of City Planning, 1996).

Massey, Douglas, and Nancy Denton, *American Apartheid* (Cambridge: Harvard University Press, 1994).

James Mittelmann, ed., *Globalization: Critical Reflections, International Political Economy Yearbook*, vol. 9 (Boulder, Colo.: Lynne Rienner Publishers, 1996).

McDonnell, Lorraine, and Paul T. Hill, *Newcomers in American Schools: Meeting the Educational Needs of Immigrant Youth* (Santa Monica, Calif.: RAND, 1993).

McNickel, Chris, *To Be Mayor of New York: Ethnic Politics in the City* (New York: Columbia University Press, 1992).

Mollenkopf, John, *A Phoenix in the Ashes: The Rise and Fall of the Koch Coalition in New York City Politics* (Princeton, N.J.: Princeton University Press, 1992).

Mollenkopf, John, and Manuel Castells, eds., *The Dual City: Restructuring New York* (New York: Russell Sage Foundation, 1991).

Nasaw, David, *Going Out: The Rise and Fall of Public Amusements* (New York: Basic Books, 1993).

O'Neill, Hugh, and Mitchell Moss, *Reinventing New York: Competing in the Next Century's Global Economy* (New York: New York University Urban Research Center, Robert F. Wagner School of Public Service, 1991).

Patterson, Orlando, "Ecumenical America: Global Culture and the American Cosmos," *World Policy Journal* 11, no. 2 (summer 1994).

Portes, Alejandro, "Global Villagers: The Rise of Transnational Communities," *American Prospect* (March-April 1996).

Portes, Alejandro, and Ruben Rumbaut, *Immigrant America: A Portrait* (Berkeley: University of California Press, 1991).

Powers, Mary G., and John J. Macisco, eds., *The Immigration Experience in the United States: Policy Implications* (New York: Center for Migration Studies, 1994).

David Rieff, "A Global Culture?" *World Policy Journal* 10, no. 4 (winter, 1993–94).

Roche, Edward M., *Managing Information Technology in Multinational Corporations* (New York: Macmillan, 1992).

Rosecrance, Richard, "The Rise of the Virtual State," *Foreign Affairs* 75, no. 4 (July/August 1996).

Rothstein, Stanley, ed., *Urban Schooling in America* (Westport, Conn.: Greenwood Press, 1993).

Rowe, Peter, ed., *Manufacturing in New York City* (Princeton, N.J.: Princeton Architectural Press, forthcoming).

Rusk, David, *Cities without Suburbs* (Baltimore: Johns Hopkins University Press, 1993).

Salacuse, Jeswald, *Making Global Deals: Negotiating in the International Marketplace* (Boston: Houghton Mifflin, 1991).

Sassen, Saskia, *The Global City: New York, London, Tokyo* (Princeton, N.J.: Princeton University Press, 1991).

Sassen, Saskia, *Losing Control? Sovereignty in an Age of Globalization*, the 1995 Columbia University Leonard Hastings Schoff Memorial Lectures (New York: Columbia University Press, 1996).

Sassen, Saskia, *Cities in a World Economy* (Thousand Oaks, Calif.: Pine Forge/Sage Publications, 1994).

Saxenian, Anna Lee, *Regional Advantage: Culture and Competition in Silicon Valley and Route 128* (Cambridge: Harvard University Press, 1994).

Schlesinger, Arthur, Jr., *The Disuniting of America* (New York: Norton 1992).

Shefter, Martin, ed., *Capital of the American Century: The National and International Influence of New York City* (New York: Russell Sage Foundation, 1993).

Smith, Peter, ed., *The Challenge of Integration: Europe and the Americas* (New Brunswick, N.J.: Transaction Publishers, 1993).

Stevens-Arroyo, Anthony, with Segundo Pantoja, *Discovering Latino Religion: A Comprehensive Social Science Bibliography* (New York: Bildner Center Books, 1995).

Sudjic, Deyan, *The 100 Mile City* (New York: HarperCollins, 1992).

United Nations Research Institute for Social Development (UNRISD), *States of Disarray—The Social Effects of Globalization: An UNRISD Report for the World Summit for Social Development* (New York: UNRISD, 1995).

Verba, Sidney, Kay Schlozman, and Henry Brady, *Voice and Equality* (Urbana, Ill.: University of Illinois Press, 1994).

Waldinger, Roger, *Still the Promised City? Blacks and Immigrants in Postindustrial New York* (Cambridge: Harvard University Press, 1996).

Internet Sources

Many sites on the Internet aim to provide useful information about cities for decision makers and planners. To get a useful international perspective, contact the Commission on Communication Networks and Telecommunications of the International Geographical Union at *http://alor.univ-montp3.fr/netcom_labs/*. This site includes many French resources. Many cities in the United States maintain websites; a list of these can be found at *http://www-unix.oit.umass.edu/~abhu000/localgov.html/*. These sites are listed both by city size and alphabetical order. A wealth of research on the impact of high technology on regional centers can be found at the Institute of Urban and Regional Development's site at the University of California in Berkeley: *http://www.ced.berkeley.edu/iurd/*. William J. Mitchell's entire "City of Bits" is available at *http://www-mitpress.mit.edu:80/City_of_Bits/index.html/*. Finally, an in-depth listing of information can be found at the New York Information Technology Center's site, *http://www.55broadst.com/*.

Participants in the Study Group

Name	Affiliation
Name	*Affiliation*
Najilaa Abdus-Samad	Brooklyn College
Ajamu Abraham	John Jay College
Dooley Adcroft	Council on Foreign Relations
Sarita Ahuja	Ford Foundation
Richard Alleyne	Council on Foreign Relations
Peter Andreas	Brookings Institution
Willa Appel	New York City Partnership and Chamber of Commerce, Inc.
Ana Arana	journalist
Diana Ayton-Shenker	Human Rights Program, Hunter College
Naomi Azrieli	Oxford University
Joshua Baron	Lehman College
Linda Basch	Wagner College
Peter Benda	International Center for Migration, Ethnicity and Citizenship, New School for Social Research
Nancy Bodurtha	Council on Foreign Relations
Andrea Bonime-Blanc	Community Energy Alternatives, Inc.
Erika Burk	"America and the World"
Paolo Calza Bine	Columbia University
Mark Lincoln Chadwin	Weissman Center for International Business, Baruch College
Dana Chasin	Calvert Emerging Europe Fund
Rodolfo D. Cifuentes	Hunter College
Mauricio Claudio	Hunter College
Nomi Colton-Max	Council on Foreign Relations
Hector R. Cordero-Guzmán	Center for Puerto Rican Studies, Hunter College

Martha E. Cruz	Brooklyn College
Lourdes F. Davila	Hunter College
Marcia De Filippi	Hunter College
Josh DeWind	Social Science Research Council
Rafael Docavo-Malvezzi	Council on Foreign Relations
Joel Dreyfuss	*Information Week*
Cristina Eguizabal	Ford Foundation
Cesar Espejo	Plymouth Church After School Program, Brooklyn
Irina Faskianos	"America and the World"
Ana Figueras	Council on Foreign Relations
Matthew Findlay	Ford Foundation
Albert Fishlow	Council on Foreign Relations
Arturo Linda Fuentes	*El Café al Día*
Sergio J. Galvis	Sullivan & Cromwell
Robert S. Gelbard	U.S. Department of State
Nina Glick-Shiller	University of New Hampshire
Charlynn Goins	Prudential Securities
JoMarie Griesgraber	Center for Concern
James F. Hoge, Jr.	*Foreign Affairs*
Ken Irish-Bramble	Medgar-Evers College
Jay Kaplan	New York Council for the Humanities
Phillip Kasinitz	Hunter College
Darren Kew	Council on Foreign Relations
Clifford Krauss	*New York Times*
Gloria Lee	Asian/American Center, Queens College
Arun Peter Lobo	New York City Planning Department, Population Division
Anthony Marcus	City University of New York, Graduate Center
Ann Markusen	Council on Foreign Relations
Armando Martínez Bravo	Ford Foundation
Daniel Mato	Columbia University
Kenneth Maxwell	Council on Foreign Relations
Christopher Mitchell	New York University
John Mollenkopf	City University of New York, Graduate Center
José Mauricio Montoya	Hunter College
Carol Nichols	Global Kids, Inc.
Carol O'Cléireacáin	Brookings Institution

Marifeli Perez-Stable	State University of New York, Old Westbury
Michael Peters	Council on Foreign Relations
Enid Rivera	Andrew W. Mellon Foundation
Elizabeth Robinson	Brincar, Inc.
Alina Rocha Menocal	Americas Society
Edward Roche	Institute of Urban and Regional Development, University of California, Berkeley
Martha Rodriguez	Caribbean Exchange Program, Hunter College
Edward Rogowsky	Baruch College/CUNY-TV
Rae Rosen	Federal Reserve Bank of New York
Daniel Rubey	Lehman College
Karen Rutberg	American Planning Association
Joseph Salvo	New York City Planning Department, Population Division
Arturo Ignacio Sanchez	Columbia University
Hema Sareen	Hunter College
Saskia Sassen	Columbia University
Susan Scott	Council on Foreign Relations
Michael Simmonds	Medgar Evers College
Robert Smith	Barnard College
Richard Smithey	Yale University
Anthony M. Stevens-Arroyo	PARAL, City University of New York, Graduate Center
Karen M. Sughrue	Council on Foreign Relations
Constance Sutton	New York University
Sharon R. Thompson	Ford Foundation
J. Michael Turner	Hunter College
Frank Vardy	New York City Department of City Planning, Population Division
Marta Varela	New York City Commission on Human Rights
Sheldon Werdiger	architect
Aristide R. Zolberg	New School for Social Research

Index

Hispanics, 102–5, 105, 123, 142, 153
Hollywood, 60, 167
Hong Kong, 31, 48, 49
Hudson County, 101

IBM (International Business Machines), 9
Illinois, 134
Image processing, 54, 55
i.MAGIC Cyber Star Awards, 62
Immigration, 1, 6, 17, 22, 39; and assimilation, 110–32; and the changing demographic profile of New York City, 88–109; and cultural production, 159–60, 166, 167, 168–69; and family reunification, 91, 96; illegal, 79–81, 96–97; and the Immigration Act of 1990, 96; and the Immigration and Nationality Act, 89–95; and the Immigration Reform and Control Act, 95, 96, 114, 130*n*32; policy, and immigrant flows, 89–90; and population growth, 97–99; and racial and ethnic diversity, 102–6. *See also* Migration
Immigration and Naturalization Service (INS), 82, 97
Income tax, 3, 28, 30
India, 47, 58, 64, 136, 137
Industrial policy, 64
Innovation, pace of, 53
Institute for East European and International Studies, 84
Insurance sector, 41, 46, 133. *See also* FIRE (finance, insurance, and real estate sectors)
Interest rates, 22
International High School, 140
International Interactive Communication Society, 62
Internet, 34, 55, 59, 61
IRCA (Immigration Reform and Control Act), 95, 96, 114, 130*n*32
Ireland, 22, 39, 88, 105, 117
ISDN (Integrated Services Digital Network), 60

ISPs (Internet Service Providers), 61
Israel, 22, 124
Italy, 22, 117–20

Jackson Heights, 5, 72, 74, 172
Jacksonville, 54
Jamaica, 16, 95, 105, 136–37, 142
Japan, 10, 39, 47, 56–57, 181
Jehovah's Witnesses, 149

Kallstrom, James, 80
Kearney, Michel, 112
Kennedy Airport, 15
Kentucky, 54
Kiosks, 54, 55
Korea, 22, 136, 137
Kuala Lumpur, 64

Labor Department, 3
Lagos, 71
Lasch, Christopher, 168
Latin America, 2–3, 5, 70–78
Latinos, 155, 153
Lau v. Nichols, 141
Lazard Frères & Co., 13
Legislation: Glass-Steagall Act, 48; Immigration Act of 1990, 96; Immigration and Nationality Act, 89–95; Immigration Reform and Control Act, 95, 96, 114, 130*n*32; McCarran-Walter Act, 91
LEP (limited English proficiency), 141
Liberation theology, 156
Linares, Guillermo, 16, 120–23
London, 10, 49, 73, 177–78, 183
Los Angeles, 41, 54, 76, 99, 100, 181–82

McCarran-Walter Act, 91
McDonalds, 9, 63
Mafia, 71
Malaysia, 56
Manufacturing jobs, 3, 24–26, 133
Market economies, conversion to, 46
Massachusetts, 121
Media industry, 63, 59–60, 162. *See also* Communications